OUR CONNECTION WITH
THE ELEMENTAL WORLD

Kalevala—Olaf Åsteson—The Russian People
The World as the Result of Balancing Influences

OUR CONNECTION WITH THE ELEMENTAL WORLD

Kalevala—Olaf Åsteson—The Russian People
The World as the Result of Balancing Influences

Seven lectures, including one public lecture, six addresses and one question and answer
session given in Hanover, Helsinki, Berlin and Dornach in 1912, 1913 and 1914

TRANSLATED BY SIMON BLAXLAND-DE LANGE

INTRODUCTION BY SIMON BLAXLAND-DE LANGE

RUDOLF STEINER

RUDOLF STEINER PRESS

CW 158

The publishers gratefully acknowledge the generous funding of this publication by the estate of Dr Eva Frommer MD (1927–2004) and the Anthroposophical Society in Great Britain

Rudolf Steiner Press
Hillside House, The Square
Forest Row, RH18 5ES

www.rudolfsteinerpress.com

Published by Rudolf Steiner Press 2016

Originally published in German under the title *Der Zusammenhang des Menschen mit der elementarischen Welt* (volume 158 in the *Rudolf Steiner Gesamtausgabe* or Collected Works) by Rudolf Steiner Verlag, Dornach. Based on shorthand notes that were not reviewed or revised by the speaker. This authorized translation is based on latest available (fourth) edition (1993), edited by Edwin Froböse

Published by permission of the Rudolf Steiner Nachlassverwaltung, Dornach

© Rudolf Steiner Nachlassverwaltung, Dornach, Rudolf Steiner Verlag 1993

This translation © Rudolf Steiner Press 2016

A catalogue record for this book is available from the British Library

ISBN 978 1 85584 488 9

Cover by Mary Giddens
Typeset by DP Photosetting, Neath, West Glamorgan
Printed and bound by Gutenberg Press Ltd., Malta

CONTENTS

KALEVALA

PUBLIC LECTURE
HELSINKI, 9 APRIL 1912

The Essential Nature of National Epics, with Particular Reference to the *Kalevala*

Recollection of ancient times through the folk-epics. Herman Grimm's studies of the *Iliad*. The influence of divine-spiritual impulses within the human soul in ancient times through the example of Achilles (*Iliad*) and Siegfried (*Nibelungen*). The legendary figures of the *Kalevala* and the Sampo. Christian impulses at the end of the *Kalevala* (Marjatta and her son). Insights of spiritual science concerning the evolution of mankind and of the animal kingdom. Imagination as a clairvoyant power in olden times; man as a vessel for supersensible forces. Achilles and Siegfried as representatives of a former humanity, Agamemnon and Gunther as representatives of modern humanity. The treasure of the Nibelungen. Brunnhilde. The anger of Kriemhilde and the anger of Achilles. The first stage of a modern clairvoyance that is imbued with intellectual powers: a perception of one's own ether body. The three members of the inner life of soul (consciousness soul, intellectual or mind soul, sentient soul) and their sheaths. The capacity that the clairvoyants of olden times had to behold these three soul-members as creative forces; their manifestation in the *Kalevala* in the form of Väinämöinen, the bringer of culture, the creator of the astral body; Ilmarinen the smith, the transformer of matter, creator of the ether body; Lemminkäinen, the bearer of bodily forces, creator of the physical body. The Sampo as an image of the ether body and, hence, as the bearer of folk consciousness. The individual and the universally human. An example of the congruence between spiritual science and the folk-epics (Väinämöinen's instrument).

earthly aspect in the British Isles. The solid land as the skeleton of elemental nature. The land configuration of Russia in connection with the development of the Spirit Self. The relationship between land and water in Southern Europe: the physiognomy of Italy, Greece and France.

LECTURE 3
DORNACH, 15 NOVEMBER 1914

Man's Connection with the Elemental World. Finland and the *Kalevala* III

Two important truths for our times: the soul belongs to a world lying behind the sense-world and goes from life to life. The inclination towards these truths in the case of certain people in the cultural environment of modern times illustrated through the example of Ralph Waldo Emerson's book *Representative Men*. Emerson's understanding of the truth of repeated earthly lives in sleep in connection with his relationship to Montaigne. The forgetting of the contact with elemental beings that one has in sleep in the case of most people; Albrecht Dürer's *Hercules*. The relationship between human soul-members and the elements. The interaction between Earth and man as ensouled and spirit-imbued organisms in connection with evolution. The Finnish people as the 'conscience' of the European East. The forming of the physical body through water-forces in the West, the forming of the physical body through earth-forces in the East in modern times. The impulses working upon the ether body from the Celtic element (genii of the sea) and from the Romance element (historical impulse) in the European West (France). The impulses of the fluid and earthly elements upon the physical body in Central Europe (Franks and Saxons). The relationship between Central Europe and the British Isles: the same impulses, borne in the former case within the physical body and in the latter case within the etheric body; harmony in the spiritual world, battle on the physical plane.

THE WORLD AS THE RESULT OF BALANCING INFLUENCES

LECTURE 4
DORNACH, 20 NOVEMBER 1914

Fundamental Experiences of the Fourth and Fifth Post-Atlantean Epochs

The perception of the world of Imagination through the ether body. Feeling oneself separated from one's own physical body as an ever stronger experience of human beings in the future. Two fundamental experiences: the riddle of the Sphinx in the Greek cultural epoch (the involvement of Lucifer in the human breathing process, his immersion in the blood; expansion of the ether body; the experience of being strangled in a nightmare or in a more subtle way in doubt, in questioning); the riddle of Mephistopheles in modern times (Ahriman's habitual existence in the nervous system, his longing for blood; contracting and drying out of the ether body; the torment of being bound through enchantment to one's own prejudices. Mephisto as one who accompanies man; a future phenomenon already appearing in childhood). Themes of riddles and enchantment in legends and fairy stories. Theology as a quest for wisdom through the nervous system. The conquering of the Sphinx through the development of the ego-nature, of Mephistopheles through imbuing the ego with knowledge of the spirit. The club feet of Oedipus; Faust as the opposite of Oedipus. Oedipus and the Sphinx, Faust and Mephisto in relation to Lucifer and Ahriman.

pages 85–99

LECTURE 5
DORNACH, 21 NOVEMBER 1914

Battles Waged by Lucifer and Ahriman in the Human Organism

Regarding the apprehending of spiritual-scientific truths. Materialistic prejudices of our time: soul-processes as an accompanying phenomenon to physical processes. The transition from a thinking based on anatomy and physiology to one founded upon spiritual science as a task of modern times. Man as a spatial being; the influence of Lucifer and Ahriman in the three dimensions of space: (1) The symmetry of the organs of perception; the arising of the sense of the ego in the experience of intersection. Man as a surface-being poised between Lucifer battling from the left and Ahriman battling from the right; the struggle between stomach (Lucifer) and liver (Ahriman). Ether body lighter on the left, darker on the right. (2) The influence of Lucifer from in front to the breast bone, the influence of Ahriman from behind to the spinal column; the free space in between. The influence of Lucifer and Ahriman: in the right and left dimension through thoughts, in the forwards-backwards dimension through feelings, in the upwards-downwards dimension through the will. (3) Lucifer's influence from above until the cervical vertebra, Ahriman's influence from below as far as the diaphragm. The forms of the Dornach Building: the principle of the 'Gugelhupf cake-tin'; the sense of 'being in-between' as a principle of modern art. The free space between the influences of Lucifer and Ahriman; Yahweh's breath.

pages 100–116

OLAF ÅSTESON

Address, New Year Festival
HANOVER, 1 JANUARY 1912

ADDRESS, INTRODUCTION TO A LECTURE FOR MEMBERS

BERLIN, 7 JANUARY 1913

Olaf Åsteson, the Awakening of the Earth Spirit

The occult significance of the time between Christmas and Three Kings Day: the change in dream life, strong connection with the spiritual world. Greatest emancipation of the soul from the cosmos at high summer. The significance of the name Olaf Åsteson; the description of experiences at the threshold of death in the Dream Song. The close relationship of the old Norwegian language to occult secrets. The sleeping (summer) and waking (winter) of the spirits connected with the Earth in the cycle of the year; Christmas as a festival of the awakening of the spirit; regarding the outward position and the spiritual state of the Sun.

pages 148–153

ADDRESS, NEW YEAR'S FESTIVAL

DORNACH, 31 DECEMBER 1914

Cosmic New Year. The Waking of the Human Soul from the Spiritual Sleep of the Age of Darkness

The influence of the cosmos upon the spirit of the Earth at Christmas and at St John's Tide. The immersion of the microcosm in the macrocosm at Christmas time: the Dream Song of Olaf Åsteson; his state of being immersed in the elements. The need to rediscover the lost wisdom of ancient times and the development of a mood of reverence and devotion towards these revelations. Words from the Book of Exodus (chapter 33, verse, 18): man as a thought of the higher hierarchies; the nature of the spiritual world's perception; the mystery of initiation in the words of Yahweh to Moses. The reason for the chaotic feelings that people have today about cosmic existence: the lack of any awareness of the various aspects of human nature. The concepts of freedom, equality, brotherhood: a true understanding arises only from knowledge of the threefold being of man. The polarities between these concepts in the example of freedom and brotherhood. The ideal of brotherhood for man's physical nature, of freedom for the soul, of equality for the spirit-world. The need for materialistic culture on the one hand and for a reawakening of spirituality on the other.

pages 154–168

Address for a Recitation of the Dream Song of Olaf Åsteson
(Undated Manuscript)

The experience of people living in rural areas of the cycle of the year. The withdrawal of the soul and its immersion in the spiritual world at Christmas time; particular dream experiences. The Dream Song of Olaf Åsteson: experience of the soul's destiny after death; partly pagan, partly Christian conceptions. The life of the Folk-soul in this poem.

pages 169–171

THE NATIONAL CHARACTER OF THE RUSSIAN PEOPLE

Address for Russians Attending the Lecture Cycle *Spiritual Beings in the Heavenly Bodies and in the Kingdoms of Nature*
HELSINKI, 11 APRIL 1912

The need for theosophy out of a sense of responsibility towards the cultural life of modern times. The revelation of the greatest wisdom through the essentially childlike personality of H.P. Blavatsky on the basis of her at once selfless and self-possessed nature. Her aspiration for the European West, for England. The suppression of Eastern occultism by the West. The revenge of the East: infiltration of the occultism appearing in the West with national, egotistic interests. Receiving of the Christ impulse into the progressive stream of humanity as a consequence of the victory of the Western world, though only at a superficial level. Taking possession of Christ's name; the continuing domination of the old warlike cultures in modern industrialism. Chivalry as the noblest flowering of materialistic culture. The superiority of Eastern peoples in their knowledge of the mysteries of existence. Chinese culture as a successor to ancient Atlantis; its future dissemination. Theosophy in Central Europe: impersonal, free from all narrow interests, hence a somewhat aloof spirituality. The task of the Russian Folk-soul: ensouling of this impersonal theosophy; uniting of theosophy with the heart.

pages 175–188

ADDRESS FOR RUSSIANS ATTENDING THE LECTURE CYCLE *THE OCCULT FOUNDATIONS OF THE BHAGAVAD GITA*

HELSINKI, 5 JUNE 1913

Becoming conscious of the theosophical impulse. The overemphasis on the dead Christ in the Russian Easter service. Christ's association with mankind through a death that is the source of life-forces. Individual soul and Folk-soul; the old Western European and the youthful East European Folk-souls; the mediating role of Central European culture. The receiving of significant impulses by primitive peoples in the example of the Christ impulse. The interweaving of Indian 'head culture' and the European soul-quality of the heart in Western culture; example of two incarnations of one individuality and its affinity first to one and then another stream (Spinoza-Fichte). The furtherance of the theosophical impulse through the life-force of Russian souls. The North American people, who are rooted in materialism, as an opposite pole to the spiritual affinities of the Russian people. What is freedom? In America it is like a product that can be used or consumed, in Western Europe, it is an ideal; while through theosophists freedom is 'ensouled'. Theosophy as a salvation for Russia.

QUESTION AND ANSWER SESSION

HELSINKI, 7 APRIL 1912

Regarding the future of Finland. The element of repetitions with respect to evolution and the cultural periods. The heroes of the *Kalevala*; the connection of the Finnish mysteries with the old European mysteries.

EDITOR'S PREFACE

The present volume contains the results of Rudolf Steiner's research on the two great Northern folk-poems, the *Kalevala* and *The Dream Song of Olaf Åsteson,* together with the three lectures directly relating to this research on the *Kalevala* which he gave in Dornach on the theme 'The World as the Result of Balancing Influences' and two addresses about the national character of the Russian people.

The lecture of 9 April 1912 entitled 'The Essential Nature of National Epics with particular reference to the *Kalevala*' was one of the two public lectures that Rudolf Steiner gave during the first lecture cycle in Helsinki, *Spiritual Beings in the Heavenly Bodies and in the Kingdoms of Nature* (GA 136). He took up this theme again in November 1914 in Dornach in the lectures 'Man's Connection with the Elemental World. Finland and the *Kalevala*'. These three lectures were directly linked to the lectures on 'The World as the Result of Balancing Influences'. Extracts relating to the *Kalevala* and Finland from a question and answer session after the lecture of 7 April 1912 (GA 136) in Helsinki have been included for the first time in the present fourth [German] edition of this volume.

The second main focus of this volume consists of the addresses and lectures that Rudolf Steiner gave about the Norwegian Dream Song of Olaf Åsteson. Among these were an introduction to a lecture for members that he gave in Berlin on 7 January 1913 (this lecture can be found in the volume *Life between Death and New Birth in Relationship to Cosmic Facts*, GA 141), while the lecture of 31 December 1914 was the fourth lecture from the cycle entitled *Art as Seen in the Light of Mystery Wisdom* (GA 275).

In the last part of the volume there are two addresses that Rudolf Steiner gave for the many Russians who attended the two Helsinki lecture cycles *Spiritual Beings in the Heavenly Bodies and in the Kingdoms of Nature* (GA 136) and *The Occult Foundations of the Bhagavad Gita* (GA 146). The second of these cycles was to have been held in St Petersburg, but the Holy Synod of the Russian Orthodox Church—as the relevant authority—refused to grant entry permits. The lecture cycle therefore took place in Finland, which—despite being part of the Russian Empire at the time—was bound by less strict laws than Russia itself. At the express indication of Rudolf Steiner, these notes were made available at the time only in exceptional circumstances.

INTRODUCTION

Although this volume of Rudolf Steiner's Complete Works centres around a particular theme as opposed to comprising a cycle of lectures given in a specific temporal context, it is nevertheless helpful to be aware of the circumstances surrounding the period in November 1914 when most of the lectures—as distinct from the addresses—in this volume were given.

After the period between the end of July and the early part of August when one declaration of war followed another, thus precipitating Europe and the world into the First World War, Rudolf Steiner increasingly centred himself in Dornach, where the construction of the first Goetheanum had become a very particular focus; and between 10 and 25 October he gave a series of lectures entitled 'The Building at Dornach'. During this time his travels—such as they were—were necessarily confined to Germany and its allies; and on 1 September he gave what was to be the first of 14 lectures in Berlin (the last was given on 6 July 1915) on the theme of 'The Destinies of Individuals and of Nations'. Other lectures were also given in, for example, Munich and Stuttgart on the spiritual origins of the war and on the tasks and destinies of the various peoples involved and the impulses of the Folk-souls associated with them. Shortly before returning to Dornach in time to give the first of the November lectures in this volume, he also gave two public lectures in Berlin on Goethe, Schiller and Fichte in the light of the conflict in which Europe had become engulfed.

Already from the first of these lectures, it is apparent that Rudolf Steiner envisaged that the Goetheanum would—and needed to—become a place where people would not only gain insight into matters pertaining to national and racial identity and conflict (and, hence, the causes of the war) but also into wider themes of individual, spiritual identity. Thus at the beginning of the third of these lectures (15 November) he indicates that humanity has reached a point where people need to emancipate themselves from the earthly influences underlying phenomena such as national and racial groups and open themselves up to influences from the world of spirit, pre-eminent amongst which in our time are those emanating from the Mystery of Golgotha; and he specifically draws attention to two things of which we need to become conscious today, namely, that we cannot find our true, essential being in the sense-perceptible world and that the human soul is not confined to the body in which it lives between birth and death but goes from life to life.

And yet, Rudolf Steiner seems to be reiterating in these and other lectures given in the early period of the war, we will not get very far with this essential exploration of our true, spiritual individuality unless we can in addition acquire a greater understanding of the elemental forces that are responsible for the configuration of our earthly nature as human beings, forces which influence us through our membership of a particular racial, national or geographical group and which, if not recognized and understood, will cause conflict and chaos rather than, as intended, work together in a spirit of colla-boration; and indeed, this endeavour to understand these elemental forces constitutes the principal aim of the present volume. One inherent problem of such an endeavour is, however, that these are 'difficult truths' that would really require a year's explanation, whereas 'I am having to explain [them] in an hour' (p. 75). And yet a reader who carefully considers the initially baffling statements and sketches in the first three of these November lectures may feel a sense of utter wonder at the way in which the elemental beings or spirits responsible for the balance of land and sea in any particular area have created conditions where the various peoples of Europe are enabled to bring their particular gifts and fulfil their destinies. (Other regions of the world are mainly referred to in terms of their contrast to the European or European-based situation.) Thus, for example, we have Finland as the ancient conscience of Europe and Russia as the nascent bearer of the Christ-imbued Spirit Self of the future, the contrast and potential conflict between the (Russian) East and the quintessentially French West, the need for the sea-girt peninsula of Italy (and also, in a different way, of Greece) and the larger land-mass of France, and the differing but complementary elemental environments of Germany and Britain, so that, 'from a spiritual point of view, no souls on Earth love one another more than those living in Central Europe and those living in the British Isles' (p. 80). And behind all of this and interwoven through these lectures is the Finnish *Kalevala*, whose ancient runes tell of the mystic origin of the human soul's threefold nature (sentient soul, intellectual or mind soul and consciousness soul), whose evolutionary drama is being engineered, whether blindly or no, by elemental beings at the behest of Folk-spirits. (It can be helpful to read the public lecture placed first in this collection, which is a model of clarity, before proceeding to the lectures of 9, 14 and 15 November.)

In the last three lectures from November 1914 a further theme is introduced and explored at some length, although the imaginative figures of the *Kalevala*—together with the geographical counterparts with which Rudolf Steiner associated them—reappear at intervals as if to indicate that this is simply another aspect of the work of elemental beings beneath or behind the veil formed by the physical world. This theme has to do with the activity of Lucifer and Ahriman and their attendant forces in our physical, etheric and astral sheaths. Rudolf Steiner emphasizes that in this context these beings are acting in a legitimate and, indeed, necessary way; for 'these powers are hostile influences in the world only where they are working outside their own territory' (p. 117). After an introductory lecture which characterizes the respective influences of Lucifer and Ahriman in the fourth and the present fifth post-Atlantean epochs through the figures of the Sphinx and Mephistopheles, we learn that the apparently solid spatial forms of our physical bodies are—except for the cuboid inner space which furnishes the physical foundation for our individual, soul-spiritual essence—the result of the collaboration between luciferic and ahrimanic powers; and that these influences also extend in differing ways to our etheric body and astral body, enabling our thinking, feeling and will to be imbued with the appropriate degree of, respectively, life and consciousness.

Whereas the *Kalevala*, together with the lectures in this volume that Rudolf Steiner gave out of the background of this great folk-poem, speaks to us of the elemental spirits who created the conditions for our earthly incarnation in modern times, the *Dream Song of Olaf Åsteson* (on which there is an extensive commentary in the notes to the text) has to do with the drama of excarnation, with the journey of the individual human soul after death. Linking the vast themes of these great folk-poems, of which Rudolf Steiner thought so highly, is that of the spiritual impulses of the Russian Folk-soul and the tasks of the Russian people. Nowhere, perhaps, did Rudolf Steiner speak so incisively and intimately about the capacities, tasks and struggles of this people, its direct contrast to the North American people (who are 'dominating the Earth for a brief period of increasing splendour', p. 196) and its distinctive and crucial relationship to the future development of anthroposophy. However, his remarks need to be viewed in the context of that remarkable lecture of 9 November 1914 where, uniquely, he explains the elemental origin and significance of the Russian soul. Not least for this reason, it seems important that the three hitherto unpublished lectures of 9, 14 and 15 November are now available in published form in English for the first time and can be viewed as an integral part of the whole volume.

Simon Blaxland-de Lange, September 2016

KALEVALA

PUBLIC LECTURE

HELSINKI, 9 APRIL 1912[1]

The Essential Nature of National Epics, with Particular Reference to the *Kalevala*

I must first apologize for the fact that I am unable to give the lecture which I am about to present to you in one of the languages that are in habitual use in this country. That I am able to speak to you now arises from a wish on the part of the friends of our Theosophical Society[2] who invited me here to give a series of lectures over the coming fortnight;[3] for they had the idea that it might be possible to insert the two public lectures that have been announced into the programme.[4] A further apology that I have to make is that, because of my ignorance of the language, my pronunciation of several of the names and other words derived from the national epic of the Finns[5] may not be altogether correct. Next Friday's lecture will lead us more directly into spiritual science itself. This evening's lecture will be mainly concerned with a closely related area which can be illuminated by spiritual science. I shall be speaking of a subject which is one of the most interesting aspects of historical research and of the thoughts that are stimulated by it.

National epics! We need only to consider some of the more well-known national epics such as those of Homer,[6] which have become the national epics of the Greeks, the Nibelungen legend of Central Europe and finally the *Kalevala* to realize at once that these national epics lead us more deeply into the inner life and aspirations of human beings than any amount of historical research; for through them ancient times of great significance become alive within us as a present experience, touching us no less than the lives and destinies of those living around us now. From a historical point of view, the times of the ancient Greeks of whom the Homeric epics speak belong to the twilight realm of uncertainty; and when we immerse ourselves in the *Iliad* or the *Odyssey* we gain a real insight into the souls of people who have become completely oblivious to ordinary historical observation. It is not surprising that those who study these national epics from the point of view of academic literature are perplexed by them. We need only to call to mind a particular aspect of the ancient Greek epics, to which a brilliant student of the *Iliad* has repeatedly referred in a very beautiful book about Homer's *Iliad* which appeared a few years ago.[7] I am speaking of Herman Grimm, the nephew of the great researcher into German language, legends and myths, Jakob Grimm.[8] When Herman Grimm allowed the characters and events of the *Iliad* to exert their influence upon him, he felt himself ever and again moved to say:[9] Oh, this fellow Homer—we do not need today to enter into the question of who Homer actually was—when he is describing something that has to do with a craft or an art appears to be an expert in that specialized field of activity. If he is describing a battle, he seems to have full knowledge of the strategic and military principles involved in conducting a war. Herman Grimm rightly points out that Napoleon,[10] who was a strict judge of such things, was an admirer of Homer's matter-of-fact descriptions of battles; and Napoleon was someone who was doubtless entitled to judge whether or not military exploits are realistically and vividly portrayed by Homer. We know from a generally human standpoint to what extent Homer was able to depict the characters in his narrative as though they stood directly before our physical eyes.

How is interest in such a national epic maintained over the years? Anyone who studies these things in an unprejudiced way will not receive the impression that the interest in the *Iliad* and the *Odyssey* that has been maintained until our own time has been artificially contrived by some kind of inbred academic institutionalism. This interest speaks for itself, it has a universally human quality. However, these national epics present us with a task; and as soon as we seek to study them we come to see that it is a quite definite and, moreover, interesting one. They want to be studied quite precisely in all their details. We feel at once that there is something about such national epics that is incomprehensible to us if we try to read them as we would a modern work of art, a modern novel for instance. From the first lines of the *Iliad* we can feel that Homer is speaking with absolute precision. What is he describing to us? He tells us right at the beginning. From other accounts not contained in the *Iliad* we know a lot about events that led up to what is described in it. Homer's sole wish is to make us aware of what he expresses so concisely in the first line[11]—the anger of Achilles. And if we now peruse the entire *Iliad* and consider it with an open mind, we have to admit that there is nothing in it that cannot be construed as following from the anger of Achilles.

There is also something else that becomes apparent right at the beginning of the *Iliad*. Homer does not simply begin with facts, nor does he begin with some kind of personal opinion. Rather does he begin with something that in the modern age might be regarded as a meaningless cliché: 'Sing to me, O Muse, of the anger of Achilles!' But the more deeply we explore this epic tale the clearer it becomes to us that we cannot understand its meaning, essential quality and significance if we do not take its initial words seriously. We then need to ask ourselves: what do they really mean?

Just consider the nature of the description, the way that the events are brought to our awareness! These words, 'O sing to me, Muse, of the anger of Achilles', have posed a question for many people, not only academic, literary specialists but also those of a truly artistic inclination such as Herman Grimm. This has been a question that went right to their hearts. How do the deeds of divine, spiritual beings (and in Homer's poetic writings these are the deeds, intentions and passions of the Olympic gods) interact in the *Iliad*, and equally in the Song of the Nibelungen or in the *Kalevala*, with the deeds, intentions and passions of human beings who—like Achilles—are in

a certain sense remote from the ordinary run of humanity and, furthermore, with the passions, intentions and deeds of human beings
who, like Odysseus or Agamemnon, are closely related to ordinary
humanity?

When we become inwardly aware of Achilles, he appears to us as
someone who, with respect to his fellow human beings, lives in
solitude. As the *Iliad* proceeds, we very soon come to feel that, in
Achilles, we have a personality who is unable to speak of his innermost concerns with all the other heroes. Homer also shows us that
Achilles has to sort out his most intimate concerns with divine,
spiritual beings who do not belong to the human kingdom, that
through the entire course of the *Iliad* he relates in solitude to the
human kingdom but is closely affiliated to supersensible, super-
earthly powers. And the strange thing is that if we summon forth all
the feeling and thinking as they have been refined in the development of human culture and direct our attention towards Achilles, he
seems to us to be so egotistic, so personal! A being with divine-
spiritual impulses dwelling in his soul is acting entirely out of personal considerations. For a long time this legendary Trojan War,
which was so important for the Greeks, continued to be waged—
thus bringing about the particular episodes described in the *Iliad*—
because Achilles was settling personal accounts with Agamemnon.
And we see constantly that super-earthly powers become involved.
We see Zeus, Apollo and Athene sharing out impulses and, as it
were, putting human beings in their place.

Before I came to have the task of approaching these matters from
the standpoint of spiritual science, I always found it strange how a
person of great brilliance with whom I often had the good fortune to
discuss these things on a personal level, namely Herman Grimm,
dealt with this sort of issue. He had a lot to say not merely in his
writings but frequently—and with far more precision—in personal
conversations. He said that if we take into account only the influence
of historical powers and impulses on human evolution, we will not be
able to make sense of what is living and working in the great national
epics. Hence for Herman Grimm, a truly erudite student of the *Iliad*

and of folk epics of every kind, there was something that goes beyond the ordinary faculties of human consciousness, beyond reason, understanding and sense observation, something that transcends ordinary feeling and becomes a real power, a power that is creative like other historical impulses. Herman Grimm spoke of a true creative imagination pervading human evolution, speaking of it as one speaks of a being, of a reality, of something that has held sway over human beings and which, in the earliest stages of the times that we are able to observe, when the individual folk-groups were coming into being, had more to say to them than their ordinary human soul-forces. Herman Grimm always spoke of this creative imagination in terms of the irradiating light of a world that goes beyond ordinary human soul-forces; and he therefore regarded it as having attained a co-creative role in the process of human evolution.

But the strange thing is that, when we focus upon this battlefield of the *Iliad,* this evocation of the anger of Achilles with all the interplay of divine-spiritual, supersensible powers, we will not be satisfied with the kind of study that Herman Grimm has provided of it; and in his book on the *Iliad* we find many references to a sense of resignation, which show us that the ordinary standpoint that an academic literary historian has to adopt today cannot give an adequate account of these phenomena. What does Herman Grimm have to say about the *Iliad* or about the Nibelungen legend? His conclusion is that the historical ruling dynasties were preceded by other similar dynasties. This is Herman Grimm's actual, even literal view. He thinks that Zeus, together with his whole retinue, represents a kind of ruling dynasty which preceded the ruling dynasty to which Agamemnon belonged. Thus his view of human history is that it has a certain uniformity, and that the gods or heroes portrayed in the *Iliad* or the Nibelungen legend are human beings from a bygone age whom people of a later time dared to portray only by clothing their deeds and character in the garb of superhuman myths. There is much that cannot be accounted for if one begins with such a supposition, especially the particular way in which the gods intervene in Homer's epic story. I beg you to consider how Thetis, the mother of Achilles,

Athene and other gods intervene in the events of Troy. They intervene by taking on the form of mortal human beings, inspiring them
and inciting them to accomplish their deeds. Hence they do not
appear in their own right but instead they pervade living human
beings. Living human beings feature not merely as their representatives but as sheaths pervaded by invisible powers which are
unable to appear on the battlefield in their own form or as they really
are. It would certainly be a strange thing to suggest that ordinary
people from long ago should have been portrayed as needing to
adopt representatives from the race of mortals as their sheaths. This is
only one of the many indications that can prove to us all that we
cannot make sense of the ancient national epics in this way.

It is no easier if we consider the characters in the Song of the
Nibelungen—for example, Siegfried from Xanten in the lower
Rhine, who went to the court of Burgundy in Worms to court
Kriemhilde, the sister of Gunther, and then courts Brunnhilde for
Gunther with his special powers. How strangely are figures such as
Brunnhilde from Issland and also Siegfried described to us! Siegfried
is described as someone who has overcome the so-called Nibelungen
race and has acquired or conquered the treasure of the Nibelungen.
Through what he has acquired as a result of his victory over the
Nibelungen, he receives quite special powers which come to
expression in the epic where it is said that he can make himself
invisible and is in a certain sense invulnerable. Furthermore, he has
powers that an ordinary person like Gunther does not possess; for he
cannot win Brunnhilde, who cannot be conquered by an ordinary
mortal. Siegfried conquers Brunnhilde through the special powers
that he has as the possessor of the treasure of the Nibelungen; and
through his capacity to conceal the powers that he has developed he
is able to lead Brunnhilde to Gunther, his brother-in-law. Then we
find that Kriemhilde and Brunnhilde, whom we experience at the
same time at the Burgundian court, are two very different characters,
who manifest influences that cannot be explained in terms of powers
residing in the human soul. Because of these influences they come in
conflict; and this leads to Brunnhilde's being able to induce the

faithful servant Hagen to kill Siegfried. This is indicative of a feature that is so characteristic of Central European legends. Siegfried has higher, superhuman powers. He has these superhuman powers because he possesses the treasure of the Nibelungen. Ultimately, they do not make him into a figure who is necessarily victorious but into one who stands tragically before us. The powers that Siegfried has through the treasure of the Nibelungen at the same time represent the undoing of human beings. Everything becomes even stranger if we also consider the related Nordic legend of Sigurd, the dragon slayer, though it is illuminating. Sigurd, who is none other than Siegfried, immediately appears to us as the conqueror of the dragon and has therefore acquired the Nibelungen treasure from an old race of dwarves; while Brunnhilde appears to us as a figure of superhuman nature, as a Valkyrie.

Thus we see that in Europe there are two ways of portraying these things. One way is where everything is connected to the divine, supersensible domain, where it becomes apparent to us that Brunnhilde belongs directly to the supersensible world, and the other way is where the legend is humanized. Nevertheless even here we can recognize that the divine world reverberates through everywhere.

Now let us turn our attention from these legends, from these national epics, to a realm of which I am only qualified to speak as someone who is able to view these phenomena from outside, that is, as someone who can recognize them without speaking the relevant language. I ask you to allow for the fact that, as a Western European studying the *Kalevala*, I am only able to speak as someone who is aware of the spiritual content and its great, mighty figures, and that the more subtle details that the epic doubtless contains, which only emerge if one has really mastered the language in which it was written, will inevitably elude me. But even a study of this nature reveals a threefold quality in the three … well, one is really in a quandary trying to find a name for them; one cannot call them gods, or heroes, so we shall simply say the three beings, Väinämöinen, Ilmarinen and Lemminkäinen. These figures speak a strange language, if we compare their characters with one another—a language from which we can clearly recognize that what is being said to us goes far beyond what can be achieved with ordinary human soul-forces. If we consider them purely outwardly, these three figures grow into monstrous proportions. But what is so strange is that, even though they grow to so vast a degree, every single characteristic appears graphically before us, so that we never have the feeling that these immense proportions have something grotesque or paradoxical about them but have the sense that what needs to be said must necessarily manifest itself on a superhuman scale and with super-human significance. And then the content itself is so full of riddles. There is something about it that spurs us on to think about the very essence of man's being but nevertheless reaches beyond what our ordinary soul-forces are able to grasp. Ilmarinen, who is often called the blacksmith and who is first and foremost an artist, at Väinä-möinen's instigation forges the Sampo for a foreign land, a region where those people who may be called the older brothers of humanity live, people who are at any rate more primitive than the Finns. And we see this remarkable circumstance that a lot takes place far from the scene where the main events are enacted, and that as time passes Väinämöinen and Ilmarinen are after a certain period obliged to retrieve the Sampo which was through them placed in a foreign land. Anyone who allows this strange language of the spirit that evokes this forging of the Sampo, its state of separation and recovery, to work upon him—and as I have said, I ask you to bear in mind that I am speaking as a foreigner and can therefore only speak of the impression that I receive—immediately has a sense that the most essential and most significant aspect of this epic poem is the forging, state of separation and regaining of the Sampo.

I find the conclusion of the *Kalevala* particularly moving. I have heard that there are those who believe that this conclusion is perhaps a later addition. For my feeling, this ending involving Marjatta and her son,[12] where one sees the interweaving of a very distinctive form of Christianity—and I say this quite explicitly—belongs very much to the whole. Because of this conclusion, the *Kalevala* acquires a quite particular nuance, a quality that enables us fully to penetrate what it is all about. I would even say that, for my feeling, the conclusion of the *Kalevala* has no parallel as a delicate and miraculously impersonal portrayal of Christianity. The Christian principle is freed from all geographical limitations. Marjatta's approach to Herod, whom we encounter in the *Kalevala* as Rotus, is formulated in so impersonal a way that it is barely reminiscent of the places and personalities in Palestine. Indeed, we are, I would say, not reminded even to the slightest degree of the historical Christ Jesus. At the end of the *Kalevala* we find a delicate reference to the immersion of the noblest cultural pearl of humanity into Finnish culture as an intimate concern of the human heart. With this is linked the tragic episode that can affect us so deeply, namely that at the moment when Christianity makes its mark—when Marjatta's son is baptized—Väinämöinen takes leave of his people in order to go to an unspecified destination, bequeathing to them only the substance and the power of what he has, through his art as a singer, been able to tell them about the events in far-off times that form part of their history. I find this withdrawal of Väinämöinen when the son of Marjatta appears so significant because we can discern in it the living interplay of what was living in the depths of the Finnish people and the Finnish Folk-soul—and had done so since ancient times—in the moment when Christianity found entry into Finland. Everything that lived in people's souls through the way that this ancient wisdom related to Christianity can be felt with a wonderful intimacy. I am saying this as something of whose objectivity I am thoroughly conscious; I am not saying it to please or flatter anyone. In this national epic we Western Europeans have one of the most wonderful examples of how the members of a folk stand bodily before us with their entire soul in the immediate present, with the result that the acquaintance that we have in Western Europe with the Finnish soul through the *Kalevala* can enable us to become thoroughly familiar with it.

Why have I said all this to you? My object has been to characterize how something speaks in national epics that cannot be explained by the ordinary powers of the human soul, even if one regards the imagination as a real power of cognition. And even though to many people what is being said sounds purely hypothetical, I may now be allowed to indicate what spiritual science has to say about the nature of these national epics. I am of course aware that what I have to say concerns matters with which very few people today are able to agree. Many will regard what I am saying as some sort of dreamy fantasy; others, however, will accept it alongside a variety of hypotheses that are proposed regarding the evolution of mankind. Nevertheless, for someone who enters into spiritual science in the way that I intend to explore it in my next lecture, what I am saying is no mere hypothesis but the result of real research which can be placed alongside the results of other scientific research. The things that I need to speak about sound strange because present-day science, which believes that it stands firmly on the ground of real facts, of what is true and uniquely attainable, limits itself to what our outward senses perceive, to what an intellect that is bound to the senses and the brain is able to discover. Hence it is generally considered unscientific today if one speaks about a method of research that makes use of other soul-forces, which have the capacity of beholding the supersensible world and the interweaving of this world in the sense-perceptible domain. The research method of spiritual science leads one not merely to the abstract fantasy that leads Herman Grimm to say what he does about national epics but, rather, to something that goes far beyond fantasy and portrays a completely different state of soul or con-sciousness than is possible for man to have in the present period of his evolution. Hence we are led back by spiritual science to a former time in human evolution in a completely different way than occurs in ordinary science.

Ordinary science is accustomed today to look back at the evolu-tion of humanity in such a way that what we now call human beings have gradually developed from lower, animal-like creatures. Spiritual science does seek to combat this modern research but fully acknowledges the great and mighty achievements of this nineteenth-century science; it recognizes the significance of the idea that animal forms have undergone a transformation from the least perfect to a perfected form and that the outward human form has an affinity to the most perfect animal form. But spiritual science cannot remain content with a view of human evolution and of the evolution of organisms in general such that what has taken place in the course of earthly evolution in the organic world until the appearance of man could be encompassed within a survey of a purely outward, sense-perceptible nature. For spiritual science, man today has a close affinity to the animal world. In the world that surrounds us we behold the diversity of animal forms; and we see spread out over the Earth a human race which has a certain degree of uniformity. In spiritual science we also have an unprejudiced view of how as regards outward forms everything is indicative of man's relationship to other organisms; but if we trace the evolution of mankind backwards we cannot go back to some dim, distant past when the stream of humanity was inserted directly into animal development. What we actually find when we reach back from the present into the past is that we are never directly able to derive the present human form from any animal form that we know from the present.

If we reach back into human evolution, we initially find in ever more primitive forms the same soul-forces—the powers of understanding, feeling and will—that we also have in our present time. We then arrive at far-off, ancient times of which old documents can tell us very little. Even when we go back as far as the Egyptians or the peoples of the near East, we find ourselves amidst an ancient humanity which, in a somewhat primitive but also larger-than-life form, had the same powers of feeling, thinking and will that have—to be sure—only attained their present form in recent times but which we are able to regard as the most important impulses of humanity and of human history, in so far as we are able to take man's present soul-configuration into account in our backward survey of human history. Nowhere do we find it possible to establish a relationship even on the part of the earliest human races with present-day animal forms. What spiritual science is obliged to assert in this way is acknowledged by the more thoughtful scientists today. But as we reach back into the past and observe how the human soul has changed, if we compare how people think today (whether scientifically or otherwise), how they use their intelligence and powers of feeling, with how people thought in the past (which we can establish with a certain precision), we find that this faculty first appeared amongst mankind at a particular time, namely in the sixth or seventh century before Christ. The entire configuration of present-day feeling and thinking cannot be traced further back than those times when the first Greek philosophers were said to have lived.[13]

If we go further back and consider what we find in an unprejudiced way without referring to spiritual science, we discover that not only is there no trace of modern scientific thinking but the human soul is constituted in an entirely different way—much less personal but also with attributes of a far more instinctive nature. It would not be true to say that the people of that time acted out of the same instincts as animals do today, but the guidance through reason and intellectual capacities that is characteristic of modern times did not then exist. Instead people had a certain immediate, instinctive certainty. They acted out of direct, elemental impulses, which they did not control through a brain-bound intellect. What we find is that the soul-forces which have in our time been carefully separated into intellectual powers, on the one hand, and imaginative faculties that we make every effort to distinguish from the intellectual powers that gave rise to science, on the other, still exist as a coherent whole. Imagination, intellect and reasoning power were all mixed up with one another in those ancient times. The further we go back, the more we find that the quality that lived then in people's souls as an inseparable combination of imaginative and intellectual faculties was one that we would no longer associate with the soul-faculty that we call imagination today.

When we now speak of the imagination, we are well aware that we are speaking of a soul-faculty which, in the way that it comes to expression, is not recognized as a means of attaining to reality. In this regard people today are very diligent, they take great care not to mix up what they derive from their imagination with what the logic of reason imparts to them. When we consider the expressions of the human mind in those prehistoric times before imagination and intellect became separate from one another, we are aware of a primordial, elemental and instinctive power that resided in people's souls. We can find in it certain characteristics of the modern imaginative faculty, but what the quality of imagination endowed the human soul with at that time had something to do with a reality. Imagination was not mere fantasy, it was—if I may be so bold as to use the appropriate word—a clairvoyant power, it was a particular soul-faculty or endowment that enabled people to see things and facts which in the modern epoch of evolution, when intellect and reason need to be especially developed, are hidden from them. Those forces that were not mere fantasy but powers of a clairvoyant nature penetrated deeply into hidden forces and forms of existence lying behind the sense-perceptible world. This is the conclusion to which an unprejudiced assessment must lead, that if we reach back into the history of human evolution we must say: we must indeed take the words 'evolution' and 'development' seriously.

That mankind has in our present age, in recent centuries and millennia, arrived at what may be described as its present advanced stage of intellectual development is the result of an evolutionary process. These soul-forces have evolved from others. And whereas our present soul-forces are limited to what can be perceived in the outer world of the senses, there was a primordial humanity which, while not having the benefit of modern science and intellectual development, had an insight residing in the depths of all individual peoples into the very foundations of existence, into a supersensible realm that lies behind the sense-perceptible domain. Clairvoyant powers formerly belonged to the human souls associated with all folk-groups; and our present intellectual faculties and reasoning powers, together with our modern way of thinking and feeling, have been formed from these clairvoyant powers. The soul-forces that we may in a certain sense refer to as clairvoyant powers were such that a person would feel: it is not I who is thinking and feeling in me. Human individuals felt themselves to be dedicated through their entire bodily nature and soul to higher, supersensible powers working and living within them.

Thus human beings felt themselves to be like vessels through which supersensible powers spoke. If one considers this, one will also understand the significance of human evolution. Human beings would have remained dependent beings who would have been able to feel themselves merely as vessels, as the sheaths of higher powers and beings, if they had not advanced to the point of using their own powers of reason and understanding. Man has become independent through the use of these powers, but he has also at the same time been cut off for a period of his evolution from the spiritual world, from the supersensible foundations of existence.

In the future all this will change. The further back we go, so much the more deeply do clairvoyant powers enable the human soul to see into the foundations of existence whence those forces emerged which exerted a creative influence upon man in prehistoric times, to behold a time when all earthly conditions were completely different from those of today, when the forms of living beings were far more mobile, much more subject to a certain kind of metamorphosis. We have to go back a long way from what is called the present period of human culture, tracing human evolution alongside the evolution of animals. Indeed, the separation of the animal from the human lies much further in the past than is generally supposed today. Animal forms then became rigid and less mobile, whereas the human form was still thoroughly soft and flexible and could be formed and moulded by what was being inwardly experienced within the soul. We have by now reached back to a time in human development to which our modern consciousness has no access; but there was another consciousness available at that time, a consciousness associated with the clairvoyant powers that have been characterized. Such a consciousness, which was able to behold the past and saw human evolution as deriving from the past in complete separation from all animal life, also saw how human forces were in living interplay with the instreaming influence of the supersensible powers. It saw what still lived as a faint echo in the times when, for example, the epics of Homer arose and what had existed to a much greater degree in even earlier times than this.

If we were to go back beyond Homer, we would find that people had a clairvoyant consciousness which had a recollection of pre-historical events in human development and was able to relate a memory of what had happened in this early time. By Homer's time the situation was that, although there was an awareness that the old clairvoyant consciousness was waning, people continued to feel its presence. This was a time when they did not speak out of themselves as egotistical beings but when gods, supersensible spiritual powers, expressed themselves through them. Thus we must take it seriously when Homer does not speak out of himself but says: 'Sing to me, O Muse, of the anger of Achilles!' Sing in me, higher being, a being who speaks through me, who takes possession of me when I sing and speak. This first line of the *Iliad* is a reality. We are not referred to ancient ruling dynasties similar in nature to our present-day humanity; rather does Homer indicate to us that in former times there were other people in whom the supersensible realm was living. Achilles is clearly a figure from the time of the transition from the old clairvoyance to the modern form of perception, which we find in Agamemnon, Nestor and Odysseus but is then led on to a higher way of seeing things. We can only understand Achilles if we know that Homer wants to present him as belonging to an ancient humanity, as someone who lived at a time between the period when human beings still directly reached up to the ancient gods and the present age of humanity, which begins approximately with Aga-memnon.

We are in a similar way linked to a prehistorical period in the Central European Nibelungen legend. The whole way that this epic is recounted shows us this. We are dealing there with people of our present time in a certain sense, but they have nevertheless still retained something from the time when the old clairvoyance pre-vailed. All the qualities possessed by Siegfried—that he can make himself invisible, that he has powers enabling him to overcome Brunnhilde, who could not be overcome by an ordinary mortal, and also other things that are said about him—show us that he is someone who has, as though in his inner memory, carried over into present-day humanity the achievements of the ancient soul-forces that were linked with clairvoyance and a deep affinity with nature. On which threshold does Siegfried stand? This is indicated to us by Brunnhilde's relationship to Kriemhilde, Siegfried's wife. It is not possible here to enter into the significance of these two figures in greater detail. However, we will be able to make sense of all these legends if we view the characters that are portrayed as pictorial representations of inner clairvoyant, or recollected clairvoyant, circumstances. Thus in Siegfried's relationship to Kriemhilde we see his relationship to the soul-forces working within himself. His soul is in a sense one of transition, in that with the Nibelungen treasure, that is, with the clairvoyant secrets of ancient times, Siegfried is carrying over into the modern age something that at the same time makes him unfit for the present. Thus the people of olden times were able to live with this hoard of the Nibelungen, that is, with the old clairvoyant powers. Earthly conditions have changed since then. As a result, Siegfried, who bears in his soul an echo of these olden times, no longer fits into the present and thereby becomes a tragic figure. How can the present relate to what is still a vital force in Siegfried? For him something of the old clairvoyant powers remains alive, for when he is overcome Kriemhilde remains behind. The Nibelungen hoard is brought to her and she can use it. We learn that this treasure is subsequently taken from her by Hagen. We can see that Brunnhilde too, in a certain sense, is capable of working with the old clairvoyant powers. In this respect she is at odds with those people who do fit into that age: Gunther and his brothers but especially Gunther, for whom Brunnhilde has no time whatever.

Why is this? We know from the legend that Brunnhilde is a kind of Valkyrie figure—an image of something in the human soul with which people in olden times were still able to unite through clairvoyant powers but which has withdrawn from them, become unconscious and is accessible to those living in the present age of the intellect only after death. This is why there is a union with the Valkyries at the moment of death. The Valkyrie is the personification of the living soul-forces residing within people today to which the old clairvoyant consciousness had access but which can be experienced by human beings in our time only once they have passed through the gate of death. Only then are they united with this soul-force represented by Brunnhilde. Because Kriemhilde still knows something of the old clairvoyant times and the powers that the soul receives through the ancient clairvoyance, she becomes a figure whose anger is described in a similar way to the anger of Achilles in the *Iliad*. This is clearly indicated to us in that those people who were still endowed with clairvoyant powers in ancient times did not accept the guidance of their intellectual faculties but acted directly out of their most intense, elemental impulses. That is the source of the strikingly egotistical, personal element that is apparent in both Kriemhilde and Achilles.

This aspect of the study of national epics becomes especially interesting if we add the *Kalevala* to those already mentioned. Although because of the shortage of time today it is possible to give only some indications of this, we shall be able to show that the only reason that spiritual science is able in our present time to shed light on the ancient clairvoyant conditions of mankind is that it is again possible today—albeit in a more elevated way, imbued with an intellectual rather than a dreamlike consciousness—to call forth clairvoyant states of consciousness through spiritual schooling. People in our time are gradually preparing for a time when, from the depths of the human soul, hidden forces—guided now by reason instead of being bereft of its control—will blossom forth and lead them again into the supersensible domain. In this way we will again come to know the realms whence the ancient national epics speak to us out of the dim consciousness of olden times. Hence we can say that there is a recognition that it is possible to experience a revelation of the world not merely through the outward senses but through a supersensible essence that underlies the physical human body.

There are methods—which are to be discussed in the next lecture—whereby a human individual is able to make the spiritual-supersensible, inner aspect of his being, whose existence is so often denied today, independent of the sense-perceptible, outward aspect of his body, so that he does not live in a state of unconsciousness as in sleep (when he becomes independent of his body) but perceives the spiritual world around him. In this way modern clairvoyance shows him that it is possible to live as a cognitive being in a higher, supersensible body for which the ordinary sense-perceptible body serves as a vessel. In spiritual science this higher body is called the etheric or ether body. This ether body resides in our body of senses. If we inwardly separate it from the physical, sense-perceptible body, we enter a state of consciousness through which we become aware of supersensible facts and of two in particular. Firstly we begin to realize at the initial stage of this clairvoyant state that we are no longer seeing by means of our physical body, we are no longer hearing by means of it and, moreover, we are no longer thinking by means of the brain that is bound to the physical body. In this situation we initially know nothing about the outer world. (I am speaking of things that will be properly explained only in the next lecture.) But for this very reason the first stage of clairvoyance leads us all the more to a perception of our own ether body. We see a supersensible bodily aspect of human nature that underlies it; and the only way of describing this is that it is something that works and creates like a kind of inner architect or master builder that permeates our physical body with life. And then we become aware of the following.

We come to realize that what we perceive within ourselves here, what we perceive as the truly living aspect of our ether body, is confined and modified by our physical body, that it is clothed in accordance with the physical aspect. To the extent that the ether body disrobes eyes and ears and also the physical brain, we belong in a sense to the earthly element. In this way we come to see that our etheric body becomes a quite particular, individual, egotistical human being who is incorporated into the sheath of the physical body concerned. On the other hand, however, we perceive how our etheric body leads us again into those regions where we stand impersonally face to face with a higher, supersensible dimension, something that is not us but which is fully present within us and works through us as a spiritual, supersensible power. Our spiritual-scientific observation then perceives our inner life of soul as divided into three parts, which are as it were enclosed within, and fully occupy, three outward bodily sheaths. We conduct our soul-life in such a way that we experience within it what our eyes see, what our ears hear, what our senses are able to apprehend and what our mind can grasp. We live with our soul in our physical body. Inasmuch as our soul lives in the physical body, our term for it in spiritual science is the consciousness soul, because only through becoming fully immersed in the physical body in the course of human evolution has it become possible for man to advance to ego consciousness. Then the modern seer also comes to know the life of the soul in what we have called the ether body. The soul indwells the ether body in such a way that its forces are its own, but we cannot say that they are our own personal forces. They are universally human forces, through which we are much closer to all the hidden mysteries of nature. In so far as the soul perceives these forces in an outward sheath and specifically in the ether body, we speak of the intellectual or mind soul as a second soul-member. So just as we find the consciousness soul in the sheath of the physical body, we have the intellectual or mind soul enclosed in the etheric body. And then we have an even more refined body, through which we reach up into the supersensible world. Everything that we inwardly experience as our intimate secrets, as what is hidden today from consciousness and was experienced at the time of the old clairvoyance as the creative forces in the evolutionary process emerging from the events of the dim and distant past, all this we ascribe to the sentient soul, which is enclosed in the most refined human body, in what—if you will excuse the technical term—we call the astral body. It is that part of man's being that forms a connection between the outer earthly environment and what lives as an inspirational element in his inner being. This latter is something that he cannot perceive through his outer senses, and neither can he perceive it when he looks into his own ether body; rather does he perceive it when he becomes independent of himself, independent of his ether body, and is united with the forces of his origin.

Thus we have the sentient soul in the astral body, the intellectual or mind soul in the etheric body and the consciousness soul in the physical body. In the times of the old clairvoyance these things were more or less instinctively familiar to people, for they had insight into themselves and perceived this threefold nature of the soul. It is not that they analysed the soul intellectually, but their clairvoyant consciousness enabled them to perceive this threefold nature of the human soul: the sentient soul in the astral body, the intellectual or mind soul in the etheric body and the consciousness soul in the physical body. As they looked back they saw how the outer aspect of man's being, his outward form—which had long been hardened into animal forms—evolved out of what the threefold soul-forces are the present-day result. They experienced that the sentient soul had its origin in supersensible creative powers that endowed man with the astral body, that body that he does not only possess between birth and death—as is the case with his etheric and physical bodies—but that he takes it with him when he passes through the portal of death and which he already had before he was born. Thus the seers of olden times saw the sentient soul as united with the astral body; and they viewed the inspirational power working upon man from out of the spiritual world and creating his astral body as a creative power that fashions him out of the universal whole.

They saw a second creative power in what has resulted in the intellectual or mind soul and which has fashioned the etheric body in such a way that it transforms all outward substances, all outward matter, so that they permeate the physical human form in a human rather than in an animal way. The old clairvoyants viewed the creative spirit for the etheric body—whose fruits appear in our intellectual soul—as a superhuman cosmic power that exerts an influence upon man comparable to that of magnetism upon physical matter. They looked up into the spiritual worlds and saw a divine-spiritual power which constructs, forges man's etheric body, so that this etheric body becomes the master builder that can transform outer matter, brings it into a state of confusion, pulverizes and grinds it to pieces, so that what otherwise exists as matter disintegrates within man, enabling him to acquire his human faculties. The ancient clairvoyants saw how this creative power transforms all material substance in an artistic way, so that it could become human matter.

Then they beheld the third creative power, the consciousness soul, which actually makes man egotistical and represents the transformation of the physical body; and they ascribed those forces that hold sway in this physical body solely to the hereditary line, to what derives from father and mother, grandfather and great-grandfather—in short, to the result of human love, human powers of reproduction. They saw in this the third creative power, the power of love working from generation to generation.

The ancient seers looked up to three powers. They looked up to a creative being who ultimately calls forth our sentient soul by fashioning the astral body, which can be inspired by supersensible powers because it is the body that man had before he became a physical being through conception, the body that he will have when he has crossed the threshold of death. This structure of forces or, rather, heavenly organism within man which endures while the ether body and physical body pass away was for the ancient clairvoyants at the same time—and they knew this from their direct experience—what has been able to bring culture of whatever kind into human life. Hence in the bringer of the astral body they saw that power that is the bearer of the divine world, which itself consists only of duration, the power through which the eternal aspect of the world sings and weaves its sounds. And the ancient clairvoyants from whom—I can clearly state—the figures in the *Kalevala* have arisen have presented a living, graphic expression of the creative power which we now find in the sentient soul, where the divine world indwells human nature as an inspirational force, in Väinämöinen. Väinämöinen is the creator of that part of human nature which endures beyond birth and death and brings the heavenly into the earthly world.

Let us now consider the second figure in the *Kalevala:* Ilmarinen. If we go back to the old clairvoyant consciousness, we find that Ilmarinen creates everything that is a reflection of the etheric body in its living form out of the forces of the Earth and out of what belongs not to the sense-perceptible Earth but to its deeper forces. We see him as the one who brings about the transformation, the pulverization of all matter. We see him as the forger of the human form. And in the Sampo we see the human ether body that Ilmarinen has forged out of the supersensible world, so that sense-perceptible matter can be pulverized and then carried forward from generation to generation in order that, amidst the forces emanating from the third divine supersensible being, the human consciousness soul may continue to function in the physical human body from generation to generation through the powers of love. We see this third divinely supersensible power in Lemminkäinen. Thus we can discern deep mysteries of mankind's origins in the forging of the Sampo, deep mysteries welling forth from the old clairvoyant consciousness and finding expression in the *Kalevala*; and with this we are gazing into the prehistory of mankind, a time of which we can say: this was not a time when it would have been possible to analyse natural phenomena with our intellect. Everything was primitive, but in this primitive consciousness there lived a clear perception of what lies behind the sense-perceptible world.

Now when these human bodies were forged, and specifically when man's etheric body, the Sampo, was forged, there was a period when he did not have the use of the forces that had been prepared for him by the supersensible powers. Once the ether body had been forged, it first had to become inwardly attuned to its circumstances, just as a machine that we are making must not only be completed but must then be properly run in before it is put to use. In the course of human evolution—and this is apparent in evolution of any kind—there have always had to be intermediary stages between the creation of the respective members of man's being and their use. Thus man had forged his etheric body long ago in a distant past. Then there was an episode when this ether body was sent down to human nature. Only later did it shine forth as the intellectual soul. Man learnt to use its powers as outer forces of nature, he brought forth the Sampo which had hitherto remained hidden from his own nature. We see this mystery of human evolution portrayed in a wonderful way in the forging of the Sampo, in its hidden state, its period of inactivity and then its rediscovery. We see how the Sampo is first implanted into human nature and then made available for creative cultural energies, which are initially manifested as the primitive cultural forces described in the second part of the *Kalevala*.

Thus everything in this great national epic acquires a profound significance if we see it as containing clairvoyant descriptions of ancient events in human evolution, of the formative process of human nature out of its various members. I can assure you that I became familiar with the *Kalevala* long, long after these facts regarding the evolution of human nature had become clear to me; and it was a wonderful surprise for me to find in this epic what I was able to describe more or less theoretically in my book *Theosophy*,[14] which was written at a time when I did not know a single line of the *Kalevala*. Thus we see how secrets are unveiled to humanity through Väinämöinen, the creator of supersensible inspirations—namely, the story of the forging of the etheric body. But another mystery lies hidden here. I must emphasize that I do not know a word of Finnish, and I can only speak out of spiritual science. The only way that I would be able to make sense of the word Sampo is to make the following attempt to understand its background. We see how in animals the etheric body becomes the master builder for the most diverse forms, from the least perfect to the most perfect. In the human ether body something was forged that combines all these animal forms into a single entity, though with the qualification that the ether body—that is, the Sampo—is forged throughout the Earth in accordance with climatic and other circumstances, so that it has within its forces the particular folk characteristics and distinctive qualities that enable it to form one folk-group in one way and another in a different way. For each people the Sampo is what constitutes the particular form of the ether body that breathes life into any particular ethnic group, so that the members of this ethnic group have a similar appearance with respect to what irradiates their living, physical form. To the extent that a similar outward appearance in the human form is the work of the etheric body, the forces of the ether body reside in the Sampo. Hence in the Sampo we have the symbol of the cohesion of the Finnish people; we have what, in the depths of human nature, causes the Finnish people to have the particular form that they do.

However, the same is true of every national epic. National epics can arise only where the culture is still encompassed within the forces of the Sampo, of the etheric body. To the extent that the culture is dependent on the forces of the Sampo, so does the people bear its particular stamp. Hence the etheric body is the bearer of the characteristics of the nation or etheric entity within the entire culture. When could the stream of the cultural development of a nation or ethnic group be interrupted? This could happen where something entered into the cultural development of humanity that is intended not for one person, racial group or people but for the whole of mankind, something that emerges from such depths of human nature and is incorporated into cultural development that it applies to all people irrespective of nationality, race or whatever. This is what occurred when human beings were addressed by those powers which spoke not to one people but to the whole of mankind and which— albeit impersonally in the sense of popular culture—are hinted at so delicately and tenderly at the end of the *Kalevala*, when Christ is born of Marjatta. When He is baptized, Väinämöinen leaves the country; for something has happened that brings the particular national element together with the universally human. Here at this point, where one of the greatest, most significant and succinct of national epics ends with the entirely impersonal and—if you will excuse the paradoxical word—non-Palestinian description of the Christ impulse, the *Kalevala* attains its fullest significance. We are in a quite particular way led to what can be experienced when the beneficial influence and blissful happiness of the Sampo are livingly experienced as continuing to work through all human evolution in conjunction with the Christian idea, with the Christian impulse. This is what is so infinitely tender about the end of the *Kalevala*. It is also what makes it so clear to us that the events preceding this conclusion in the *Kalevala* belong to the pre-Christian era.

But just as it is true that everything of a universally human nature will continue to exist only if it preserves the individual element, so likewise will individual national cultures, which derive their essential nature from former clairvoyant states of the peoples concerned, live on on a universally human level. Similarly, the Christian element that shines through at the end of the *Kalevala* will find its perpetual place and maintain its particular legacy through the eternal influence of what is represented by the inspirations of Väinämöinen. For Väinämöinen stands for something that belongs to that part of man's being that transcends birth and death, something that accompanies him through every stage of his evolution. Thus epics such as the *Kalevala* represent something that is eternal and can be imbued with a Christian conception, but which will begin to show itself as having an individual impulse, consistently demonstrating that, just as white sunlight splits up into many colours, what is universally human will continue to live in the many folk cultures. And because this universally human quality in the national epics penetrates the individual element, shining into and addressing each person, the individualities of the peoples live so strongly in the essential nature of their national epics. Hence the people of ancient times stand so full of life before our eyes; for in their clairvoyance they have beheld the essence of their own folk as it is described to us in all national epics, where—as in the *Kalevala*—we can have a wonderful opportunity of learning how humanity in all its intimate details is surrounded by the circumstances pertaining to Finnish culture and where this is portrayed in its innermost depths in such a way that it can be directly compared with what modern spiritual science is able to reveal concerning the mysteries of mankind.

In this way, ladies and gentlemen, such national epics also by their very nature represent a living protest against any kind of materialism, against anything derived from purely outward forces, states or beings of a material nature. National epics, and especially the *Kalevala*, tell of how man has his origin in the soul-spiritual domain. Hence any renewal or re-enlivening of ancient national epics can contribute immeasurably to a truly spiritual culture. For just as spiritual science seeks in our time to bring about a renewal of human consciousness, bearing in mind that humanity has its source not in matter but in the spirit, so does a precise study of an epic such as the *Kalevala* show us that the best that man has, and also the best that he is, originates from the realm of soul and spirit. In this sense I found it interesting that one of the runes concerning the kantele directly protests against a materialistic interpretation of the events in the *Kalevala*. That harplike instrument with which the ancient singers of olden times accompanied their singing is portrayed in a picture as if it were formed from materials taken from the physical world. However, the old runes protested against this (one might say that they protested from a spiritual-scientific standpoint), taking issue with the idea that the string instrument for Väinämöinen was constructed from products of nature which can be beheld by the senses. In truth, says the old rune, the instrument on which people played the melodies that came to them directly from the spiritual world has its origin in the world of soul and spirit. In this sense the old rune should be interpreted in a spiritual-scientific sense as a living protest against the ideas of which people with a materialistic interpretation are so capable, as an indication that what man possesses as regards his essential nature and which is symbolically expressed through an instrument such as the one ascribed to Väinämöinen, that such an instrument originates in the spirit, as does man's being in its entirety. This old folk rune,[15] in which I can discern the fundamental mood or nuance of what I have sought to present in this lecture regarding the essential nature of national epics, may serve as a motto for the whole standpoint of spiritual science:

> Words of falsehood do they utter
> And their judgement deep in error,
> Those who think that Väinämöinen
> Shaped for us the fair kantele,
> Our string instrument so cherished,
> From the jawbones of a pike,

And that he has spun the strings
From the tail of Hiisi's steed.
It was fashioned from dire hardship,
Sorrow bound its parts together,
And its strings by tears of longing
And deep suffering were woven.

Thus everything in existence is born not out of material substance but out of the realm of soul and spirit—not only this old folk rune but also spiritual science, which seeks to play an active part in the living cultural development of our time.

LECTURE 1

DORNACH, 9 NOVEMBER 1914

TODAY I should like to open up a theme which will enable us to gain a better understanding of what I have been saying in several lectures recently with regard to the further development of our Building and which will, moreover, be a basis for much that may be added in future.

We know that man's soul nature appears to us as having the distinct aspects of the sentient soul, the intellectual or mind soul and the consciousness soul. We know too that, as described in my book *Theosophy*, man's ego is active within these three soul members. Now a great deal happens in human nature that does not enter one's consciousness. It is a feature of spiritual-scientific knowledge that much that resides in the depths of the human soul can gradually be illumined by the light of consciousness. But if the human soul is active in this way, it is only able to shed light upon a small part of its inner horizon; whereas below this horizon there is much that, while it does not normally become conscious, is of the deepest significance for the soul and is, indeed, far more significant for its whole configuration than anything of which it is conscious.

We shall now turn our attention primarily to something that does not normally come to consciousness; and indeed it is greatly to the benefit of people today that it does not do so. However, we shall come to see that this was not always the case for all people. If ordinary everyday human consciousness were only deepened to a small extent and were able to bring to the surface what is one degree less conscious than ordinary consciousness, the human soul would very soon discover that there is a threefold aspect to it such that it is not simply a unity but has a triune nature. I have indicated in my book *Knowledge of the Higher Worlds: How is it achieved?*[16] that if a person begins to approach the spiritual worlds he as it were separates out into a threefold soul nature. If—as has been suggested—one begins to observe the hidden part of consciousness, one very soon comes to see that this threefoldness of sentient soul, intellectual or mind soul and consciousness soul is a reality. Beneath the threshold of consciousness—and not to any great depth for people today—there is a soul-domain of such a kind that it is not pervaded by a unity but is irradiated by a threefold quality; so that the moment that a person suppresses what he has actually only fully acquired since the second half of the fourth post-Atlantean period[17] (and, hence, with full clarity only since the beginning of the fifth post-Atlantean era) he can distinguish with some precision between three worlds or regions in his soul. One region is one that is to a greater degree inspired by dreamlike inspirations. The second is a realm whereby man is in a certain sense ensouled, formed in his various physical aspects. And the third region is where he becomes conscious of the world.

The first region is, therefore, one into which inspirations enter, dreamlike inspirations with which the soul that is affiliated to the sentient soul is filled. A second realm, where the soul builds up its body through its own inner forms and shapes, is associated with the intellectual or mind soul. This is the inner architect or master builder—we might also say the smith or forger—of the physical body. And the third realm, that of serving as the mediator of outward knowledge, which is connected with the world of the senses, is associated with the consciousness soul. Thus this latter member has, one could say, a connection with physical powers.

Something akin to a triune soul-quality lives in man's soul, and in contrast to this threefold aspect there is a prevailing tendency towards oneness. I should like to indicate this by contrasting one particular soul-region with another [see the following drawing]. *This* soul-region functions in a certain respect wholly as a unity. It is of course quite natural for the soul as regards its temperament, character and fundamental nature to have a quality of oneness or one-foldness. I should like to characterize it as the onefold soul, in contrast to the threefold soul.

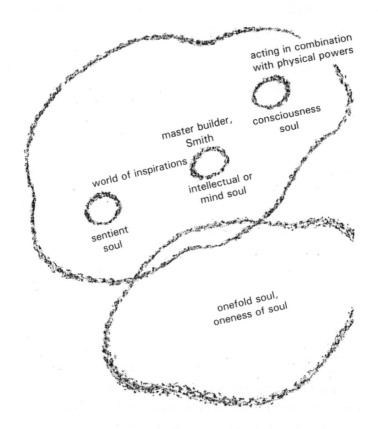

As our soul is presently constituted, this onefold soul is unable to emerge from a somewhat apathetic kind of existence unless it is illumined or irradiated in some way; and in our time this results in one form or another from the Mystery of Golgotha. I shall therefore make you a symbolic representation of the way in which the Mystery of Golgotha irradiates the onefold soul [see drawing 2].

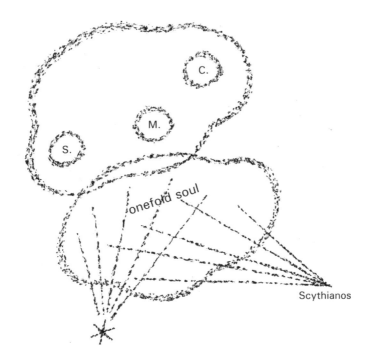

We have in the course of recent years been making considerable efforts gradually to form some idea of the infinite implications of everything associated with the Mystery of Golgotha. You will therefore realize that when the Mystery of Golgotha illumines the human soul in some way this is only a certain stage, a certain level of the Mystery of Golgotha. But let us suppose that, because the onefold soul is of a dull and brooding nature (even though it has something of the greatest value for our time), this quality of oneness needs in some way or other to be illumined by the Mystery of Golgotha.

Now every soul receives influences emanating from various centres of inspiration and initiation in the world, and that also includes the subconscious influences upon the human soul. The influence of the Mystery of Golgotha is of an all-encompassing, universal nature; but an individual human soul can receive this Mystery of Golgotha only in a particular way. The centre of initiation which exerts a particular influence upon the inner regions of the soul in order that it may be properly prepared to receive the illuminating influences from the

Mystery of Golgotha is one of which I have often spoken as being under the guardianship of the initiate Scythianos.[18] Let us therefore assume that the soul has been prepared in the onefold soul for what emanates from the Mystery of Golgotha and is ready to receive it through the influence that streams unconsciously into every soul from Scythianos.

Thus we see the human soul divided as it were into two realms, one of which has a threefold quality and the other a quality of oneness—one that has more of a soul character and one of a more elemental, brooding kind, a realm that receives into the very depths of its nature on the one hand the forces of the Mystery of Golgotha and, on the other, the influences of Scythianos.

Now this onefold quality cannot so readily be merged with man's threefold nature; that would be impossible. For this reason this threefold nature remains below the threshold of consciousness; it must in a certain sense be numbed, the consciousness of it has to be extinguished. If the soul were really able to enter into the state of threefoldness, it would immediately feel itself as three rather than one. It would say: there is something in me that inspires me, something that builds me, that welds and forges me, and something that connects me with the outside world. But this threefoldness has to be blotted out or overshadowed by what leads a person to say to himself: I do not distinguish the three. Thus something needs to radiate into the three that causes the soul not to have an awareness of them but blots them out, so that they relate to one another like clouds of mist.

You see, it is possible for there to be a connection between what needs to live in the soul as a single entity and the soul's threefold nature if there is a means of communication or exchange, a kind of interconnecting link within the soul extending to the obscured threefold aspect from the single entity, which is irradiated from two sides, so that there is not only a dull, vague sameness about its character and mood but that it is illumined as a whole by a sense of man's potential, by a consciousness of the human soul's connection with divine-spiritual existence.

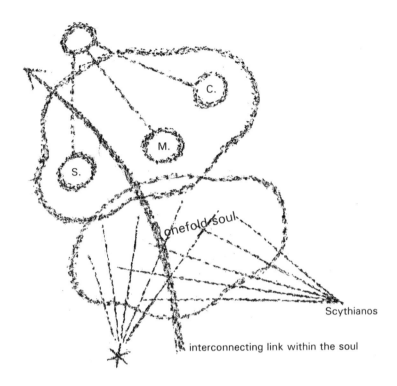

What I have drawn here is a picture of what lies at the foundation of every human soul. No human soul can exist in our time without these elements being present within it.

But now consider the following. As a means of demonstrating what our Building needs to become, I have often reiterated that what lives in the human soul and also manifests itself outwardly comes to expression in the outward evolution of the Earth. If there is a realm in the human soul that indeed manifests a kind of threefold nature and which in people today is veiled by ordinary consciousness, we must find a stage in evolution where this becomes outwardly apparent to us, where the soul really feels itself as having a threefold nature and as being separated into three soul members. In other words, there must have been a people who experienced these three soul members as separate, such that the oneness in the soul was actually experienced far less vividly than its triune nature, on the grounds that this threefoldness was still thought of as being in conjunction with the cosmos. Such a people did indeed exist in Europe, and they have bequeathed a remarkable cultural legacy of which I have previously spoken.[19] This people, who experienced this threefold nature in that part of Europe which they needed to occupy, is the Finnish people; and the expression of this stage of culture is set forth in the *Kalevala*. In what is described in the *Kalevala* there is a clear consciousness of the threefold nature of the soul. For the seers of olden times whose visionary clairvoyance underlay the *Kalevala* felt that there is an inspirational quality in the world with which one of their soul-members—the sentient soul—had a connection, in that all its forces were oriented towards this source of its impulses. This people, or rather its ancient seers, experienced what inspired the sentient soul as something of a divinely human, or heroically human, nature. They called this Väinämöinen. This is none other than the inspiring force of the sentient soul in the cosmos. All the destinies that are described in the *Kalevala* as the destinies of Väinämöinen are evidence of the fact that this consciousness formerly existed in a people who extended widely over the north-eastern part of Europe and who experienced the three soul-members as separate entities and the sentient soul as inspired by Väinämöinen.

Similarly this people, these seers of olden times, experienced that the intellectual or mind soul is an additional soul-member that receives its impulse to forge, what it builds within the human soul, from another elemental being of a heroic nature called Ilmarinen. Just as Väinämöinen corresponds to the sentient soul, so does Ilmarinen correspond in the *Kalevala* to the intellectual or mind soul. If you read the lecture about the *Kalevala* you can find it all there.[20]

Moreover, in that this people—and this must be clearly stated—experienced the consciousness soul as that which first enabled man to achieve conquests on the physical plane, these ancient seers experienced Lemminkäinen as a being who is connected with the forces of the physical plane, an elemental, heroic being who inspires the consciousness soul. Thus these three figures whom one might well—by analogy with other epics—refer to as being in the heroic mould derive from the ancient Finnish people; and they inspire the threefold nature of the soul.

What is so wonderful is the connection between Ilmarinen and the fruits of his forging activity. I have already pointed out that man is forged out of the elements of nature. This being who is fashioned from all the atoms of nature, first reduced to dust and then welded together again, is portrayed in a magnificent tableau in the forging of the Sampo in the *Kalevala*. It is also related in the *Kalevala* that once this process of forming man from these three soul-members has taken place, this formative process had to go into a pralaya and then be re-engendered; for it is described how the Sampo is lost and then found again, just as the light of consciousness that is initially veiled in darkness is then rediscovered.

And now we need to imagine that to the south or, rather, to the south-east of the Finnish people there is another people, which has in olden times cultivated those qualities of soul of which I have spoken—the onefold aspect of the soul which brings the quality of oneness to the character, feelings and temperament. This is a Slavic people, in contrast to the Finnish people who were mentioned earlier. This Slavic people receives its influences from Scythianos, who also lived for a while in olden times surrounded by the ancient Scythian people. It is not at all necessary that a highly evolved people should be living around a centre of initiation; but it is nevertheless the case that in the course of evolution the necessary developments should occur. What happened here was that a particular form of the Mystery of Golgotha arose as a result of the influence of Graeco-Byzantine culture upon the Slavic world. What I have shown here as a centre of Graeco-Byzantine can, if you will, be identified on the map of Europe as Constantinople; for it is indeed Constantinople.

Thus we now have souls of a fundamentally Slavic nature who are on the one hand connected with an influence from the Mystery of Golgotha which can lead to a onefold nature and can prepare souls with this quality of oneness for Christianity and who, on the other hand, receive the Mystery of Golgotha in a quite particular form, as

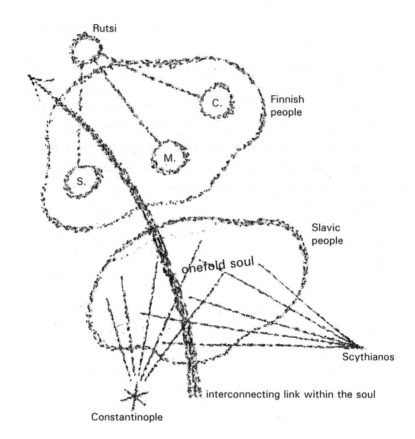

an inspiration from the Mystery of Golgotha imparted through Graeco-Byzantine culture.

However, something further needs to be added which can only come from a particular quarter. The separation or division of the soul into three members which we have observed in the Finnish people and whose fundamental principle is so beautifully portrayed in the *Kalevala* must be obscured; and this can only happen if an influence comes from outside, through there being a people or a part of a people who are predisposed to have inner experience not of three-foldness but of onefoldness—not the sense of oneness that one receives from the Mystery of Golgotha but, rather, a quality that one can imbibe from the natural world. When we study the Finnish people, we find a particular predisposition to develop a threefold consciousness; and there is no clearer expression of this threefold quality in its relation to the cosmos than in the *Kalvala*. But it was then necessary for what was thus developing in the north to be covered over or veiled by the process leading to the loss of this consciousness of this threefoldness. A race asserted its presence which quite naturally bore in its soul the aspiration towards oneness, an aspiration which—albeit in a completely different way and on an altogether different level—comes to expression in Goethe's *Faust* and explicitly in the figure of Faust; and the impulse underlying this, in its ignorance of threefoldness, strove towards the oneness or single-ness of the ego. At what was still at a primitive level, it served to obscure the three members of the soul.

Now the Finns were a people who still quite naturally felt these things, otherwise they would not have experienced the three soul-members. They were aware of what was thus flooding in and obliterating all trace of threefoldness in the soul as r r r. And because they experienced this in-flooding tide as something that could best be expressed in occult language through the letters u u o (as if they wanted to say: 'It is coming near, we must be filled with awe at its approach'), what was lightly aspirated in 'rruo' was given firmer substance through the Tao, t when it penetrates the human soul. Just as in the days of Jehovah the pervading of the human soul was expressed by the sound s, the Hebrew 'Shin', this reaching right into the soul comes to expression through the sound s. This, then, links up with what approaches and becomes firmly rooted in the soul; and in the Finnish people everything connected with the rruu mood reaches towards the i [English 'ee'], whose significance is well known. So the Finnish people experienced this whole process as rutsi or ruotsi, and they called the people from whom it came the Rutsi or Ruotsi. The Slavs gradually took on this name, and because they associated themselves with what the Finns referred to as working its way down from above, they called themselves Rutsi or, later, Russians.

So you see that everything that is related in historical accounts had to be, that these peoples living further south called in the

Varangians,[21] who were actually of Norman-Germanic origin, to form an alliance with the Slavic races. This was brought about by what was necessary because of the particular constitution of the human soul. And so there came into being what later became incorporated in the east of Europe as the Russian element of the European peoples. Thus in the element of Russia there really lives all that of which I have been speaking, and especially the Norman-Germanic element; moreover, what I have been telling you also lives very much in the name 'Russian', for it came about in the way I have indicated.

The *Kalevala* makes it very clearly apparent that the greatness of the Finnish people lies in that it fosters unity within a threefold context, that through the obscuring of threefoldness it prepares for the receiving of that unity which is now no longer merely a human unity but the divine unity, wherein lives the divine Hero of the Mystery of Golgotha.

In order that a group of people may be able to receive what is approaching them, they must first be prepared. In this way we may gain an impression of all that has to happen inwardly in order that what approaches one from without may come to fulfilment in evolution. I said that the Finnish people's task to provide this preparation comes to expression in a wonderful way in the *Kalevala*, in that at the end of the *Kalevala* the Mystery of Golgotha is introduced in a remarkable way. Christ makes an appearance at the end of the *Kalevala*, but as He casts His impulse into Finnish life Väinämöinen leaves the country, from which we are to understand that the primordial greatness and significance of what entered Europe through Finland was a preparatory stage for Christianity, which it received as a message imparted from outside.

Just as we see in the case of an individual human being that it is necessary for him to be prepared in highly complicated ways in order that his soul may receive from all manner of different directions what it needs to live in a particular incarnation, the same is also true of peoples. A people does not have this degree of uniformity or homogeneity but is, rather, a context where many influences meet.

Amongst the people that dwelt in those eastern regions, all the influences of what I have spoken flowed together. Moreover, everything of an inner, spiritual nature was reflected outwardly, even if only indistinctly. I indicated that in this people there had to be an interconnecting link within the soul leading from below upwards and also from above downwards. This actually existed in the form of a great road leading from the Black Sea to the Gulf of Finland where it was possible for exchanges to take place between the Graeco-Byzantine cultural element and the native element of the Rutsi.

In the course of his various incarnations a human individual has to undergo a variety of experiences. Any particular incarnation must be based on the previous one. This is only possible for the individual human being because the forces necessary for the further course of human evolution are brought together into the substance or material out of which all the various peoples and those belonging to them are formed. A human soul must on one occasion in its incarnations find a bodily constitution that has been forged out of the forces that I have described here. It is a simple thing to say that someone is born a Russian; but it has the deepest possible significance. That a person is born as a Russian means that in the course of his various incarnations he has arrived at the point where he experiences during his life's journey what can only be experienced by living a life between birth and death in a body which has been formed in such a way. If one were not to experience this in such a body, something would be lacking in what one acquires from one incarnation to another. Foolish people— I say this merely as a statement of fact rather than as a means of casting aspersions—are fond of quoting the proverb: 'The world is best understood in its true essence if it is seen in its full simplicity'. This is not true; it is merely convenient to think in this way. Deep thinkers have always emphasized—and Ralph Waldo Emerson[22] is probably the most impressive recent example—that one only penetrates to the essential truth of facts when they are understood in their full complexity. There is actually nothing simple about the world, or about anything connected with world evolution.

And just as in the eastern half of the European continent souls were prepared to experience something special, the same is true of all other parts of the Earth's surface, where individual national characteristics are prepared in complicated ways. At this point we need to recall one thing in particular with which we have become familiar in the course of our spiritual-scientific studies.

When a human individual has passed through the portal of death, he looks back on his last earthly life; and he is as a result dependent in a certain sense on what he experienced in that life. We know that for several years the links with the former life are a contributory factor to the life after death. This has to be the case. A person must pass through a physical incarnation so that in this period between death and a new birth he has particular memories of this previous incarnation, certain impulses which extend from this former time on Earth. Because this person had been a quite particular human being with a particular organism which had been subject to certain influences as a result of earthly circumstances, there are some impressions engraved in the memory that also continue to have an influence after death and which have a certain colouring. This is responsible for the characteristics that a soul acquires as a result of having passed through a particular nationality, that it receives from a certain nationality. This is increasingly stripped away the more that the national is submerged by the international; but it is still an omnipresent factor today, otherwise the events of modern times would not be able to occur. People still to a certain extent look back upon what they experienced through their organism—in so far as it is determined by national factors—in their previous life between birth and death. Now the souls which pass in the manner described through bodies that have been prepared in this way are given a quite particular preparation for the life that they encounter once they have gone through the gate of death. Of course, it is not the individuality that is influenced, only its outer garments or sheaths. But these sheaths with which the nationality is connected still provide something that the soul retains after death, something that it knows formed part of its journey through earthly life.

When the soul has undergone life in a body that has been thus prepared (exoterically one would say that in a particular incarnation it passed through a Russian body), it naturally has the characteristics of the outer sheaths, which after death become an idea, such as one has of oneself in the way one ordinarily forms such ideas. Into these sheaths it has received everything that I have indicated in this drawing [see page 38]; and if one is seeking to express what the soul inwardly experiences through having a body that is constituted in this way, one can say the following. We know from our previous studies that our consciousness changes in a certain way after death; it reaches a higher level, it becomes clearer and more intense after death than it is in a physical body. To have passed through what I have previously described prepares the soul for entering into a particularly intimate relationship after death with those beings who live as guardian spirits of actual human individualities and belong to the next higher hierarchy, that of the Angels. In the life after a death following a Russian incarnation, the soul is enabled to identify itself in consciousness with its Angel, to view the spiritual world with—to put it rather crudely—the eyes of this Angel.

Man is ever aspiring towards the higher self. This higher self comes to expression in the most diverse ways. If you read the recent Munich cycle about *The Secrets of the Threshold,* [23] you will find an explanation of how consciousness changes, how the soul is wholly imbued with the Angel. It must be so imbued and prepared for being thus imbued by the Angel as a result of passing through the portal of death into the spiritual world after a life in a Russian body, which has been prepared as I have described. Thus we can say that someone who has passed through a Russian body actually feels how everything has been coloured after his death as a result of his being pervaded throughout his whole being by an Angel, by the genius of the next highest hierarchy who protects all human beings.

On the other hand, the situation with peoples affiliated to Western culture is that one is less strongly impregnated, less strongly imbued after death with the being of the Angel. If one passes through a Western incarnation, one tends, rather, to have an experience after death that one could express in the following words:

'I still feel as I have always felt, I still look at the world as I did before.' People experience it as a particular art to grow together with their Angel; whereas for Russians it is perfectly natural to be always together with their Angel. On its path through incarnations, the soul passes through all possible nationalities and must also experience this incarnation where it receives the impulse to be completely absorbed in the Angel, to grow together with him and to behold the spiritual world with his spirit-eye.

This does of course relate not so much to the whole period between death and a new birth but specifically to the time immediately after death, the first few years or from one and a half to two decades; for in the main period before and after 'midnight', of which I have previously spoken,[24] the soul wipes away such images. Thus it relates to the time when the human individual is still influenced by what he has experienced in the physical body, where this continues to exert an influence.

And now, on this basis, let us direct our attention to the spiritual world, to what is actually the inner aspect of the world in which we are living; for we must realize that it is only a limited understanding of human nature that believes that one is surrounded only by physical human beings. We are also surrounded continually by those who have died and who live in the spiritual world. Thus we have around us dead souls who have passed through physical, Russian bodies and who have a strong inclination to live, so to say, more as an Angel in their present soul-condition than as a human being.

After such an incarnation, what is particularly characteristic is that the ether body dissolves very rapidly in the surrounding ether world. In the case of Western peoples, on the other hand, the ether body is more compact and cohesive and dissolves less easily in the surrounding ether world. Now as I have often pointed out we live at a time—I am referring specifically to the time since the last third of the nineteenth century—since the beginning of Michael's rulership[25] in the spiritual world, which succeeded that of Gabriel. We are living at a time when these conditions—and especially what I have been describing—manifest themselves particularly strongly in the spiritual world. For it is the responsibility of our time to prepare for the great event to which I have referred in my first Mystery Play *The Portal of Initiation*[26]—Christ's appearance to man in a spiritual form. This event of the appearance of Christ referred to by Theodora[27] can be brought about only if Michael's rulership is extended more and more widely. This is still a process that is being enacted in the spiritual world, where on the plane that adjoins our world Michael fights for the coming of Christ. For this he needs his hosts, those who fight on his behalf; and those souls who have been in a Russian body in their present incarnation are important fighters for him in this regard. So we can perceive in the spiritual world a kind of Michaelic campaign of conquest for the coming of Christ, a campaign for which he recruits a host of important fighters from the souls who have passed through Russian bodies and are predisposed to identify themselves with their Angel. As a result they are particularly suited to summon forth the forces to provide, in purity, the image or form through which the Christ will appear. The purpose of Michael's battle, as I have indicated it, is that He does not appear in a false form in accordance with subjective human imagination, but in a true form. He can best wage this battle through those souls who naturally bear within themselves this Angel consciousness and have thereby been specially prepared. A further factor which aids this preparation is that, because their ether bodies dissolve particularly easily, they have nothing in their ether body that would make the Christ appear in a false form, in erroneous imaginations.

In order that everything that has to happen in the world can happen in the right way, various parts or aspects of the world order need to interact with one another. To be specific (and this should be understood in a purely objective way), in order that what I have described might come about there is a need to combat a characteristic which is more prevalent in the West, and especially in souls that have passed through a French incarnation. These souls acquire from their nationality the characteristics of clinging firmly to their ether body, of keeping firm hold of a quite particular imaginative form in the ether body. This cannot be combated by Western souls alone; these

Western souls must, shall we say, be helped, efforts must be made as regards the dispersal of these ether bodies in the universal ether so that no false picture of Christ's appearance is evoked. Hence the hosts fighting under Michael must become involved by combating those souls that have passed through French bodies.

This is what clairvoyant consciousness has been able to perceive in the last third of the nineteenth century and until our own time as the fundamental aspect of our present evolution. A struggle of a spiritual nature has been developing in the spiritual world, in the astral world, between Russia and France (I am of course referring to what spiritually underlies these peoples); and this struggle has been intensifying to an ever greater degree. Strife in the spiritual world actually signifies a combining of forces in the physical world, but this is in itself a picture of struggle and opposition; and anyone who has insight into the spiritual world has since the last third of the nineteenth century until our time been aware of a spiritual struggle of an ever growing intensity between West and East being waged throughout Central Europe. It might well be called the war in heaven, in that the hosts in the East have been increasingly assembling under Michael's rulership to counteract everything that is being done in the West—where materialistic forces are growing ever stronger—to prevent the appearance of Christ.

Yes, my dear friends, where there is an advanced culture, one that is so developed and has reached such a stage of culmination as in France, the soul has adopted certain imaginations. These imaginations remain after death, and they prevent anything completely new from coming, and specifically what must come through Christ. Thus it is of primal importance in the spiritual world to combat what human souls receive from a fully mature culture. Michael cannot choose the members of his hosts from a fully mature culture which has embraced a specific imagination; such imaginations must first be obliterated. Hence behind the scenes in the spiritual world there emerges the majestic picture of the struggle of the East against the West, the host of Michael against the independent souls of the West.

And yet the outward physical expression of a spiritual battle is a physical bond or alliance. An alliance on the physical plane is the outward manifestation of a struggle on the spiritual plane. People become allies on the physical plane when on the spiritual plane there is a need for them to fight. From this you may again see how seriously we must take what is said about maya and truth. Again and again people speak of maya and truth, but it remains mere theory; for anyone who has insight into the spiritual world and sees there what underlies the physical world is overwhelmed by a feeling of immeasurable shock as he endeavours in all seriousness to penetrate from maya to truth and finds the truth that lies behind the veil of maya. Truth often has to be expressed with completely different words from those used on the physical plane.

What is called an alliance on the physical plane often signifies war on the spiritual plane. Of course one should not build on this a series of false assumptions, so that one seeks the opposite of what one finds in the physical world in the spirit; for this does not apply in every case. Things must be sought in their full reality in the spiritual domain. In many cases what takes place on the physical plane may indeed be a direct reflection of what is going on in the spiritual world. In other cases there is a huge contrast, just as in the present instance between East and West, where on the physical plane there is an alliance in the realm of maya and in the world of spirit a battle of infinitely greater significance; for through this battle a true picture gradually needs to emerge from the ether world of the being who shall in our time, in the course of the twentieth century, approach mankind in the person of the Christ.

At our next opportunity we shall continue with these reflections. But I must ask you to take what I have said today very seriously, for I can assure you that it has a very disturbing effect when encountered for the first time.

LECTURE 2

IF we merely concern ourselves with the physical body, it is very difficult to arrive at experiences of the kind that we spoke about last time. This is especially so in the case of the peoples represented by the nations of the modern world, those of Europe and America.

The physical human body in these areas is formed from within to far less a degree than, for example, in Asia and Africa. Amongst the populations of Asia and Africa the physical body is fashioned to a greater extent from inner resources, from forces residing in the ether body. In the case of the peoples of Europe and America, the forces that form the physical body are derived to a greater extent from external influences.

We could put it this way. If we would seek the forces that form man's physical body, we will find them in etheric forces. For the inhabitants of Africa and Asia these etheric forces lie more within their own ether body, whereas for those living in Europe and America they lie to a greater extent in the ether world that surrounds man.

People in Africa and Asia are therefore related more to inner ether forces, while those in Europe and America have a stronger connection with external ether forces and, hence, with nature spirits.

To express what has become clear to us from a spiritual-scientific study as simply as possible, we can say that the physical body of African and Asiatic peoples is moulded more from within through the agency of inner formative forces. The bodies of European and

American peoples, in contrast, are fashioned more through a response to the conditions of the outside world, which impress themselves upon these mouldable forms and, hence, shape the forms of the physical body.

In my book *The Threshold of the Spiritual World*[28] I pointed out that as soon as we take account of man's ether body we find that he has a much closer connection with the whole organism of the Earth than we would believe if we were to confine our attention to the physical body alone. The Earth itself is a kind of living being. However, whereas man is a living being who appears to us as a self-contained entity, so that we cannot help experiencing him as such, we must necessarily view the Earth as a living organism of such a kind that we see in it a multiplicity of natural beings in constant interaction with one another.

The Earth consists first and foremost of the solid earthly substance itself that forms the continents. However, what we regard as this material solidity of the Earth is nothing but maya. True reality consists of a large number of nature spirits, who are in turn under the guidance of spirits of the higher hierarchies. That it is massed together and compressed and functions as solid earthly substance is an aspect of maya. The Earth is spirit through and through. I have frequently emphasized this.

Now the Earth does not merely consist of solid earthly substance but also the water that permeates it; and in so far as the substance of the Earth finds expression in fluid matter, we are in a similar way dealing with water as maya. The reality is that here again there are a large number of nature spirits. It is the same with air and also with the warmth that pervades and envelops the Earth. Everything consists of a multitude of nature spirits; while matter as such is merely the outward illusion that is maya.

In the case of Europeans (we will confine ourselves to them for the moment) there is—to a far greater extent than in Asia and Africa—a continual exchange of impulses between their own inner ether forces and the elemental beings residing in fire, water, air and earth. These elemental beings influence human ether bodies from without, and these ether bodies thereby receive the formative forces which are then manifested in the appearance and functions of the physical body including the faculty of speech and language. For speech is wholly a function of the physical body; and yet the impulses for it reside in the ether body.

Now to the extent that—from the way man lives on the Earth and is, through the mediating power of his ether body, an earthly being—one regards him as belonging to the Earth, one has to consider the various ways in which the distinctive beings of earth, water, air and so forth exert their influences upon the human ether body. For the elemental and etheric beings of earth are completely different in nature from the etheric and elemental beings of water, so that we can say that the mere fact that someone lives as a physical being in the mountains or by the sea means that different beings exert a greater influence on his etheric body. In the case of someone who lives by the sea the elemental beings who have their maya expression in water have a much greater influence than with a person who lives in the mountains. Where someone lives in the mountains, the beings who live in earth have a greater influence than those who have their maya expression in water.

Now I must emphasize that this process of the forming and fashioning of man's being—and I am referring especially to Europeans here—is the result of a collaboration between the elemental spirits; and the way in which these elemental spirits of nature work manifests something of the process that forms man from the spiritual world, in so far as he is an earthly being.

I spoke to you last time of how the culture of Eastern Europe was preceded by a cultural environment where people were so constituted that they still had something in their souls which in modern human beings has been thrust back into their subconscious minds, namely a division of the soul into sentient soul, intellectual or mind soul and consciousness soul. I pointed out to you that the Finns, the great Finnish people of olden times (for its present representatives are no more than a remnant of a people that was formerly widespread), had souls which, through a certain ancient clairvoyance that they possessed, had in their direct daytime experience something of the nature of a division of their souls into their sentient, intellectual or mind soul and consciousness components.

I also told you that in the great epic of the *Kalevala* we have in the three figures of Väinämöinen, Ilmarinen and Lemminkäinen a portrayal of how this tripartite soul is directed and determined from out of the cosmos.

How could something of this nature come about? How was it that at a particular place in Europe—for it is valid to ask this—a great people was able to evolve which had the kind of soul that I have described?

Now the way that man develops his own ego, the gift of the Earth, depends on the influence upon him of the spirits of the Earth from below upwards through the maya of earthly matter. These spirits of the Earth work from below upwards, as it were through the solid earth; and in our present age these spirits of the Earth essentially have the task of summoning forth the ego-nature within a human being.

If something of what lies beneath the ego-nature, something more spiritual and more closely connected with divine forces (for when the soul experiences itself as split up into three it is more closely linked to the divine forces than where this is not so), were to shine into the souls of a race such as the ancient Finnish people, then it would not merely be the earth with its elemental spirits that would be raying upwards from below into man's earthly nature but something else must be streaming into this earthly aspect of man, another elemental influence.

Now just as man's physical existence (in so far as it is an earthly existence, where man develops his ego) is intimately connected with the spirits of the earth element, that is, with the spirits who work from the Earth itself from below upwards, so does man's soul nature, which is proclaimed through inner qualities of temperament and character, have a connection with everything that lives on the Earth as a watery element. Thus the spirits of the watery, fluid element must pervade these souls that are divided in this threefold way.

In our present age it is the earthly element, which has a formative influence upon the ego, that is of importance. When another element—for example, the watery element—exerts an influence, it works more from the spiritual world. It is not to be found in man himself. It must as it were become embodied within man as a spiritual being in order that he receives into his earthly nature something that leads him into the spiritual world.

Let us suppose that the surface of the blackboard represents the place whence the elemental forces of the Earth proceed. If a spiritual element wants to find a kind of embodiment there it must proceed from the organism of the Earth, from something that is in itself spiritual. There must be a being, a real being who is not man himself and who inspires him to experience this threefold division of the soul. A being must be present whose influence upon the soul from the spirituality inherent in nature is such that the sentient soul, intellectual or mind soul and consciousness soul are separated out, so that the human souls are able to say: my sentient soul is being influenced from nature by something that I can call Väinämöinen, streaming towards me like a being of nature and giving me the forces of the sentient soul.

But there is also an influence of the nature of Ilmarinen which gives me the forces of the intellectual or mind soul, and then the further influence of Lemminkäinen, something that gives me the forces of the consciousness soul. If we postulate a being that stretches out its feelers into nature from a kind of neck [see diagram], a being that has its main body here and then extends its feelers in this direction, so that we can associate one of the feelers with the sentient soul, while a second tentacle is extended here and the third one here, the nature being has a body and thrusts out its soul in the form of feelers as a source of inspiration, with the result that ether bodies are able to form which give the soul the capacity to feel itself as having a threefold nature.

The inhabitants of ancient Finland said: we live here, but we can feel something like three mighty beings that are not beings of the physical plane but nature beings. They are unveiled from the West,

they are three parts—or organs—of a great being that has its body over yonder but it extends its tentacles (Väinämöinen, Ilmarinen and Lemminkäinen) in this direction. A mighty sea being spreads itself out from West to East, stretching out its feelers and endowing this race with the threefold soul.

The peoples who still experienced this felt it in the way that I have explained and also spoke of it in the *Kalevala*. People today, who live only on the physical plane, say: here is the Western Sea extending in this direction; this is the Gulf of Bothnia, this is the Gulf of Finland and here the Gulf of Riga. But if we would penetrate to the spiritual aspect of the outward physical phenomena, we need to put together what is presented to us in the form of a kind of cross-section of nature. Down there it is all water, up above is air. People breathe the air, and the watery world of sea is a great, mighty being that is merely differently formed from what we are accustomed to. It is a mighty being that is spread out over that region, and the people of an earlier race had a quite particular and distinctive connection with this being. And as for the Folk-spirits, they have the elemental beings that live in countless such expressions of soul conditions as instruments for their work. They are organized like an army for the purpose of working right into the ether body, and from the ether body they make it possible for man's physical body to be a fitting instrument for what is to be his special mission on the Earth.

Only when we are able to view the forms that we encounter in nature as the expression of the spiritual dimension will we understand nature itself in its connection with man; for it is not enough simply to look thoughtlessly at where land and sea meet but rather do we need to understand what comes to expression in these forms. It could even occur to someone looking at a person's face to say: yes, I can see certain forms, this is where human flesh and air meet. If someone says such a thing, it makes little sense.

The form only begins to mean anything when one understands it as the expression of a human being, as a countenance. In a similar way one can only understand what is being described here if one conceives of it as the physiognomy of a mighty being who stretches out certain parts of its body from the ocean.

There is much that goes on below the threshold of consciousness, and it is not for nothing that the Spirits of Form have created the forms that we find in nature. These forms can be understood. They are the expression of an inner essence. And when we become pupils of the Spirits of Form, we ourselves create forms that express what lives in the inner essence of the worlds of nature and of the spirit.

Thus, for example, forms will be carved in our architraves,[29] in what lies above the columns, which really are the expression of that spiritual quality which is to be brought into connection with all that goes on within the Building. Man is essentially a being who emerges with his outward form from a sea, from a sea of reality—of hidden reality—in which he is submerged.

This is another example of how we must penetrate behind maya if we really want to understand what confronts us in the world and especially if we want to understand man in all his manifestations. Hence it is often necessary for us to immerse ourselves in what lives within man without his being aware of it and which he only gradually learns through knowledge being imparted to him.

Whenever we turn our eyes, we cannot help initially beholding this outer maya; and we then need to be clearly aware that behind this outer maya lies something of the greatest complexity.

If we had the inclination to probe everywhere into what lies behind maya, an infinite harmony would prevail in the whole of man's being; for this human essence is related by means of an infinite wealth of sub-earthly impulses to a harmonious onefold essence; and everything that exists in the world can only be understood if one examines it in relation to what lies beneath the surface of existence.

There is always a one-sided aspect to anything viewed in terms of maya. I should like to illustrate this in the following way. After all, such things as we have been speaking about can only be understood in their entirety by degrees. I should like to show you how difficult it is in ordinary life to make a proper investigation of everything that lies beneath the surface of the phenomena that we encounter. Thus, for example, it is highly possible that very few of our dear friends have noticed that in a recent lecture I spoke quite intimately about Switzerland, about some fundamental aspects of the Swiss character. I do not know how many of you still have any recollection of what I am referring to. You may perhaps recall that after the four lectures that I gave on *Occult Reading and Occult Hearing*[30] I added a lecture in which I spoke at length about Herman Grimm[31] from a purely historical point of view. This was a lecture when I had a great deal to say about Switzerland. However, one must go back to the inner aspect of this question, to what lies below the surface. Why is this?

To repeat what you already know very well, man consists of his physical body, ether body, astral body and ego or 'I' nature. We know that the ego and astral body leave a person's physical and ether body as he sleeps and reside as it were in the periphery in the spiritual world. So this is a world of which we can say that at night we dwell within it, a world where elemental, etheric beings also live. Here, too, are those spiritual, elemental beings who are connected with the whole process of forming our physical existence. They are all living and active there. A number of elemental beings are associated with the entire development of our physical existence. In a lecture cycle that I held in Kassel[32] on the connection of St John's Gospel with the other Gospels, I spoke of how a human individual is connected through his ancestors with the beings of an elemental nature. As you can read in this lecture cycle, I indicated that, if we picture his four bodily members in this way [see diagram], a person inherits what lives more in his physical body and his ego from his father's side. Anyone who has read this lecture cycle carefully will recall that what lives more in the ether body and astral body is inherited from the mother's side. Now when we fall asleep, our physical and etheric bodies—that is, a paternal and maternal element—are lying in bed. Our ego and astral body are in the periphery. The astral body contains what is impressed upon our feelings and our whole disposition and temperament, everything that gives us our character; and into this that endows us with our soul disposition there work the

ether body | astral body | maternal element

physical body | 'I' or ego | paternal element

elemental beings who, in the course of time, bring from the ancestors to their descendants the forces that can enable them to fulfil their potential.

In a personality such as Herman Grimm something quite distinctive was going on; for the influence of his immediate ancestors can be observed in him. His immediate ancestors, his father and his uncle, were the collectors of fairy tales, which they heard people telling. They would simply listen while they were being related to them, and they wrote them down. But one cannot do this unless one has an astral body which has a predisposition for having a particular inclination for this. Such factors need to be deeply rooted in the whole background to what happened.

Herman Grimm has a particular way of expressing himself with a certain intellectual finesse which almost approaches spiritual science. He has this quality because there was in his family background a strong inclination towards fairy tales and towards any spirituality deriving from nature. We see how the nature spirits conveyed something to him that they allowed to continue to resound when Herman Grimm's ego and astral body were outside his physical and ether bodies. Who was it who first told fairy tales to his father and uncle with such clarity and vividness, as though intimately in tune with an elemental being? The wife of Herman Grimm's father, in other words his mother. Herman Grimm's mother was the enlivening element in the way that these fairy tales were transmitted. She had a particular joy in listening to these fairy tales as they lived amongst the people, and she imbibed them in such a way that the two brothers Grimm, Herman Grimm's father and uncle,[33] were able to write them down.

Who was this mother? Dorothea Grimm,[34] whose maiden name was Wild, was from an old Bernese family. She herself was a citizen of Bern; and her ancestors had fought in the battle of Murten. All the feelings that she had acquired there among the elemental spirits then came with her to Hesse, for her father—Herman Grimm's grandfather[35]—had migrated there from Bern and had trained as a pharmaceutical chemist, thereafter moving to Kassel and founding the 'Sonnenapoteke' there. So if we want to understand the nature of the influence of elemental spirits upon Herman Grimm and what was responsible for the particular configuration of his intellectual faculties (for these spirits were active within him while he was asleep), we must think of Switzerland; and if we are speaking of what is really characteristic of Herman Grimm, we are actually speaking of the Bernese part of Switzerland.

Thus sometimes we can gain an insight into the essential significance of a phenomenon, even though outwardly it is wholly veiled with maya. We need to be aware of the particular soul-qualities of Herman Grimm's mother if we are wanting to understand the distinctive configuration of his mind. Thus in emphasizing the spiritual element lying beneath the threshold of consciousness I spoke of something directly Swiss in nature, and when I spoke of Herman Grimm I was referring specifically to a Bernese Swiss quality. Hence it is not difficult to see why this way of presenting indications should have given rise to a particular warmth of feeling among many of our friends.

It is therefore not simply a question of what we encounter in an external sense but of what is really living in these outward phenomena. The Earth with all that it contains—the Earth as a onefold essence—is indeed in intimate connection with what man can be upon it, with what is formed or fashioned around man through the mediating function of the ether body.

Now that I have made it clear to you how we must penetrate the veils of maya if we want to understand what is really there, let us return to the sea-dragon who is in a certain sense the inspirer of European humanity and who made its passage from the Atlantic Ocean so as to take on this inspirational role. If we take account of the totality of its elemental, etheric beings, this dragon contains everything that is spiritual in European humanity. If we were fully able to understand this dragon and give ourselves up entirely to it, we would all be clairvoyant. But European humanity does not have the task of merely being clairvoyant; its task is to develop that part of man's soul-nature that rises up above clairvoyance, just as islands rise up out of the sea. Thus that which had to evolve quite particularly in the form of the basic types of the fifth post-Atlantean cultural period had to have the particular character of raising itself up in its consciousness from what is purely of soul nature. This had to be inspired by the nature spirits that work through the Earth. There had to be the possibility of everywhere forming connections with this inspiring being through countless flowing impulses. But the earth element had to raise itself up and emerge amidst the watery element; and this happened when the British Isles, together with the totality of their nature spirits, were lifted up from the surrounding sea that gave them inspiration.

When a true spiritual science becomes a reality, people will come to know that in such a continental region the bearers of man's soul, his physical and ether bodies, must be formed in a manner that accords with the relationship between sea and land. Just as this is conditioned by the elevation of the land above the sea, so in a similar way does man have to fill out certain spaces in his organism through ensuring that they become not muscle but bone, with the result that the soft and hard elements have a particular relationship to one another.

This is how the formative process in the great earthly mother proceeds, that out of the fluid element the element of solidity appears. One can therefore say that the Earth sends up from its depths the elemental spirits that form the Earth in a particular configuration, at a specific place of spiritual inspiration, so that a land comes into being where bodies are able to live within which the consciousness soul can evolve.

Solid land amidst the sea is indeed like a skeletal structure in the world of elemental being. Just as our bone system is embedded in the solid muscular system, so is the solid part of the Earth positioned through a particular configuration in the sea. Moreover, the regions of dry land do not arise in the arbitrary way that geologists suppose but are just as regular in the way that their forms come about as are the forms of our bones—even though this does not occur through cellular activity, as is the case with bones. We need merely to learn to understand why the individual continents have this or that particular form.

I should like to make a further comparison, which I hope you will not misunderstand. In order that among this ancient Finnish people the perceptive faculties of which we have spoken could arise, it was necessary for there to be a land configuration of this nature arising amidst the gulfs of the sea. Just as the human lung lets in the air, so in this configuration of the land can be discerned—as though inserted into it—tentacles of that great being that has to do with the whole configuration of Europe.

We spoke last time about the bodies that are made available for the Russian soul, when this soul incarnates in a Russian body. We showed both on the previous occasion and in the course of other studies that in a Russian body the Russian soul has a gesture of expectation, that it has an inner conception of some future gift and potential. It is therefore necessary for this soul to remain in a certain sense in contact with the world of spirit. Otherwise the Spirit Self could not come into being. On the other hand, this soul must be prevented from evolving too early in those regions that are envisaged for it.

Let us imagine that where the Baltic Sea is now there was land, and that where Russia lies was all sea, into which peninsulas projected rather as Italy does, for example. The gulfs of Bothnia, Finland

and Riga would extend to the Caspian Sea instead of the land of Russia that we have now. We would then have a seafaring people here navigating these inlets of sea. But that would mean that the bodies could not be formed as they should be in this region. In such a case the being that stretches out its tentacles here would breathe out what these seafaring folk would receive, and they would develop what they have as a predisposition prematurely, that is, before the time that is right for it. They would develop too early what needs to await a later time. The Spirit Self must wait for a certain time, it should not be developed too early. Hence instead of there being sea here the land must manifest its presence so that the Spirit Self is not developed too early, while nevertheless the possibility remains of receiving the inspirations of this great being. There must not be high mountain ranges like the Alps, and also not flat plains, just enough elevation so that the Spirit Self is not received too soon. There has to be sufficient land to engender the Spirit Self, extended areas that are more flat than hilly. If there was a seafaring folk here they would have developed the Spirit Self long ago. But that would mean that it had evolved before its time and would be inadequately prepared.

And now we come to the cosmic intelligence of the Earth. The Earth has a cosmic intelligence which determines its form, so that it raises up land wherever and to the extent that it is necessary in order that the right elemental spirits enter into a connection with the beings on the Earth, and on the other hand allows the water to have its place to the extent that this is necessary for the inspiring geniuses to be able to be active.

As we really look at our Earth, we have the impression that—in instances where land has been uplifted in this way—we are able to see something similar to a facial expression of one kind or another, where the soul-nature becomes manifest in this or that configuration. It is the Earth's soul-nature that is appearing before us in the particular earthly configuration. Moreover, as we come to consider the human ether body, this essence of man's ether body extends over the entire organism of the Earth and is everywhere associated with it. Everywhere we find that the earthly element as such—which is therefore maya for the earth-spirits—is for human beings of our time connected with their ego-nature, with outward physical nature. Every aspect of water and air is—if viewed spiritually—connected with what man develops that is at variance with his ego-nature. For the whole of the Earth is there in order to form earthly man. The other aspect has the object of qualifying and varying his nature, which is what can be achieved through the mutual relationship between land, water and air.

When we focus upon the southern part of Europe and especially the Greek and Italian peninsulas, we find that, through the way that land and water are distributed in this region, the Earth is prepared for the bodies that were able to carry the fourth post-Atlantean culture, when the intellectual or mind soul comes pre-eminently to expression.

If the regions of dry land in the south of Europe had been bigger and the inlets of sea smaller, something would inevitably have arisen in Greece and Italy that was supposed to emerge only later; in other words, it would have come about in a way that made it fruitless for the evolutionary process. In order that Greek culture might be able to be repeated—as I have previously indicated—in the Romance culture, a broader land-mass had to be extended towards the sea than is the case in Greece. However, this is so in France; and you can discern the relationship that exists between France and Greece precisely expressed in—on the one hand—the physiognomy of Greece, which is everywhere indented by the sea, and—on the other—that of France, where there are much larger projections of land into the sea.

I wanted today to give you some hints in various directions which will be developed further in our time together. We shall build upon these initial indications when we meet tomorrow.

LECTURE 3

DORNACH, 15 NOVEMBER 1914

YESTERDAY I gave some initial indications of the extent to which the Earth itself is an inspirer for human beings; for in so vast a realm of enquiry it is of course impossible to do more than this.

It is important quite especially in our time to be aware that such connections as we have been considering exist, for man is currently at the point in his earthly evolution where he is emancipating himself from this earthly influence and needs to open himself up to those influences that come not from the earthly world but from the spiritual world that surrounds the Earth.

This determination to imbue human faculties, man's thinking and feeling, with something that transcends purely earthly phenomena lies at the foundation of our anthroposophical endeavours. Indeed, the whole tendency of modern cultural development is in harmony with these aims of spiritual science. In this respect, there are two things of which people in our time need to become conscious.

The first is that, as regards his own soul-being, man belongs to a world which does not reveal itself to the outward senses but lies behind this sense-perceptible world, that in his innermost soul-nature he belongs to a world which he can approach neither by means of sense-observation nor by drawing logical conclusions based upon such observation. It will be the task of our time to develop great clarity about this point, that all knowledge which the outer senses impart and a philosophy that has its foundation solely in such knowledge cannot come near to the true mystery of the human soul.

The second is a truth which is familiar to you from your involvement in spiritual science, even though you know that it is still remote from the general awareness of people today. I refer to the important truth of repeated earthly lives, that the human soul is not confined to the body in which it lives between birth and death and to everything connected with this body but goes from life to life.

Because these two questions—that the soul belongs to a world that lies behind the sense-perceptible world and that it goes from life to life—are among the most important issues for our time and therefore need to be understood, I have added a chapter in the second volume of my *Riddles of Philosophy*[36] where I have considered these two truths in the context of the evolutionary journey of mankind; for there is an urgent need in our time that increasing numbers of people learn to understand both these truths. As this book *The Riddles of Philosophy* is one that is not specifically directed towards anthroposophists but to all who can read and understand what they have read, the attempt had to be made, however briefly, to examine these two truths with the greatest precision. It may be true to say that at a deeper level of consciousness people in our time do direct their thoughts towards these truths (and I am initially saying no more than this). Such tendencies to direct thoughts towards these truths can indeed be observed everywhere. I have tried on occasion to name modern cultural figures who do have an inclination towards these thoughts. I should like to cite another example.

One of the greatest figures of the nineteenth century is without doubt Emerson,[37] who writes in a language which, while not being philosophical in a pedantic sense, is particularly impressive. Whether he is speaking about nature or about the human race, Emerson shows again and again how the outward structure of the world, which man perceives with his senses and understands with his intellect, is merely an outer sheath, a phantasmagoria, and that one only arrives at truth if one tries to reach behind this phantasmagoria.

But a mind such as Emerson's goes beyond this. In order to

exemplify what I mean, I should like to refer to one of his many remarkable books, *Representative Men*.[38] In this book he cites Plato as the representative of all of humanity's philosophical endeavours, Swedenborg as the representative of mankind's mystic strivings, Montaigne, a remarkable figure from the sixteenth century, as the representative of scepticism, Shakespeare as the representative of the realm of poetry, Goethe as the representative of the skill of writing and Napoleon as the man of action, the representative of the will. Emerson achieved something highly significant with this book. Particular human qualities are singled out and related to certain individuals. It would be an interesting study to try to discern how Plato is the representative of philosophical endeavour and Montaigne similarly the representative of scepticism. This book is one of the greatest achievements of the human mind.

Now it is remarkable that Emerson gives a particularly affectionate picture of Montaigne, although one discovers this only if one reads this chapter on Montaigne with quite some thoroughness. This is, moreover, highly significant with respect to Emerson's inclination towards a spiritual-scientific conception of the world. Anyone who seriously embarks upon a study of this world-conception will be aware that everything has two sides, and that when one tries to express a truth what one says is somewhat one-sided and the other aspect inevitably has to lurk somewhere in the background.

The sceptic, who is acutely aware that whenever one formulates a truth in strict terms one is inevitably in the wrong, is deeply affected by the soul-spiritual fluid that is constantly present in the human soul and prevents one, from the moment of one's contact with the spiritual world, from advancing a sharply outlined truth without also indicating that there is some justification for the opposite point of view.

It is this sense of being affected by a feeling that derives from the world of spirit that makes Montaigne a person of real significance. But this is not what I was wanting to say. I wanted to draw your attention to the way that Emerson relates how he came to know about Montaigne.[39] He says that he had found a volume of Montaigne in his father's library but didn't understand it at the time. When he had graduated from college, he read the book again and then had the overwhelming urge to acquaint himself sentence by sentence with what Montaigne had written. And he did so, following the call of this great urge. Now we see in the chapter that Emerson wrote about Montaigne that he was searching for a way of expressing why he was suddenly so taken up with him and had begun to be wholly immersed in his work. He finds no better way of expressing this than to say: 'It seemed to me as if I had myself written the book, in some former life.'

From this you can see how someone who was a contemporary spirit in the fullest sense of the word, a man who was wholly in tune with the demands of the present time, felt compelled to express what lived most intimately in his soul by writing something that is fully in accordance with the spiritual-scientific truth of reincarnation. He can find no better way of expressing himself and is obliged to avail himself of the idea of repeated earthly lives.

Something of this kind is remarkably characteristic and enormously significant; and this leads us to form a connection with the thoughts that we formulated yesterday. If we consider the foremost minds of our time—and Emerson is one of them—we have on the one hand (if they are people of the rank of Emerson) the earthly knowledge that they have assimilated, in so far as they are involved with the evolutionary process of the Earth. They know what one embraces today as a human being. They know that if one is placed in a certain location of the Earth one speaks a particular language and so forth, that wherever one is it is customary to pass on these things to children and young people and, hence, to foster what is referred to as education. This knowledge which is handed down in this way to a people or national group is a knowledge of a broad perspective. One can well say such a thing if one sees how Emerson actually carries out what he undertakes.

We know that when he had to give a lecture, it was as though what he said poured forth directly from his mind as he was saying it. Everything appeared to be improvised. If he was visited on a day when he was to be giving a lecture, the visitors were able to see that he strewed throughout the room all the notes from which he had gathered together what he had to say about the external aspect of his subject. But behind what he imparted in this way to mankind there were some more intimate aspects—such as the instance that I have mentioned, when the idea of repeated earthly lives shone through in a very genuine way.

One can see that when even the leading representatives of our time have a deep feeling about such truths and are, moreover, able to express them, they do so very modestly and are as yet reluctant to introduce these truths to the realm whence outward knowledge has its origin.

If we now approach this matter in a spiritual-scientific way, we would have to look at it with different eyes; for our time is entrusted with the task of bringing what has hitherto been held back within the soul and only hinted at occasionally to the full clarity of understanding, of embodying it in appropriate forms of knowledge, so that what formerly welled forth from the souls of those with the greatest insight can become a self-evident truth that can be easily understood. So we can see very clearly how in his deeply meaningful lectures Emerson would speak a few words that demonstrated his knowledge about the individual life of his immediate surroundings and then a little later said something about Shakespeare. Thus he assembles a great store of earthly knowledge and then a remark slips out in the middle of it all that comes from the intimate depths of his soul.

What is the source of such a remark? This question can only be answered if one considers all aspects of human nature. In his life on Earth a human individual is aware only of the most insignificant part of his nature, he knows only that part of his life which is spent between waking up and going to sleep. The other part of his life is spent in sleep, and this part of human life has many, many aspects.

It would be true to say that for a great number of people this life during sleep entails that they come in contact with elemental cosmic beings who are connected with lower manifestations of human nature than the manifestations associated with the day. Between falling asleep until waking up—that is, in the realm of elemental life—people engage in all sorts of antics which would for them be unheard of in normal life. It is not an unfamiliar idea that dreams are often something to be ashamed of. This is a common experience that anyone can have. People do all sorts of undesirable things when they are asleep, in company that is not exactly good and which appeals to their passions and lower impulses and is far worse than the company which they have cultivated during waking life. When one understands this, one has a much better understanding of historical events.

In order that this habit of larking about is not extended to physical life, it is necessary that people today cultivate the ability not to attribute too much value to their dreams. They will therefore very easily forget their dreams, forget all that they have been up to in their dreams; and this will be beneficial to them, in that they need to be prepared for entering into the spiritual world while they are awake (whereas in former times the idea was that people were enabled to enter the spiritual world during sleep).

As a matter of fact it is not so long ago as is generally thought that there was a stronger awareness of this world. Again, I shall give you an example. There is a picture by Albrecht Dürer[40] which has puzzled many people and especially experts in the field. The theme of this etching is essentially that a satyr-like, faun-like figure is depicted who is holding a female figure in his embrace. From the background another female figure appears, approaching this pair with a punishing gesture; while close by stands a Herculean-looking male figure who holds a club in his hand, which keeps the aggressive female figure away from the group comprising the woman and the satyr, so that she cannot come near them. It is quite astonishing, to say the least, what trouble learned scholars have taken to understand this picture, which is generally called 'Hercules'. However, there is nothing in the familiar legend of Hercules that is suggestive of what is depicted here. So people ask themselves: 'How did Dürer come to portray this scene?' The strangest ideas have been put forward. One can see how helpless Herman Grimm was, for example, when confronted by this picture. He could not make head or tail of it and proposed the most curious ideas as ways of explaining it. How can we understand this situation? Why is it that people can make nothing of this picture? Because neither Herman Grimm nor the other scholars know what Albrecht Dürer still knew, that in sleep human beings are still able to enter a spiritual world. Today this awareness has disappeared. But Dürer still knew that there are, for example, men who get up to all sorts of mischief when they are asleep in company with the elemental world, men who are generally perfectly well-behaved but who during sleep fall back into the world of desires and engage in all sorts of frivolous and pointless activities.

In this picture by Dürer we see the satyr and Hercules with the club. The good Hercules, as he stands by, would very much like to be this satyr. But he lives in the physical world, in a moral world on the physical plane, and his wife will not let him. So she comes and tries to drive him away. However, he rather likes what he sees, and holds her back.

We see here an inner soul-process and know that Albrecht Dürer still knew something about all this. Much in the art of centuries not so very distant from our own can therefore be explained because there was then an awareness of man's connection with the elemental world of the spirit that borders directly upon the physical world.

But if we now turn our thoughts to individuals who are as worthy as Emerson, we should make it quite clear that they are not larking about when they are asleep but that what they do is above reproach. When they are in the spiritual world with their ego and astral body, they have a relationship to truths, to what is to live amongst mankind as true anthroposophy; they become aware of what is to become the physical knowledge of the future. One could say that Emerson receives something of this kind in sleep. This is why it finds expression in what he has to say about physical life, as he surveys the full extent of earthly life with his physical senses and intellect, in so modest and intimate a way.

Now it would not be in accordance with the rightful path of human evolution if it were simply to remain the case that human beings should perceive what lies behind sensory appearances, the phantasmagoria of the senses, only while they are asleep; for it is of evolutionary significance that sleep life will increasingly cease to have a part to play in the quest for knowledge. It takes a great spirit such as Emerson to arrive at an idea such as repeated earthly lives from one's sleep life. Nevertheless, it must be possible for spiritual insights to come to humanity, to gain entry to human lives. Thus whereas these truths have hitherto been proclaimed—as if in a kind of dawning light through individuals such as Emerson—in connection with the innermost life of the soul, there needs now to be a more earthly basis for understanding such truths in clear waking consciousness. The earthly aptitude must exist for feeling that it is perfectly natural to recognize these truths. You will be well aware from the fact that there are still only a handful of anthroposophists that this is not as yet perfectly natural, and all those who stand outside the anthroposophical movement regard us as fools or something of the kind.

Our modern culture is not capable of recognizing these truths. People's natural temperament goes against it. The logical arguments that are put forward against spiritual science are by and large of little value; for people do not resist it on logical grounds but, rather, because the forces of the Earth have rendered them in their nature to be in general ill-disposed to receive such truths today.

However, a time must come when human nature will be constituted in such a way that it will be possible to perceive these truths directly, just as mathematical truths can be perceived today. Man must be so organized that he can quite naturally perceive these truths. For this it is necessary that for the time between birth and death he is physically constituted, and his brain configured, in such a way that he is able to have such insights.

In the sense of yesterday's deliberations,[41] a relationship needs to be established between the spirits working within the Earth and human beings whereby the constitution of human beings is such that they are able to apprehend these truths; and this comes about in the way that I indicated yesterday through descriptions and drawings, namely that a stretch of land reaches out from East to West towards the three gulfs that I spoke of yesterday. This stretch of land is outwardly only a phantasmagoria, and is in reality made up of spirits of earth. It is indeed the case that the spirits of this stretch of land exert an influence upon the human beings and form them physically in such a way that they perceive the truths of man's soul-spiritual constitution and repeated earthly lives. What minds of a more Western inclination have to struggle to acquire from sleep will necessarily become a more self-evident truth in waking life for those approaching from the East whose inclinations are oriented towards the evolution of mankind. The earth element prepares their bodies for what they need for evolution. This earthly realm is to the fullest extent what I explained to you yesterday: a wide-ranging organism which is ensouled and which, from its soul-life, sends forth the earth spirits from time to time that so form and organize the human bodies that they are able to play their allotted part in evolution.

You see, these things are extraordinarily deep and meaningful, and they will need to be studied very carefully if one is to be able to understand them. If one compares the Earth as an ensouled and enspirited organism with man's status as similarly being an organism with a soul and a spirit, there is a great difference between them. Through the outward aspect of his physical body, in which he does not actually live at all but within which he is placed, he is related to the spirits of earth. Through his ether body he is related to the spirits of water, through his astral body to the spirits of air; and through being united with the ego he is related to the spirits of fire.

When a person goes to sleep and leaves his physical and etheric bodies, he is living with his ego and astral body alone in relation to the warmth that pervades the Earth and the air that flows and wafts through it. He is wrested from everything that forms and fashions earth and water in his physical body; when he is asleep he is actually wrenched away from everything that his physical and ether bodies accomplish as earthly essences. Air and warmth do, of course, also belong to the Earth; they belong to the Earth but not to parts of the earth. Now for man as a being of soul and spirit, warmth is the element in which he dwells as in his own elemental space. In the higher animals a preparatory stage for this can be discerned. They have warmth of their own, not merely the warmth of their surroundings. They live in their soul-domain, in their own warmth. Man has developed to a particular degree this living in his own warmth and having his own temperature. This is something that shuts him off from the varying conditions in the surrounding world. Warmth is, so to speak, something of which every human being has within himself his quantum, his particular portion, which he carries about with him. Here he dwells in his own ego, he is at home in warmth. In the element of air this is already less the case; and indeed, here the respective relationship to the Earth is a significant factor. It makes a difference whether he is in the air of the heights, in the air on water, or on land. Here he enters into a relationship with what influences him from without. This, then, is how it is with man as an ensouled and enspirited organism.

The very opposite is the case with the Earth as an organism imbued with soul and spirit. What warmth is for man, earth is for the Earth, the solid, earthly realm. Warmth is for the Earth the outermost realm, and its relationship to the ensouled Earth is equivalent to the relationship that we have to the domain of earth. The Earth is earth through and through, just as we are warmth through and through. The Earth is outwardly differentiated with respect to warmth. To the extent that it stretches forth its limbs into ice-bound regions or into the sultry regions of the tropics, so does it open out its soul-being towards the warmth, just as we adapt our physical body to the region in which we are living. The Earth is in this respect the exact opposite of man, and this is the basis of the cooperation between the Earth and man as organisms endowed with a soul and a spirit. As a result of this cooperation, a process is enacted within the physical human body whereby this physical body of man is able to participate rightly in the evolution of Earth existence through the succession of nations and peoples. Specifically in those peoples who participated in mass migrations from East to West there was a pronounced relationship of the earthly to the human elements; and this relationship could be envisaged by imagining a mighty being within the Earth itself, a being who would make the resolve to intervene in evolution in the appropriate way, say, from the twentieth century onwards. At this point it has to say: I must guide certain spiritual beings up to my surface, I must enable them to become active in preparing physical bodies which are able to receive through the brain the truths that are needful at this time in the evolution of mankind.

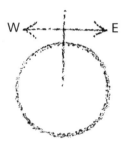

What I have just expressed should be seen as a thought that the Earth has. This thought can be rightly understood only if it is grasped with genuine piety and reverence, if one apprehends it not as one does the thoughts of ordinary science but if one regards it as something holy, as something that cannot be mentioned without a sense of reverence; for one is reminded of man's connection with the spiritual world, in that when such things are expressed one is directly involved in the interrelationship between the human and spiritual worlds. Care therefore needs to be taken that the necessary atmosphere of feeling and receptivity is present when such things are expressed. This is of immense importance in this context. It would even be appropriate to say that things such as this should not be expressed unless they are imbued with a prayer-like feeling or mood. A vista of the spiritual worlds needs to irradiate our thinking when we approach such thoughts. It is in order that this can happen quite naturally through the mediation of external surroundings that our Building is being erected; and everything that will become manifest within it is being fashioned with this intention.

Thus in what I have just described to you, we have an example of how the Earth in its earthly aspect works spiritually through what is contained in its solid element, how it forges and fashions all that lives on it in the course of evolution.

If, on the other hand, we go more towards the West, we find different relationships. Yesterday I described to you a relationship where the West interacts with the East, where the watery element sets its course towards the East like a mighty being in the form of the three great gulfs, which are an expression of the threefold nature of the soul and which the spiritually attuned peoples of ancient Finland experienced as Väinämöinen, Ilmarinen and Lemminkäinen (and are now, more prosaically, known as the Gulfs of Finland, Bothnia and Riga). Thus in the ancient Finnish people there was an interplay between what emanates from the fluid element and what derives from the solid element. In the Finnish people the element that constitutes in particular man's etheric aspect and has a refining influence on his physical aspect, namely the fluid element, was united with the element of earth, with what derives from earth and constitutes man's physical aspect.

The question may be asked as to the significance that a people such as the ancient Finns, who accomplished such an eminent task in the course of earthly evolution, still has in later times. It indeed has a significance in the whole course of evolution that such a people continues to exist, that it does not disappear from the Earth when it has accomplished its mission. Just as an individual human being retains a living memory of the thoughts that he has had at a certain stage of his life for some later period, so must earlier peoples live on as a conscience, as a memory that can continue to exert a living influence on what happened later on: in truth, as a conscience.

One could say in this connection that what the Finnish people have preserved will be the conscience of Europe. A time must come—if human hearts are to be filled with an understanding of the tasks of evolution—when from amongst the Finnish people the ideas of the *Kalevala* will blossom once more, when this wonderful epic will be spiritualized and imbued with modern anthroposophical concepts and when it will again be brought to the consciousness of the whole of Europe in all its rich profundity.

The European peoples have venerated the epics of Homer. However, the epic of the *Kalevala* had its source in still deeper depths of the soul, even if it is not as yet possible to perceive this. It will nevertheless become possible if the teachings of spiritual science are used in the appropriate way for explaining the spiritual phenomena of Earth evolution. An epic such as the *Kalevala* cannot be preserved without being maintained in a living state of existence, without souls who—while dwelling in an earthly body—are closely related to the creative forces of the *Kalevala*. It remains there as a living conscience. It can continue to exert an influence if not its words alone but what has lived within it can go on living, if there is a centre from which it can ray forth. What matters is that there is such a centre, just as the thoughts that we have had previously can be there in our later life.

In the West it is more a question of what forms and fashions the etheric body. (These are difficult truths; and you will have to make the best of it, because I do not have the possibility—which I hope may arise sometime in the course of earthly evolution—to explain in a whole year what I am having to explain in an hour. You will have to undertake to amplify a lot of what I have said through your own thoughts and ponder it meditatively. It will then begin to make complete sense to you. I must especially emphasize that you should not try to approach these matters with rash judgements or hastily formed feelings.) In the West, then, the influence is more upon the etheric body, which had to be formed and fashioned in the same way (albeit at an earlier time) as has to occur for the East with the physical body.

You see, it is very easy at this point to allow misunderstandings to creep in, for the distinctions are extremely subtle. When, for example, one sees in the West that for its peoples the essential thing is that the etheric body has been formed more by the spirits of water, it follows that—because the physical body is an impression of the ether body—the physical body has also been formed from the forces of water. But the point is that in the East the forces have a more direct influence upon the physical body. It is therefore necessary to keep one's mind focused on what really matters. Making subtle distinctions of this kind is beyond the capacity of ordinary science. It sees that the physical body of someone from the East has a particular configuration and that the Western physical body has a different one. It cannot see more than this. Only spiritual science is able to perceive such distinctions. It often happens that when one is saying something totally different, people have the impression that one is actually saying the same thing as before. Yesterday, for example, I needed to say that the essential thing for the Asiatic peoples is that the forces that build up the physical body reside in their own ether body. Today I am saying that for the peoples of the West the ether body is formed out of the forces of water. If you take everything into account, you will understand that in olden times the situation with the peoples of Eastern Europe was that the ether body had to be formed and now, in our time, the physical body; whereas in the case of the peoples of the West the situation is that the ether body is now being formed once the physical body has already received its special character from without, that their ether body is exposed directly to the genii of the sea, the genii of water.

The peoples of the West are what they are because of impulses that enter into the ether body. Where impulses enter primarily into the ether body, the focus is more upon time than on space; and what matters is the way that impulses exert their influence in the succession of time.

If we look towards the East, we see thoughts welling up out of the earthly domain in order to prepare man for a future evolution. If we turn our gaze towards the West, we see thoughts or forces bubbling forth from the fluid element which form ether bodies in the sequence of time. And we see how already in olden times formative forces were at work upon man's ether body in the West and right into Central Europe so that it might live its own independent life in a living, outward, bodily aspect.

What does this mean? It means, my dear friends, that there were people living in former times in the west of Europe whose way of life was the outward manifestation of their ether body, just as now—when the ether body has already been exerting its influence through these old impulses—man is working out of the physical body. In those times people were living who still had a living interconnection with the spiritual world, and especially with the elemental world. This is the way it was then. These times when the genii of the fluid element spoke in such a living way to the ether body of Western man are already over. But when the ether body is being addressed in this way, things are different from how they are in our time, when man's physical body is what is primarily being called upon. Man's physical body is addressed in such a way that an impression is made upon his senses, so that in addition to certain aspects of behaviour he acquires a knowledge which is connected with sensory impressions.

As regards their habitual behaviour and what lived within their inner being, these people of the West in olden times still had a connection with the elemental world. Among the Celts there were people who knew as much about the elemental world as we know today about the physical world, people to whom the elemental world was not closed, who could speak of nature genii, water genii and earth genii in the way that we speak of trees, plants, mountains and clouds and who had direct access to these genii of nature. Indeed, the particular character of life in Europe derives from these circumstances—from the fact that, whereas in our time influences are exerted upon the physical body by way of the senses, in those ancient times they were exerted upon man's etheric body.

The influence of this formative process upon man's etheric body then continued, but in such a way that the etheric body's relationship to the genii of water became increasingly unconscious, with the result that conscious communication with the nature spirits ceased to be a significant factor.

How did this come about? The situation in France, for example, was that the wave of Celtic evolution was succeeded by a wave of Romance evolution, so that the Celtic element was pervaded by a Romance element. In the interplay between the Celtic and Romance elements we can discern two impulses: an old impulse, which fosters a direct interconnection between the elemental world and the ether body, and a new impulse, that of the Romance influence, which likewise affects the ether body but in such a way that its influence is of the nature of a historical wave, making it possible for the reawakening of ancient Greek culture to take place in France to which I have referred in previous lectures. If we want to understand the kind of human being that we find in the West, we need to evaluate the various impulses that flow into the ether body in the right way.

We have spoken about certain characteristic phenomena with respect to influences upon the physical body and upon the ether body. When we come to consider the middle region, the circumstances are somewhat different. Here we are confronted by something which is, I would say, much less defined, something that is far harder to characterize with any clarity; for both spirits of the earth element and spirits of the fluid element are in this context working directly upon the physical body.

As you can see, this is a realm of transition. In the West, spirits of the fluid element are directly influencing the ether body. In Central Europe, the spirits of the fluid element reduce their activity; and certain spirits of the earthly element join forces with them. They work directly upon the physical body, and less strongly upon the ether body. The spirits of the earthly element refine the physical body, as you will find if you go further East. So Central Europe has in one way or another to do with everything that provides Europe over long periods of time with physical bodies that are accessible to the fluid element and to the solid element; and we can therefore see the inevitable complexities of what flows into the evolution of mankind. We see how from this reservoir [in Central Europe] the people of the Franks—prepared in the way that I have described, by the genii of the fluid and the solid element—make their presence felt amongst the Celtic-Romance peoples; and only then does what we can discern as the effective force in the evolution of humanity emerge.

The Franks who remained behind (and the Saxons are also associated with them) preserved the particular attribute of receiving primarily in their physical body what derives from the watery and earthly spirits. The Franks who migrated westwards united their being with that essential quality that results from the direct influence of the genii of the sea, which becomes even more significant through embracing the historical aspect of the Romance element.

Thus the impulses become interwoven with one another; and we can therefore see that, especially if we want to characterize Western Europe, we shall never come to understand it unless we take into account everything that influences the etheric body. If we want to characterize Central Europe, we would have to say that it is more a question of what forms and shapes the physical body.

Now we may see that impulses such as I have described are concentrated in certain centres, where they manifest their particular characteristics. Two such centres, which relate to one another in a really characteristic way, are Central Europe on the one hand and the British Isles on the other. In Central Europe, where this is manifested most strongly, we find what I have referred to as the solid element, where the physical body is imbued with what comes from the genii of the liquid realm and the genii of the solid realm and, hence, where these are mingled together; while in the British Isles we find especially—and to a greater extent than in France, for example—the influence of what derives from the genii of water. The consequence of this is that in these two regions there live people who fundamentally carry the same impulses; but in the former case they bear these impulses within the physical body and are adapted to everything that is associated with the working of these genii in the physical body, while those in the British Isles bear them within the ether body and therefore have the task of enabling everything connected with the impulses of the etheric body to become a reality. If I were to formulate this in a somewhat grotesque fashion, I could say that, when comparing a German and an Englishman, one notices a difference if one observes them as physical bodies. One begins to see a similarity only if one compares the physical body of the German with the etheric body of the Englishman. Only then does it become clear that the same impulses—indeed the very same impulses—live in both.

Everything that forms part of our outward vision, of the phantasmagoria of the senses, appears as a caricature. This may seem a surprising statement. But we only see things in their true form if we consider the living source and, hence, the truth of what we behold. Because beings in the world must collaborate (and this can hardly be otherwise, since the world is a whole), it has to be so that certain impulses work, on the one hand, through the physical body and, on the other hand, through the ether body. That is how it has to be; for that is how a true collaboration comes about.

As a result of this, a very special relationship can be discerned in the spiritual world between the German world and the world of Britain. I have in a previous lecture[42] explained this very special relationship in the context of East and West, when I showed you how East and West were engaged in a struggle in the spiritual world, brought about by the difference in the souls coming from an Eastern body and the souls coming from a Western body.

What is brought about by the circumstances that I have described is of a somewhat different nature. I must also ask that you do not take what I have to say today as a theme for speculative intellectual enquiry. It is necessary to observe these things in the spiritual world, otherwise one will not be able to arrive at the truth. A harmony gradually begins to develop between what is reflected from Central Europe and the British Isles, a sense of accord, a true spiritual bond that has by degrees been gaining strength to the point where one say that, from a spiritual point of view, no souls on Earth love one another more than those living in Central Europe and those living in the British Isles. These souls, seen spiritually, are united in the strongest love, and this comes to expression in what we see before us now, so entangled have human affairs become.

I would not say such things if they were based on unsound research and if they had not been arrived at through very painful experiences. You should not now try to systematize this by imagining that every alliance in the physical world is a war in the spiritual world, while a war in the physical world represents a bond in the spiritual world. The situation is as I have described it; and the fact that it comes to expression in the form of a war is the manifestation of how difficult it is in the materialistic culture of modern times for a spiritual fact to become an actual reality.

Our age has not merely in words but also in deeds a resistance to recognizing what exists as a reality in the spiritual world. It tries to put forth the opposite of the true state of affairs in the spiritual world, because the age of materialism resists acknowledging the spiritual world also in deeds. Hence the trends evident in the spiritual world towards establishing harmony between what has been achieved physically in Central Europe and etherically in the British Isles are completely submerged in the maya of the strife and mutual hatred that confronts us now.

Those who are not anthroposophists may well feel a glow, a satisfaction in calling us fools, since the knowledge that emanates from the spiritual world is in complete contradiction to what can be observed on the physical plane. Nevertheless we may be assured that the further evolution of mankind is dependent upon spiritual truths becoming discernible and upon human beings learning to see behind the sense-perceptible world. If this is to happen, certain events of which I have been speaking over the course of these days with at least some degree of clarity need to take place.

We may be glad that karma has brought us together here in a neutral region where it is possible to speak about these matters with such complete openness; for it is not easy to speak about these things today. But it is good for anthroposophists to become familiar with these truths, since they should regard what is happening in the wider world as a stimulus to look behind the veil [of events]. There is much that must remain completely incomprehensible unless one is able to look behind this veil; for only then will things show themselves in their full significance.

THE WORLD AS THE RESULT OF
BALANCING INFLUENCES

LECTURE 4

WE have through our studies become familiar with the idea that beneath or behind the physical world we can find the gateway to other worlds. I should like today by way of an introduction to speak about certain characteristics of these spiritual worlds of which we already have some knowledge, since by extending this knowledge other aspects of this theme will become apparent to us.

As you know, the world that borders upon our world is the so-called world of Imagination. This world is far more mobile than our physical world, with its clear-cut outlines and sharply defined objects. We enter a fluid, fleeting world when we penetrate the veil formed by the physical world; and we are also aware that as we encounter this first spiritual world we begin to have the feeling that we are outside our physical body. Directly we enter this spiritual world we acquire a new relationship to our physical body—a relationship such as we have to our eyes or ears in our physical body. The physical body in its totality functions essentially as a kind of organ of perception; but we very soon notice that it is not really the physical body that is the motivating factor behind this feeling but the etheric body. The physical body merely provides us with a kind of framework for the etheric body. We look upon the etheric body from outside, while also experiencing it as the sensory organ that perceives a world of weaving, moving images and sounds. Our relationship to the ether body that is thus embraced within the physical body is similar to our relationship to our ears and eyes.

This feeling of being outside our physical body is an experience similar to that of sleep. When we are asleep, that aspect of our humanity which is of a soul and spiritual nature is outside our physical and ether bodies. However, at such times our consciousness is dulled, and we know nothing of what is happening to us or around us. It is therefore apparent that we can have a relationship to our physical body that is different from the one to which we are accustomed. This is something of which people need to be made aware through spiritual science; and in the course of evolution mankind will increasingly be directed towards such an awareness the further we go into the future.

I have emphasized on many occasions that it is no arbitrary matter that we concern ourselves with spiritual science today, but that this is demanded of us because of what is currently under preparation in human evolution at this present time. This feeling of separation from one's physical body will, therefore, increasingly be an unfathomable experience that will come over people as the future unfolds. A time will come when a great number of people will begin to feel: 'Why is it that I feel as if I were split in two, as if a second being were standing beside me?' This feeling, which will arise as a matter of course, just as hunger or thirst or other experiences, is one that people of the present and future should not fail to understand. It will become comprehensible when, through spiritual science, people manage to understand the true significance of this experience of division.

As these experiences become increasingly common, it will also become necessary for educationalists to take them into account. More careful attention will have to be paid to certain experiences of children than has hitherto been the case, when these experiences have not been present to the same degree. It is true that in the maturity of later life, amidst the impressions of the physical world, these feelings that I have characterized will not be particularly strong in the immediate future; but as time goes on they will become ever more intense. They will, to begin with, manifest themselves in the growing child, and adults will hear many things from their children that they will need to understand—the sort of things that they are liable to dismiss as absurd but which they really should not dismiss, because they are connected with the deepest mysteries of world evolution.

Children will claim that they have seen a being of some kind who told them what they should do. Someone who thinks in a materialistic way will say that this is all nonsense and that there is no such being. But anyone who wishes to understand spiritual science has to realize that this is a phenomenon of real significance. If a child speaks of having seen someone who goes away again but then keeps on returning, talks incessantly about this and that and cannot be silenced, someone who understands spiritual science will realize that something that will manifest itself with ever greater clarity in human evolution is revealing itself in the child. What is this that can be discerned here?

We shall understand it if we consider two fundamental experiences, the first of which was of particular importance for the fourth post-Atlantean, Graeco-Roman age, while the other is of significance for our own time, when it is gradually becoming a reality. Whereas the first experience reached its culmination in the Graeco-Roman age, we are slowly moving towards the second.

Experiences deriving from Lucifer and Ahriman are forever influencing human life. Lucifer had a particularly strong influence upon the fundamental experience of the fourth post-Atlantean period; while in our time Ahriman is more involved and is the determining influence upon our experience. Now Lucifer is associated with everything that has not developed into clear sense-perceptions, with what is perceived by man in a vague and undifferentiated form. In other words, Lucifer is connected with the experience of breathing, with inhaling and exhaling. A person's breathing has to have a quite specifically attuned relationship to his whole organism. The moment when the breathing process is disturbed in some way, the unconscious process to which we do not need to pay any attention is immediately transformed into a conscious process of which we are more or less dreamily aware. And when, to be specific, the breathing process becomes too vigorous and places excessive demands on the organism, it is possible for Lucifer to enter with the breath into the human organism—not necessarily Lucifer himself but the hosts belonging to him.

I am speaking here of a phenomenon which is familiar to everyone through their experience of dreams. Such experiences can arise in dreams in all sorts of ways. Nightmares when a disturbed breathing process makes a person conscious in his dream, so that experiences of the spiritual world become intermingled with it (together with all the fears and anxieties associated with nightmares), have their source in the luciferic element. Whenever an ordinary breathing process changes into choking or a feeling that one is being strangled, this is connected with the involvement of Lucifer in the breathing process. This is the crude form of the process, when as the result of a diminishing of consciousness Lucifer enters into the breathing process, becomes manifest in dream consciousness and adopts the role of the strangler. This is the crude form of the experience.

There is, however, a more subtle experience, where this experience of choking is toned down and is not so abrupt as physical strangulation. It would not generally be thought that there is such an experience as a refined form of choking or strangulation. But whenever someone has an inner question or a doubt about something or other in the world, this is actually a subtle experience of being strangled. Thus when we are obliged to question something, when we are confronted by a riddle of whatever magnitude, we are being strangled but in such a way that we do not notice it. Every doubt, every question is a subtle form of nightmare.

Experiences which would otherwise be felt as crude become subtle and more intangible when they manifest themselves in a more inward way. One might well imagine that science will eventually come to study the connection of the breathing process with the posing of questions or the sense of being assailed by doubt. But in any case, everything that is associated with questions and doubts, with a sense of dissatisfaction prompted by something in the world that is approaching us and demanding an answer, or simply because we are being forced to respond out of what we are—all this is connected with the influence of Lucifer.

If we consider this in the light of spiritual science, we can say that whenever we feel threatened by the Angel of Death in a nightmare or experience a sense of inner oppression or anxiety where problems arise, our breathing process becomes stronger and more forceful; whereas if human nature is to function as it should and life is to unfold in the right way, what lives in the breath needs to be toned down and restored to harmony. What happens when the breathing process becomes more forceful? In such a situation the ether body and everything connected with man's etheric nature expands too far and becomes too diffuse; and as this takes place in the physical body it cannot be confined to it and works upon the physical body as if it would tear it apart. An over-exuberant, too widely extended ether body gives rise to an intensified breathing process, and it then becomes possible for the luciferic element to exert a particular power.

Thus the luciferic forces can find their way into human nature when the ether body has expanded. One can also say that the luciferic forces have the tendency to express themselves in an ether body that has expanded beyond the limits of the human form, that is to say, in an ether body that needs more space than is available within the confines of the human skin and thus goes beyond the form provided.

If one were to imagine how one might respond artistically to this process, one might say something of this kind. In its normal state, the human ether body is the sculptor of the human form that appears physically before us. But as soon as it expands and seeks to create for itself greater space and wider boundaries than are available within the human skin, it tends to adopt other forms. The human form is no longer adequate; and the ether body endeavours to transcend it. In former times a solution was found to this problem. What kind of form emerges when the expanded ether body, which is not suitable for human nature but is appropriate for a luciferic being, gains recognition and appears visibly before the human soul? What will then emerge from this? The Sphinx!

Here we have a particular way of penetrating the mystery of the Sphinx; for it is actually the Sphinx who is at one's throat. When the ether body expands as a result of the energy expended in breathing, a luciferic being appears within the soul. What is living in such an ether body is not the human form but a luciferic form, the form of the Sphinx. The Sphinx presents itself as the being who fills us with doubt and torments us with questions. It therefore has a particular connection with the breathing process. But we also know that the breathing process is related in a particular way to the process of blood-formation. Hence the luciferic forces also live in the blood, seething and surging through it. By way of the breathing, luciferic beings have full access to the human blood; and if the blood is imbued with excessive energy the luciferic nature of the Sphinx is especially powerful.

Thus because man is open to the cosmos through his breathing process, he is confronted by the Sphinx. This experience of confronting the Sphinx nature of the cosmos was a particular feature of the fourth post-Atlantean, or Graeco-Roman, cultural period; and we see in the legend of Oedipus something of the nature of this confrontation, how the Sphinx binds itself to him and torments him with questions. The picture of man and the Sphinx, or of man and the luciferic powers in the universe, is indicative of a fundamental experience that people had in the fourth post-Atlantean cultural period, namely that when, however slightly, they broke through the boundaries of their normal life they came into contact with the Sphinx. At such times Lucifer approached them, and they had to cope with Lucifer, with the Sphinx.

The basic experience of our time, the fifth post-Atlantean epoch, is quite different. A particular feature of our epoch has been that the ether body is not puffed up or expanded but is compressed, so that instead of being too large it is too small, a situation that will intensify as evolution proceeds. Whereas we can say that in the normal form of a human being in Greek times the ether body was too large, in a human being in modern times the ether body is constricted, compressed and altogether too small. As the materialistic scorn that

Human being in
Greek times

Human being in
modern times

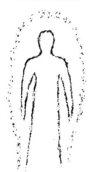

people feel for the spiritual world intensifies, the more compressed and withered will the ether body become. But because the functions of the physical body depend on the ether body's capacity to permeate it in the right way, the physical body will always have a tendency to dry up if the ether body becomes too compressed; and if it were to dry up to an excessive degree, it would have hornlike feet instead of human feet. People will not actually have such feet, but they have the tendency to do so because of this proclivity of the ether body to become dried up and bereft of etheric forces. This dried up ether body can be a particularly suitable domain for Ahriman, as is an expanded ether body for Lucifer. Ahriman will take on a form that is indicative of a poverty with respect to the ether body, which will develop insufficient etheric forces for properly formed feet and will instead produce hornlike goat's feet.

Mephistopheles is of course Ahriman; and for the reason that I have given, it is not for nothing that he has goat's feet. Myths and legends are highly meaningful. Thus Mephistopheles very often appears with horse's hoofs, where his feet are likewise dried up and have become hoofs. If Goethe had fully understood the problem of Mephistopheles, he would not have portrayed him like a modern cavalier; for it belongs to the nature of Ahriman-Mephistopheles that he does not have sufficient etheric forces to pervade and fashion a physical human form.

However, a further characteristic is brought about by the fact that the ether body is compressed and more lacking in etheric forces than is normally the case. We can see this most clearly if we consider human nature as a whole. From a physical point of view there is in a sense a duality in our nature. Just think of yourself as you are as a physical human being. And yet it is an aspect of this physical human being that there is a constant flow of breath within it. This air is, however, expelled from the body with the next exhalation, so that this aspect of the physical human being that is associated with the air that you are breathing is continually changing. You do not merely consist of muscles and bones but are also a breathing human being. This, however, is constantly changing, air is passing in and out; and this aspect of your nature is connected with the constantly circulating blood.

As though separated from this breathing aspect of your physical nature is the other pole, the nervous system, where nerve-fluid circulates; and the contact between the nervous system and the blood is of a purely external nature. Just as only those etheric forces that have an inclination towards the luciferic nature can find ready access to the blood by way of the breath, so are the etheric forces that have a tendency towards the mephistophelian or ahrimanic nature only able to approach the nervous system and not the blood. Ahriman is denied the possibility of pervading the blood; he must continually live in the nerves in a dried-up realm of bareness and austerity, because he cannot come near to the warmth of the blood. If he wants to establish a connection with human nature, he will be obliged to crave for a drop of blood; for it is so difficult for him to gain access to blood as such. An abyss lies between Mephistopheles and blood. When he is wanting to draw near to man as a living human being, when he is endeavouring to form a connection with man, he realizes that man's essential being lives in the blood. He therefore has to try to get hold of the blood.

You see, it is a mark of the wisdom of the Mephistopheles legend that the pact is signed with blood. Faust must commit himself to Mephistopheles through the blood, because Mephistopheles has no direct access to blood and has to crave for it. Just as people in the age of ancient Greece confronted the Sphinx who resides in the breathing system, so do people in the fifth post-Atlantean cultural period confront Mephistopheles, whose field of operation is the nervous system, who is cold and insipid because he suffers from bloodlessness, because he lacks the warmth of blood. It is because of this that he is a mocker of humanity, its cold and cheerless companion.

Just as Oedipus had to learn to cope with the Sphinx, so do people in the fifth post-Atlantean epoch need to find a way of dealing with Mephistopheles. Mephistopheles confronts them like a second nature. The Greeks were confronted by the Sphinx as a result of what entered into them through the intensification of the breathing process and blood circulation. The human being of the modern age is confronted by everything that emanates from his intellect, from his cold sobriety, by everything that is rooted in the nervous system. This experience of coming face-to-face with Mephistopheles has been prophetically intuited through poetic language; but it will increasingly become a universal experience the further we proceed into the fifth post-Atlantean age, and the experiences which, as I have indicated, will appear in children will indeed be encounters with Mephistopheles.

Whereas people in ancient Greece suffered from the torment of an over-abundance of questions, people today are not so much tormented by a flood of questions as suffering from being in the grip of preconceptions, from having a second body at their side which is the repository of all their prejudices. What has brought this situation about?

Let us consider human evolution with an open mind. There is so much that, in the course of the fifth post-Atlantean cultural age, has ceased to stir people's warm enthusiasm. Think of all the innumerable questions that confront us when we study spiritual science. They simply do not exist for people with a materialistic way of thinking. The riddle of the Sphinx means nothing to them, whereas the ancient Greeks were keenly aware of it. A typical modern person does, however, have to experience something else. He is very good at having an opinion about everything, he observes the world of the senses, uses his intellect to see the connections between what he observes and then believes that all its riddles are solved. It would not occur to him that he is to a large extent groping around in a world of imaginary pictures. But this has the effect of compressing and drying up his ether body so that eventually the influence of the mephisto-phelian powers becomes firmly linked to him as a kind of second nature both now and in times to come. All the prejudices and limitations of materialism strengthen the mephistophelian nature, and we can even now discern a future when everyone will be born with a second being by his side who will say that those who speak about the spiritual world are fools—'I know everything, I rely wholly upon my senses.' Of course, people will dismiss the claims of the mephistophelian riddle, as they dismiss that of the Sphinx; but they will nevertheless have a second being hard on their heels. This being will accompany them to the point where they feel compelled to think materialistic thoughts—not through themselves but through a second being who is their companion.

A materialistic outlook brings an aridity to the ether body within which Mephistopheles is able to dwell. It is essential that we understand this, and that children are in times to come given an education—whether through eurythmy or through the cultivation of spiritual-scientific ideas—which can enable their ether bodies to be enlivened, so that people adopt a right attitude and come to recognize the nature of the being who stands by their side. They will otherwise not understand this companion of theirs and will remain confronted by, and under the enchantment of, an otherness. Just as the ancient Greeks had to deal with the Sphinx, so will modern man have to meet the challenge of Mephistopheles, of the satyr-like, faun-like figure with goat's or horse's feet.

After all, every age knows how to express what is most char-acteristic of it in an archetypal legend or saga. Examples of this are the Oedipus legend in Greece and the legend of Mephistopheles in modern times. And yet phenomena of this kind need to be under-stood at a fundamental level.

You see, what is otherwise merely recounted in the form of poetry—in the drama enacted between Faust and Mephistopheles—needs to become a fundamental aspect of future education. The prelude to such a scenario is that a people or a poet have had an intuitive sense of 'the companion'; but ultimately everyone will have a companion who should not remain unintelligible to him, and this companion will appear most forcefully during a person's childhood. And if adults who are responsible for education do not know how to deal appropriately with what comes to expression through children, human nature will be corrupted by a failure to understand the enchantments of Mephistopheles.

It is very remarkable that these characteristics can be found everywhere in legends and fairy tales; for the structure of legends and fairy tales, which modern scholars find so difficult to understand, either has a mephistophelian or ahrimanic tendency or else has a Sphinx-like, luciferic quality. All legends and fairy tales owe their origin to the fact that their content was originally experienced in terms of man's relationship either to the Sphinx or to Mephistopheles. Deeply hidden within legends and fairy tales we find either the theme of the riddle, the Sphinx theme, where something has to be solved and a question answered, or the theme of enchantment, where something or someone is under a spell, that is, the mephistophelian or ahrimanic theme. For what exactly is the ahrimanic theme? We can recognize it when Ahriman is beside us, and we are constantly in danger of falling prey to him, of giving ourselves over to him and being unable to escape his clutches. When confronted by the Sphinx one is aware of something that invades one's being and tears it to pieces; whereas in the face of Mephistopheles one feels that one must immerse oneself in this influence, give oneself up to it and wholly succumb to it.

The Greeks had no theology in our modern sense, but they were closer to the wisdom of nature and its phenomena than people are today. They approached the wisdom of nature without theology, and because of this they were tormented with questions.

Man is closer to nature in his breathing process than in his nervous system. The Greeks therefore had a particularly vivid experience of this approach to wisdom in their relationship to the Sphinx. The advent of theology is a sign that man no longer believes that he can be in touch with the divine wisdom of the world by being in direct contact with nature but that he wants to study it; and his means of approaching it is not through the breathing process and the blood but through the nervous system. The search for wisdom has, in theology, become a nerve-process. But because man has shackled his wisdom to the nerve-process, he draws near to Mephistopheles; and with the dawn of the fifth post-Atlantean age this imprisoning of wisdom in the nervous system has led to the arising of the intuitive sense that Mephistopheles is chained to one's heels, that he is in close proximity.

If we strip the Faust legend down to its bare essentials, we have the picture of a young theologian striving for wisdom who is tormented with doubts and sells his soul to the devil, to Mephistopheles, with the result that he is drawn into his sphere of influence. But just as it was the task of the Greeks to withstand the onslaught of the Sphinx by fully developing their human ego, so in our time do we need to get the better of Mephistopheles by extending the capacity of the ego and filling it with that wisdom which can alone come from spiritual-scientific research, from a knowledge of the spiritual world.

Oedipus was the greatest of these conquerors of the Sphinx. Every Greek who took himself seriously as a human being was to one degree or other a lesser version of him who had vanquished the Sphinx. Oedipus merely represented what every Greek had to experience in a typical form. What did this imply? Oedipus had to achieve mastery over all that lives in the respiratory system and the blood. His task was to counterbalance this aspect of man's being by means of the nervous system with its impoverished etheric forces. How did he do this? By taking the forces that are related to the nervous system—that is, the mephistophelian forces—into his own nature but in a healthy way, so that they do not accompany him as a second being at his side but are within him, enabling him to counteract the Sphinx by means of these forces.

From this we see that Lucifer and Ahriman do actually have a beneficial influence in their rightfully allotted place, but that when they are where they are not supposed to be they have a harmful influence. For the Greeks the Sphinx was something that they had to deal with, that they had to extricate from themselves. When they cast it into the abyss and were therefore able to bring the extended ether body into the physical body, they had overcome the Sphinx. The abyss is not somewhere outside us, it is our own physical body into which the Sphinx must be drawn down in a healthy way. But the other pole—that which works not from without but from within—must here be strengthened. The ahrimanic element must be embraced within man and be put into its right place.[43]

Oedipus is the son of Laius. It had been prophesied to Laius that if he had a child this child would bring misfortune to his whole race. He therefore cast out the boy who was born to him. He pierced his feet, and so he acquired the name Oedipus, or 'club foot'. Thus we have the mephistophelian forces in the drama of Oedipus.

I have said that, when the etheric power is impoverished through these forces, the feet cannot develop normally, they become stunted and wither. In the case of Oedipus this was brought about artificially. According to the legend he was found hanging from a tree by a shepherd, who brought him up and therefore rescued him from death. But he continued through life with club feet. In a certain sense he is a sanctified version of Mephistopheles. Here Mephistopheles is in his rightful place and can give a powerful impulse to the ego in connection with the task of the fourth post-Atlantean epoch. Oedipus is deprived of everything that constituted the greatness of the Greek era, namely the harmony between the ether body and the physical body which we admire in the wonderful forms of Greek art, so that he can become a 'personality', the representative human being in whom the ego becomes strong. The ego that has now migrated to the head becomes strong, while the feet atrophy.

People in the fifth post-Atlantean cultural period have an opposite task. Just as Oedipus had to embrace Ahriman in order to confront and conquer the Sphinx, so must the people of the fifth post-

Atlantean cultural period—who have to deal with Ahriman-Mephistopheles—take Lucifer into themselves, that is, they have to go through the opposite process to Oedipus. Everything that has been accumulated by the ego in the head must be pressed down by the head into the rest of man's nature. Thus philosophy, law, medicine and unfortunately also theology have accumulated in the ego; and inasmuch as the ego lives in the nervous system they are therefore all nerve-processes! And now the urge arises to get rid of all this from the head and to impart it to the whole world through the veils of material existence.

Now think of Faust, endowed with all that the ego has built up, think of how he wants to divest his head of everything that Goethe has summarized in these words: 'Alas, I have studied philosophy, law and medicine, and unfortunately also theology with great ardour.'[44] He now wants to rid his head of it all. He does this, moreover, by giving himself up to a life that is *not* bound up with the head. He is the opposite of Oedipus, he takes the Lucifer nature into himself.

And now think of everything that Faust does to receive Lucifer into his being in order to do battle with Ahriman, with Mephistopheles who is beside him. All this shows us to what extent Faust is indeed the inverted Oedipus. Whereas everything that occurs within Oedipus as a result of the inverted Ahriman nature has to do with Lucifer, everything that happens to Faust through the inverted Lucifer nature is concerned with Ahriman-Mephistopheles. Just as Ahriman-Mephistopheles lives more in the outside world, Lucifer lives more in the inner world. All the misfortune that Oedipus encounters through being imbued with an ahrimanic nature is connected with outward phenomena. Disaster assails his race, not merely himself. Even the disaster that befalls him personally is of an external character. That he pierces his eyes and blinds himself is an outward occurrence; likewise the plague that descends upon his native land is something of an external nature. All Faust's experiences, however, are of an inner, soul nature and represent inner tragedies; so that Faust can also in this respect be seen as the reverse of Oedipus.

If we consider these two figures—or, rather, these two dual figures—Oedipus and the Sphinx, Faust and Mephistopheles, we have typical pictures of the evolution of the fourth and fifth post-Atlantean epochs.

When the time comes when history is regarded less as an impression of external happenings and rather as a record of what people experience, then and only then will it be seen how significant and important these fundamental experiences are. It will then be possible to see what actually underlies the ongoing flow of evolution, of which the outward phantasmagoria that is usually presented as history is merely an impression, a mere sequence of external events, however meaningful they may appear to be.

Whereas the ego had to be strengthened through the entry of Ahriman-Mephistopheles into Oedipus, that is, into the Greek soul, this ego has nevertheless become too strong in people today. They therefore need to free themselves once more from the ego by deepening their knowledge of spiritual events and realities of the world to which the ego belongs, if it is aware that it does not merely live in a human body but is a citizen of the spiritual world. This is demanded by the age in which we are now living. Whereas in the fourth post-Atlantean age people had to strive with all their might to become conscious of the ego in the physical body, people in our fifth post-Atlantean age need to devote themselves to becoming conscious that the ego belongs to the spiritual world. This extending of ego-consciousness to encompass the spiritual world is what spiritual science represents; and so it is connected at the deepest level with the highest demands of human evolution in our fifth post-Atlantean age.

LECTURE 5

IN a lecture[45] that I gave in relation to the *Kalevala* I said something that you will have found somewhat perplexing. Once you had thought this lecture through, you would most likely have said that I had been talking about a being that stretches from West to East, with three further extensions or limbs which the ancient Finnish people experienced as Väinämöinen, Ilmarinen and Lemminkäinen and which today, in our materialistic language, we call the Gulfs of Riga, Finland and Bothnia. However, you might well have wondered what this has to do with a being, since it is merely a surface, the surface of the sea together with its extensions. It does not have a bodily nature at all. So why had I been speaking about a being? Your thoughts will have been along these lines.

It is quite typical that a spiritual-scientific truth gives rise to thoughts such as these, for it happens again and again that truths which come from the spiritual world evoke challenges. It is absolutely right and significant that people make such protests; and the only way of dealing with issues such as these is that one makes a deeper study of the matter in question. I want to do this today with respect to certain problems of spiritual knowledge. However, I need to preface this with some introductory remarks.

We shall, to begin with, briefly consider the materialistic prejudices of our time regarding the nature of man. Thus, for example, there is the very understandable prejudice that a number of physical processes take place in man's being, including those in his nervous system and brain, and that these physical processes are accompanied by soul processes which for the materialist are merely the expression of these physical processes. The materialist studies what is going on in the human body, discerns—or presupposes hypothetically—certain finely tuned nerve processes and claims that they are the basis for all processes of thinking, feeling and will, that these soul processes are merely the concomitants of what is happening physically. This is a widely held view today; and there is no doubt that it will become even more firmly established through the materialistic thinking of modern times. But it is about as clever as the following scenario, which is a logical extension of it. Let us suppose that someone who is going for a walk finds tracks on the path, some of which are parallel ruts and others that look like feet. He then ponders and says to himself: now then, the substance of which this path is formed has undergone some changes, as a result of which it has gradually become compressed and formed these ruts; and in certain places it has subsided, thus forming impressions that resemble footprints.

Of course, this is absolute nonsense; for what actually happened was that a cart came along here and made these ruts with its wheels, and this is where someone was walking and left these footprints. It was not the ground that was responsible for these tracks but the human being with his feet and the cart with its wheels.

It is a similar situation with the processes in our nervous system. Whenever we are inwardly active in thinking, feeling and willing, we are engaged in processes of a soul-spiritual nature. For as long as we are living in the physical world, these are enacted in conjunction with the physical body, just as the cart makes its way along the path and the human being walks along it, leaving their tracks behind. These traces that they leave behind have just as little to do with physical substance as the tracks on the footpath have to do with the substance of the ground. The processes taking place in the substance of the brain, in the nervous system, actually have absolutely nothing to do with thought processes, and indeed no more than the effect of what the cart and human being have done has to do with what is going on beneath the surface of the ground.

It is highly important to take note of such things, for one then understands that an anatomist or physiologist who merely investigates processes in the organism is like a spirit-being who moves about beneath the surface of the Earth but never comes above it and has never seen people or carts. He only sees from the earthly perspective that there are unevennesses in the Earth's surface, but never comes to view them from the other side. In this limited way he then makes an investigation and believes that the Earth itself is responsible for this through its own activity. The moment such a spirit appears above the surface of the Earth he would become aware of the true state of affairs. The same is true of anatomists and physiologists working out of a materialistic background; for they are always under the Earth's surface, which is to say that they know nothing of spiritual science and, hence, inhabit a sub-earthly realm. They study merely the processes in the material world, which have nothing to do with what happens in the realm of soul and spirit. It will be a task for our time that people make the transition from this anatomical and physiological thinking to spiritual-scientific thinking. They would then be like goblins who have hitherto only been beneath the Earth's surface and who, on being raised above it, would see how the tracks in the ground had actually been made. Materialistic scientists, who concern themselves only with the sub-earthly spiritual domain (for even matter is spiritual), are actually like wild goblins; and humanity will have a great shock in store when these goblins or earth-spirits make their appearance in the realm of soul and spirit.

I needed to say these introductory words because I want to give you some kind of explanation of the anomaly referred to earlier, that the Gulfs of Bothnia, Finland and Riga, which are indeed level surfaces or plains, were described as the essential nature or attributes of a mighty being stretching from West to East.

Now we think of ourselves, do we not, as spatial beings, beings of space. But we are not really the kind of spatial beings that we consider ourselves to be; for man is actually a different being from the one whom we behold only in the maya of illusion, in the phantasmagoria of outward appearance. We do indeed perceive him as a being who manifests himself in space and is spatially enclosed within his skin. But there are actually three significant riddles or questions that lie concealed within the frame of the human form.

The first of these riddles is hidden behind all sorts of puzzling and mystifying illusions. We are indeed deceived about our own existence by the outward maya of a world of imaginary pictures. The traces of this deception can be found in modern science, particularly where science is completely at a loss and has to resort to all sorts of hypotheses. The riddle or question to which I refer is concealed behind scientific explanations or hypotheses as to why people have two eyes and two ears and yet do not see or hear double, why these organs are arranged symmetrically so that there are two of them rather than one. Merely to perceive this represents a profound problem or question for science, and if you study the relevant literature you will find everything that has been written about this question of why we see with two eyes and hear with two ears.

From a certain point of view man is very coarsely organized, and this sometimes comes to expression in the way he speaks. He actually also has two noses, although they have grown together to the extent that they cannot be discerned so readily as the two eyes and the two ears. Hence we do not speak of having two noses but, rather, one nose, even though in reality a person has *two* noses and not *one*. However, man is so coarsely organized that where something has grown together this cannot be noticed. Nevertheless, it is in any case a fact that in one's perception of human nature there is a total symmetry between left and right. If we did not have two ears, two eyes and two noses we would not have an experience of our ego. We also need two hands for this. When we clap our hands and feel one hand against the other, we have a sense of our own ego. We also do something similar when we combine what our two eyes or ears have perceived into a unity. We always perceive the world from two sides, from the left and from the right, whenever we perceive anything with our senses; and it is only because we perceive everything from these two directions and bring these images to a point of intersection that we possess our ego-nature as human beings. Otherwise this would not be the case. If, for example, our eyes were in the vicinity of our ears and we were unable to combine the lines of vision, we would always remain beings who are imprisoned in a group-soul. In order to be ego-beings, we have to bring left and right to a focal point.

We bring everything that we perceive from left and right to a point of intersection in the middle. Imagine a flat surface extending outwards from this vertical line on the blackboard. Everything comes to this line of intersection from both left and right, and we are actually in this plane. We are not in space but in this plane, within this surface. We are, as human beings, not really extended in space, we are surface-beings, on the grounds that impulses coming from left and right are intersecting [in us]. And if you want to give a real answer—as opposed to one enshrouded in maya—to the question as to where you really are, you should not say that you are in whatever space that your body occupies but, rather, that you are wherever your left and right dimensions intersect. You are actually there and there only. Just as the being to whom I referred previously has surfaces where its airy and watery halves meet (and here the two halves are different), so in man there are two similar halves of right and left. But man is also a surface-being, a plane; and it is maya that we see him as having an actual form.

So where does this 'actual form' come from? He has it because he is in the midst of a kind of battle. A being from the left is fighting with a being coming from the right. If we were to perceive spiritually the nature of this being on the left, we would perceive it as light; whereas a spiritual perception of the being active on our right side would make us aware that it has other qualities. The twofold nature of our being arises from the fact that the being of Lucifer is fighting within us from the left, and the being of Ahriman from the right.

In order to form a clear picture of this, we need to think of the luciferic being waging his battle from the left, where he builds up his fortifications; while the ahrimanic being engages in similar exploits from the right. The left aspect of your being is the fortification established by Lucifer, whereas the right aspect of your being consists of the fortifications of Ahriman. All that it is possible for you to do is to stand in the middle. The art of life consists in finding the right balance between them. We do this unconsciously when we perceive with our senses. When we hear with our left ear and with our right ear, and then unite the impulses that reach us in this way into a single perception, or when we feel something with our left hand and with our right hand and unite the two perceptions, we are always establishing ourselves in the surface that lies on the boundary of the

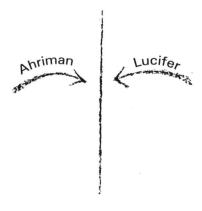

battle between Lucifer and Ahriman. The space that is left to us in the middle is as narrow as—or even narrower than—the blade of a knife. Our organism does not belong to us but is the legacy of the battle between the luciferic and ahrimanic powers and also other powers that are of a similar nature to Lucifer and Ahriman. However, this is an area that will not be investigated further at present.

Thus as surface-beings we are wedged between entities that do not concern us directly as human beings. The left aspect of our being does not concern us, nor does its right aspect; there is only the process that takes place between them.

And now you can develop further the picture that I presented earlier. You see, there is a continuous stream of processes going on within the Earth. But what happens within the Earth does not make these tracks. Similarly, what happens within you in the left or right half of your organism has absolutely nothing to do with what you experience within your soul; for these are processes that take place between Lucifer and Ahriman. What goes on beneath the Earth's surface, everything that happens there—worms creeping about, the seasonal alternations between warmth and cold—has nothing to do with the tracks that left their impressions; and it is these tracks that are comparable with what goes on within the human organism. We should therefore say that spiritual observation of physiological and anatomical processes reveals to us the battle that Lucifer and Ahriman are waging within us, but we must not suppose that our soul life is the result of these processes involving Lucifer and Ahriman. That would be an incorrect conclusion, for our soul life is enacted within the soul itself. Moreover, it is enacted in the surface, in the plane, not in the spatial organism.

Now there are different stages in the working of Lucifer and Ahriman in the human organism, and it is very interesting to study these. With regard to the human head, we find that Lucifer and Ahriman have built up roughly equal fortifications on its left and right sides. The left and right halves of the head are very similar, and their forces are such that little intermingling is possible between them, with the result that they have little effect upon the surface in

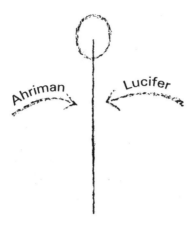

the middle. At this mid-point is the surface, Lucifer is on the left and Ahriman on the right; but because the left and right halves of the head are formed in so similar a way, Lucifer and Ahriman rebound from one another, and so man is able to develop a calm, inner activity [see drawing]. His thinking is very little disturbed by the influences of Lucifer and Ahriman, because in the head they mutually repel one another.

If one considers the lower regions of the human form, this is no longer the case. On one side Lucifer manages to enhance the stomach, while on the other side Ahriman enhances the liver. The stomach is the means whereby Lucifer wages his battle from left to right, while the liver is Ahriman's means of battling from right to left. The relationship between the stomach and the liver can be rightly understood if one bears in mind that Lucifer manages to build up the stomach as a kind of weapon, whereas Ahriman does something similar with the liver. These organs are in a state of perpetual battle, and scientists would do well to study this battle between the stomach and the liver. And if the heart has a tendency to be somewhat over towards the left, this is an expression of Lucifer's desire to seize something for himself, as does Ahriman on the other side. The whole left-right relationship manifests the way in which Lucifer and Ahriman wage their battle within man, even though from man's point of view what lies on either side of the central surface is in a certain sense alike. But we have already seen that this is only true of the upper part; for the two sides cease to be alike as we follow the human form in a downwards direction.

In the case of the being of whom I spoke previously with three outstretched feelers or tentacles associated with Lemminkäinen, Ilmarinen and Väinämöinen, the one half is air and the other half water; and so here the two halves are quite different. But once one has attained knowledge of a clairvoyant nature, it becomes clear that man is actually also a surface between two distinct halves; for as soon as one is no longer thinking of the physical body and is focusing on the ether body, one finds that the left half becomes significantly lighter than the right half. The left half shines, glistens and glimmers with radiant light; whereas the right half is overshadowed with darkness. This is how it actually is with the left and right aspects of man's being.

There are, however, other orientations associated with man's relationship to space, or—to express this in occult terms—to the battle between Lucifer and Ahriman. Thus he has a forward and backward orientation, looking in front and behind.

If instead of observing man in terms of left and right we think of him as having a forward and backward orientation (and we need to

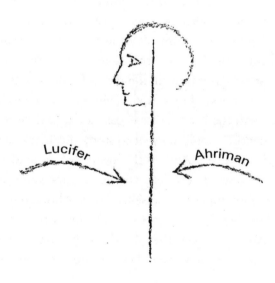

include the whole human form), we find that also in this orientation
he is not the spatial being that he appears to be; for, just as Lucifer
and Ahriman engage in combat in the left to right dimension, with
the spatial aspect merely representing the barricades that they erect
against one another, so does Ahriman fight against man from behind
and Lucifer from in front. Ahriman mobilizes his activity from a
backwards direction, while Lucifer manifests his activity from in front
in opposition to Ahriman. Man stands in the middle between them.

It should, however, be noted that as regards this forwards—
backwards orientation Lucifer and Ahriman do not succeed in
coming so close to one another that they form no more than a surface
between them. The situation is somewhat different here. Ahriman
comes only as far as the plane extended through the spinal column,
while Lucifer comes as far as the plane through the breast bone,
where the ribs meet. In between these two planes lies a space which
separates them, where the influences of Lucifer and Ahriman are
thrown into confusion. It is a region where they battle without
encountering one another directly, sending their missiles through the
intervening space. Thus Ahriman can reach only as far as the spinal
column and Lucifer to where the ribs meet the breast bone; while we

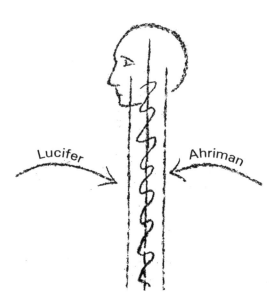

stand in the midst of this fight between Lucifer and Ahriman. Thus with respect to the forwards–backwards orientation we are a being that has space; while with respect to left and right we have no space.

In the left–right orientation Lucifer and Ahriman battle mainly through thoughts. Thoughts buzz around from left and from right and meet in the surface or plane in the middle. These are thoughts of a cosmic nature which knock up against one another and come together at the human surface in the middle. In the forwards–backwards orientation Lucifer and Ahriman do battle more with feelings; and because their forces do not approach one another so completely, there is a space in the middle where we can dwell inwardly with our own feelings. When we have thoughts that engage in mutual combat from left and right, we feel that these thoughts belong to the world. When thoughts come to us we think of things that are outside. When we form our own thoughts, they are a mere phantasmagoria, an imaginary world that no longer belongs to the actual world. In our feelings we belong to ourselves, because Lucifer and Ahriman do not encounter one another completely and we therefore have scope to play with between the two areas. This is why we are so fully within ourselves in our feelings.

You see, as human beings we have been created by the influences of beings of the higher hierarchies; and we are surface-beings in a left–right dimension because the higher hierarchies have so formed us as human beings. They do not allow Lucifer and Ahriman to come together here. We are creatures of the good Gods inasmuch as these good Gods have decreed out of their creative thoughts that, in the light of the battle that is going on between Lucifer and Ahriman, a boundary must be established to enclose a region into which they cannot enter, where they will be unable to come together. We human beings have been placed into the midst of this battle as creatures of the good Gods, and the more we stand our ground in this battle the more we are creatures of the good Gods.

With respect to the forwards and backwards dimension, the good Gods do not wholly allow Lucifer to enter into us; they have created a barricade where the ribs meet in the breast bone. And by forming this wonderful tower that encloses the spine and the brain, the good Gods have established a fortification against Ahriman. He cannot pass by there, and the most he can do is to send the arrows of his feelings across to Lucifer. This is the place where we have the scope to keep them apart from one another.

There is also a third dimension, from above to below. Here, too, we need to understand that the true state of affairs is not as it appears to be in the world of outward semblance, or maya; for Ahriman works from below upwards, and Lucifer from above downwards. Here, too, the good Gods have established a barrier against Lucifer, in that his influences coming from above are as it were resisted by a plane. You can find this plane by taking a skeleton and removing the skull from it. Where the skull rests on the cervical vertebrae you need to imagine a planar surface. This invisible horizontal plane where the skull rests on the cervical vertebrae is the barrier. When a person makes this his focus, he can resist the luciferic influences coming from above. Lucifer can only shoot his arrows from above, these arrows now being will-impulses. From left to right fly arrows of thought, from in front to behind arrows of feeling and from above downwards and also from below upwards arrows of will.

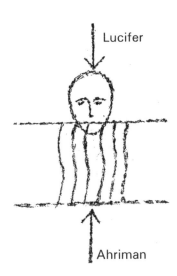

Here, too, we have a certain amount of scope; for approximately in line with the diaphragm there is a plane that has been established as a barricade against the upward pressure of Ahriman. Thus Ahriman can only reach the diaphragm in his upward movement and cannot reach any further with his will, with his missiles of will, with his essential being. Above this is our own field of action.

So you see how complicated man is! Take any part of the human form—for example, the left side of the face. As a being of thought, Lucifer can completely pervade this left side of the human countenance, and as a being of feeling he can penetrate it to a certain point; finally, as a being of will he can imbue it with his forces from above downwards. Thus in this way you can discover for every part of the human organism how Lucifer and Ahriman are active within man as a spatial being through cosmic impulses of thought, feeling and will; bearing in mind that in our thoughts we are actually surface-beings, in our feelings we have a certain free space between in front and behind and in our will we have such a space between above and below, between the plane through the upper part of the cervical vertebrae and the plane through the diaphragm. Only if you separate out what does not belong to man at all will you arrive at a true picture of the human form; and you can then construct this for yourself.

Thus you can see that the human form has been forged from without, that it receives its particular character from external forces, and that we are unable to understand it if we simply equate it with the forms that directly confront us; for we can understand it only if we know how it is connected with the entire spiritual cosmos, how luciferic and ahrimanic forces approach man from right and left, from below and above and from before and behind and how they give his being its particular character of a spatial being.

This is also the way in which you should study something else that has been formed in accordance with the true cosmic influences in the world, namely our Building.[46] If you look at it merely in terms of its outward appearance, you might well think that the most important aspect of this Building is the wooden structure that exists there in space. But that is not the case. Its most important aspect can be found where, apparently, nothing is present. If we take any one of its forms and consider the particular piece of wood [see first drawing below], what matters here is not the wood itself but where there is nothing, where air adjoins the wood. The way to arrive at a true picture of our Building would be to take an enormous lump of wax and make an impression of the interior and then study it. What really matters is what you dwell within when you enter the Building, something that you cannot see but need to feel. I once pointed out that the principle underlying our Building is one of a 'Gugelhupf'[47] cake-tin. Imagine that you have such a mould [see second drawing] and you bake a cake in it. What is the important thing about this whole operation? Clearly it is not the cake-tin but the cake, which has thereby acquired its proper shape and has been baked as it should be. The mould's significance is purely so that pouring the cake mixture into it and then baking it enables one to produce the required form of cake.

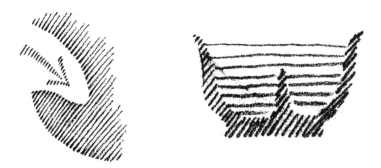

Similarly, what is important about our Building is not its sur-roundings but what is inside it; and within its walls will be the feelings and thoughts of those who are in the Building. These will arise through people directing their eyes to its extremities, feeling its forms and filling themselves with thoughts. What is inside the Building will be the 'Gugelhupf', and what we build is the sheath, the form. But this has to be of such a kind that what is thought, felt and experienced in it is right and true. This is the principle of modern art as opposed to older forms of art. What used to matter about art was what is outwardly visible in space, whereas modern art has a different emphasis. What is outside is the containing vessel, whereas the part that really matters cannot be made by the artist, for it is what is within it. This does not only apply to sculptural or architectural forms but also to painting. What matters is likewise not what is painted but what is experienced in connection with it. The painting itself is merely the equivalent of a 'Gugelhupf' cake-tin.

This, may I say, is the very essence of the step in evolution that we need to take, that we indeed—pardon the expression—make the transition from the cake-tin to the cake. To remain in the containing vessel equates with materialism; arriving at the cake itself means finding the spiritual essence, and this is what we are working towards. If we are not aware of this, we shall not be able to evaluate our artistic endeavours in the right way. If our artistic conception of our Building is in accordance with an older model, we may well say that we cannot see anything beautiful about it; but we would then be unaware that it is not the cake-tin that matters but the cake that is inside it. If we adopt this artistic principle, we will begin to understand the whole meaning and significance of the advance in evolution that spiritual science makes possible. Through spiritual science man needs to make the transition from the mould within which the 'Gugelhupf' is baked to the 'Gugelhupf' itself.

He must, therefore, free himself from the belief that, for example, the source of thoughts resides in brain processes, whereas on the contrary cosmic processes are at work in what goes on in the brain and there is an ongoing battle between Lucifer and Ahriman; and he must come to see that the thoughts and feelings of the human soul are simply the tracks that have been engraved into this battleground and have nothing to do with the so-called material processes—in other words, with the processes enacted by Lucifer and Ahriman.

I should like to offer another picture. Let us suppose that we are entering a beautiful garden, whose beauties can be attributed both to the arrangement of the trees and the layout of the flower-beds; and we are wanting to form an opinion about it. If we were then to look down a hole in the Earth, we might be approached by an elemental being who says to us: 'I will tell you why all these roses and violets are growing here, why there is a bush in one place and flowers in another. I creep everywhere down there beneath the Earth's surface and I see the soil that has enabled the trees, violets and roses to spring forth.' We might reply: 'Yes, you describe these processes very well. This is the way that everything is bound to happen in the physical world. But in order that plants are able to thrive this garden has been created, and for this a gardener was necessary. However, these are areas of which you have absolutely no knowledge and with which you have never concerned yourself.'

So we must learn to say to materialistic anatomists and physiologists: 'I find your activity only when I peep down into the Earth. You creep around and study processes that necessarily take place, but they have nothing to do with what goes on in the soul-spiritual domain. Moreover, you will only be able rightly to interpret what happens down there when you endeavour to understand the relationships that exist between Lucifer and Ahriman, on the one hand, and the other hierarchies who bring Lucifer and Ahriman into a state of balance.' If this is achieved, what has hitherto been active only as an idea fostered from within the ego will be enriched by spiritual science.

A time will come when people will say: 'We are told in the biblical story of the Creation of the breath of Jehovah that was breathed into man.' Then people of the future will ask: 'But when this breath was inhaled, in what part of man was it received?' If you recall all that I have said, you will find that the immediate regions where this breath was breathed are these intermediate spaces where Jehovah created man as a kind of cube out of the dimensions extending from in front to behind and from above to below [see drawing] and filled him with His own being, with His magical breath, in such a way that the influence of this magical breath was able to extend throughout the rest of his being into the regions dominated by Lucifer and Ahriman. Here, bounded on right and left, from above and below and from forwards and backwards, is an intervening space where the breath of

Jehovah enters directly into the spatial aspect of man's being. What I have been saying applies in the first instance to this physical, spatial being of man.

You will see that this liberates our outlook so that we can behold man as he stands within the entire cosmos; and indeed, there are also moral, soul aspects of what outwardly appears in a purely spatial guise. For in these aspects, too, even though not to so strong a degree as with man as a spatial being, we are initially confronted by a phantasmagoria of shifting images. In everything pertaining to morality and logic, in all of our soul-activity, Lucifer and Ahriman are working in combination, while man stands on the boundary between them.

We shall speak tomorrow about this highly important and significant subject.

LECTURE 6

FROM yesterday's lecture you will have come to realize that our body has the particular form that it has because it represents a result of the collaboration between luciferic and ahrimanic powers.

It is very important for our time to acquire a real knowledge of this interplay between the luciferic and ahrimanic powers, for only through this will humanity gradually be able to understand the forces that are at work behind the outward phantasmagoria of existence. We know that we need neither to hate Ahriman nor to fear Lucifer, because these powers are hostile influences in the world only where they are working outside their own territory. I spoke at some length about this in Munich last year.[48] Some indications regarding this theme have also been given here.

Our study yesterday of how the physical, spatial human body owes its form to the interaction of the luciferic and ahrimanic powers has given us an indication of the most external aspects of the way in which Lucifer and Ahriman play their part in human life. We come somewhat nearer to the more intimate side of human life when we turn our attention from the physical body to the etheric body. The ether body is in a certain sense the sculptor of the physical body. It is embedded within the etheric world as a whole and, as an etheric organism in a constant state of inner movement, lies at the foundation of our physical organism. Now as we have seen in the case of the physical body, luciferic and ahrimanic powers are also active within the etheric body; and it is important to emphasize that, also as an etheric being, man is intimately involved in the interplay between luciferic and ahrimanic forces.

In order to give some indication of the matter at hand, we shall turn our attention to the three basic functions of man's being in so far as he is not a physical being, namely willing, feeling and thinking. Of course, we do not perceive these qualities when we view man with respect to his physical body. Only inasmuch as the physical body manifests itself through a certain physiognomy, through particular gestures and so forth, are we able to glimpse these inner qualities in the physical body itself. The ether body, which is an organism in constant movement, is, however, a living expression of man's thinking, feeling and will.

Orthodox science has certain problems with studying these three soul-forces. If one surveys the views of various philosophers, one will see that there are some who emphasize the will, while others give priority to thinking; and there are yet others who regard feeling as the most important faculty. But none of these philosophers have much of an idea of how thinking, feeling and will form a unity within man. This inability to have any real conception of the relationship between thinking, feeling and will in the life of the human soul is a manifestation of the difficulties that people have in dealing with the whole question of man himself. I really do not know—say the philosophers—whether the human soul is oriented more towards will, feeling or thinking. Is it inclined more towards one or the other? This is very much like admitting that one does not really any longer know what a human being is. Thus someone may say to me that he wants to bring a person to see me, and he brings me a five-year-old child and says: this is a human being. Then someone else comes along and also says that he wants to show me a human being, and he brings a person who is much bigger than the first and is, let us say, middle-aged. Finally, a third individual appears wanting to show me a human being; and the person he brings has a wrinkled face and grey hair. And now I really no longer know what a human being is. I have been shown three different beings! Of course, they are all human beings; but one is very young, the next is somewhat older and the third is really elderly. They are all quite different in appearance. But if one looks at all three together, one knows what a human being is. It is similar with willing, feeling and thinking. The difference between them is essentially that, whereas willing is the same soul-activity as thinking, it is still very youthful or childlike in character. When willing grows older, it becomes feeling, and when it is really old it is thinking. There is merely a difference in age between willing, feeling and thinking; and what makes everything complicated is that the various ages associated with these soul-activities live in our soul together.

I have previously explained in, for example, my book *The Threshold of the Spiritual World*[49] that as soon as we leave the physical world the law of transformation prevails rather than that of rigidity or fixity. Everything is in a state of constant change. What is old suddenly becomes young, what is young becomes old and so on. Thus the three soul-activities can manifest themselves in us simultaneously: willing appears at once in its youthful form, in its older form (that is, as feeling) and also as the oldest form of willing, that is, as thinking. So the ages of life are intermingled, everything becomes fluid. This is how it is with man's ether body.

But these changes do not simply come about out of themselves. Moreover, we are not generally aware in ordinary life of a unified soul-activity, we are unable to bring this to consciousness. If we nevertheless—because we need to observe the ether body as a single entity, as something whose nature is mobile and fluid—symbolically draw the ether body as a flowing stream, this stream of soul-activity does not come to consciousness at all in ordinary life; but into this stream, into this constant movement of the ether body that flows onwards with the passage of time, there enters first a luciferic and then an ahrimanic influence.

This luciferic activity makes the will youthful. When our soul-activity is pervaded by a luciferic influence, the result is will. When the luciferic influence in our soul-activity is predominant, when Lucifer makes his forces an effective presence in our soul, then will is

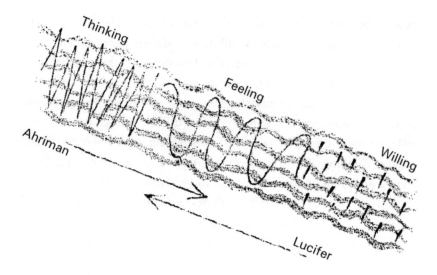

active within us. Lucifer has a rejuvenating influence upon the whole stream of our soul-activity. When Ahriman, on the other hand, is the main influence upon our soul-activity, it becomes old; and this is thinking. Thinking, having thoughts, is completely impossible in ordinary life unless Ahriman exerts his influence upon our etheric body. In so far as it comes to expression in our ether body, our soul-life cannot function without Ahriman and Lucifer. If Lucifer were to withdraw entirely from our etheric body, we would have no luciferic fire for our will. If Ahriman were to withdraw entirely from our soul-life, we would never be able to develop the coolness of thinking. In the middle, between these two is a region where Lucifer and Ahriman are in conflict with one another. This is where they interpenetrate, where their influences are intertwined. This is the region of feeling. It is indeed the case that in the human ether body one can perceive both the light of Lucifer and the hardness of Ahriman. If one were to look at the human ether body as a whole, it would not of course appear as it is symbolically depicted in the drawing but everything would be in a constant state of interpenetration. There are certain areas where the ether body appears to be opaque, as if there were traces of ice in it. Forms appear in the ether body that can be compared with patterns made by ice on window panes. These are hardened sections of the

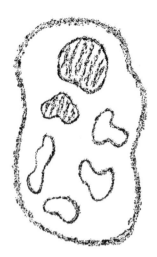

ether body, where it becomes opaque; and they are the living legacy of the life of thought. This freezing of the ether body in certain places derives from Ahriman, who transmits his forces through thinking.

There are other places in the ether body that seem to be full of light; they are transparent and have a radiant, gleaming quality. Here Lucifer sends his rays, his forces; and these are the centres of will in the ether body. And in the regions in between, where the ether body is in a state of perpetual activity, there is every now and then a hard place which is then immediately encompassed and dissolved by rays of light. A perpetual oscillation between rigidification and dissolution— this is the expression of the activity of feeling in the ether body.

Thus we can say that not only is the form of the physical body called forth by the interplay of luciferic and ahrimanic forces, alternately disturbing and creating balance, but the same forces are also active in the entire ether body. When the ahrimanic forces have the upper hand, this is an expression of thinking; when the luciferic forces are in the ascendant, this is an expression of willing; and when they are in mutual conflict, one can say that this is an expression of feeling. This is how luciferic and ahrimanic forces intermingle within our ether body. We human beings are in a certain sense the result of the influence of these forces and are in an intermediate position between them.

Now we must be clearly aware that we are not always present with our full ego in what is going on here. Our earthly ego, which we have acquired only in the course of Earth evolution, can only manifest its full activity and consciousness in the physical body. Not until the age of Jupiter[50] will it be possible for the ego to manifest itself fully within the ether body, which means that man's actual ego is not directly involved in all that takes place in the ether body. If ahrimanic and luciferic forces had not intervened in the advancing flow of world evolution, man would have been a totally different being; for he would be able to have perceptions in his physical body, but the possibility of having thoughts would be denied to him. He has thoughts because Ahriman is able to acquire an influence upon his ether body; and similarly, he has will impulses because luciferic forces can influence his ether body. These forces are therefore necessary.

We must therefore realize that as regards our earthly conscious-ness we cannot enter fully into our ether body. Only in the physical body can we come to full ego-consciousness. We cannot enter in this way into the ether body. Thus as regards the ether body we enter a world in which we are not fully present. Moreover, when Ahriman enters our ether body to form our thoughts, it is not our thoughts alone that are dwelling within it; and when Lucifer brings his for-mative forces into our ether body, it is not only our will impulses that are living within it. The same is also true of feelings, the realm where these two beings are in conflict. In so far as Ahriman lives in our ether body, we are through our ether body immersed in the sphere of nature spirits, the elemental nature spirits, the spirits of earth, water, air and fire. The only reason that we are unaware of this is that we cannot fully enter with our ego into our ether body. But it is always the case that our ether body is not only the bearer of the thoughts that we ourselves think but it is also the receptacle of the influences of nature spirits. Thus whenever someone has an encounter with these nature spirits, he is able to speak about an experience that he has had which he has not had in his ordinary ego-consciousness; and it is indeed so that these nature spirits are encountered when something abnormal happens to a person, when his ether body is loosened from his physical body.

How can something of this kind happen? The fact is that man's ether body is connected with the whole of the surrounding etheric world, thus also with the whole sphere of nature spirits. To exemplify this, let us suppose that someone is walking along a road in the daytime. When he is walking along a road with his ordinary consciousness, his ether body is residing properly in his physical body, and he perceives with his ego-consciousness what it is normally possible to perceive with such a consciousness.

But suppose that he is walking along a path by night. If one is walking along a path at night it is normally dark, and in many people this arouses sensations of horror and creepiness. Because of these feelings, one may be assailed by those distinctive sensations associated with the intervention of Lucifer, with the result that the etheric body is loosened from the physical body; and this etheric body which has thus been loosened from the physical body is enabled to enter into a relationship with the surrounding etheric world.

Now let us suppose that the person concerned comes into the vicinity of a churchyard where ether bodies are still closely associated with the graves of people who have died. With his ether body being in this loosened state it is possible that he may be able to apprehend something of the thoughts that are still residing in the ether bodies of these dead people. Suppose that someone has died recently who has incurred debts and has died with the thought that he has done so. This thought may still be present in the ether body of the person who has died. Of course, one does not perceive these thoughts in the ether body of another person if one's own ether body has not been loosened, but this is possible in the circumstances that I have described. Thus the person in question may enter into a relationship with the ether body of the other person and perceive the thought: 'I have incurred debts.' And then, because such an experience strengthens the luciferic power within him, there awakens in him the feeling: 'I must pay this debt.'

Such a person therefore experiences in his etheric body something that he would never experience in the physical body in normal life. This is not the sort of thing that is experienced every day in ordinary human life, and it therefore makes a considerable impression upon the consciousness of anyone who does. It calls forth the awareness that the person concerned knows: 'I have experienced something that I did not experience in my body, nor could I have experienced it in my body.' He feels that he is somewhere other than in his body, and this is an unfamiliar situation to be in. He then feels the urge to return to his body, and he longs for help to be able to do this.

This sense of longing to return to one's body attracts certain elemental spirits or nature spirits for whom this human feeling is a kind of food or nourishment. They are attracted because they are drawn by the feeling, 'I long to return to my physical body,' and they help people to find the way back to their physical bodies. If we are asleep in the ordinary way, we can easily find the way back; but when we are experiencing something of the kind that I have described, we find this difficult. We do not see the situation as we would perceive it in the physical body but, rather, imaginatively, in pictures. Someone comes along in the guise of a shepherd, perhaps, but who is actually a nature spirit, and gives us this advice: 'Go to a certain castle. I shall take you there on a cart'—or words in a similar vein.

There is also something else that can be linked with such imaginative pictures. The body that one has left and outside of which one had the experience in question may appear to one as an enchanted castle from which one has to release someone when one returns to it. This is how this longing for the physical body and the help of the nature spirits can be imagined. Then one returns to the physical body, that is to say, one wakes up.

People who have had such experiences then relate them because they have the feeling that they have in this way been in contact with the thoughts of someone who has died. They say to themselves: 'This was a feeling of something that was not merely within me, it was not simply something that I had dreamed; it was a feeling that communicated to me something that was going on in the world outside.' This naturally comes to expression in pictures, but it corresponds to a process. I shall now share such a picture with you, where someone has related what he has experienced;[51] and it has similarities with what I have just been telling you about. He describes it as follows: 'When I had taken leave of the soldiers, I encountered three men on my path. They wanted to exhume a dead person because he owed them three marks. I was filled with compassion and settled the debt, so that the one who had died might rest in peace and not be disturbed in his grave. I continued on my journey. Then I was approached by a strange man with a pale face who invited me to climb into a leaden carriage, and persuaded me to accompany him to a castle. In the castle there lived a princess, who, he explained, would only marry a man who came to her on a vehicle made of lead. He then turned to the coachman and said: "Drive as best you can towards the sunrise." Then a shepherd appeared who said: "I am the Count of Ravensburg!" He ordered the coachman to drive faster. We arrived at a gate, and the sound of a tumult came to our ears. The gate was opened. The princess asked the man where he came from and how it had been possible for him to drive in company with the old man; and I noticed that the person who had led me there was a spirit. Then I entered in by the gate and took possession of the castle.' That is, he came back into his body. Here you find a similar experience to the one that I described earlier.

And what do we call it when something happens to someone who then goes on to tell others about it? It is a fairy tale. In this and in no other way have fairy tales arisen. Everything else that is said about the origin of fairy tales is sheer fantasy. All true fairy tales are a proof that one can have experiences outside the physical body, if the ether body has been loosened in some way and a relationship is formed with the surrounding etheric world. This is one way in which someone can enter into a relationship with the outside world through his ether body.

But there is another way in which this can happen. A relationship can also be established with the surrounding etheric world where an activity is being undertaken in a semi-conscious state, where the ego is present only to a certain degree. This is the case with speech. When we speak, we are not so fully conscious as we think we are. It is not at all true to say that speaking is something that belongs to us, that we have in our power. Etheric forces live in speech, and much of our speaking is unconscious. The ego does not fully penetrate our speech. When we speak, our ether body is connected with the surrounding etheric world. We learn to think as individuals, but this is not the case with speech. We are taught to speak through karma, which places us in a particular life-situation. Whereas we enter into a relationship with nature spirits in abnormal conditions when our ether body has been loosened, we find that inasmuch as we speak and are not merely thinking in silence we are linked with the Folk-spirits. Thus the Folk-spirits come to dwell within our ether bodies, even though we are not conscious of this. We are just as unconscious in terms of our ego-activity of this aspect of our lives as we are of what has been recounted to us in the form of a fairy tale.

Now that we have seen how Lucifer and Ahriman make their interventions in man's ether body, we must also consider the way in which luciferic and ahrimanic forces play a part within the astral body. When we study the human astral body, we must necessarily turn our attention to the most prominent aspect of man's astral body in the way that it manifests itself on the Earth. This is consciousness. In the physical body, form and force are the essential elements; in the ether body, movement and life; in the astral body, consciousness. However, we do not have only one state of consciousness in the human body but two: ordinary waking consciousness and sleep. But the strange thing is that neither of these two states of consciousness is completely natural to us. A natural state of consciousness for us would be one that is between the two, in which we never actually live.

If we were continually awake, we would hardly be able to develop properly as human beings through the various stages of life. Only because there is always something present in us that is less awake than we are during the day are we able to develop. Ask yourselves how much you think you develop as a result of what you experience and apprehend in ordinary life. For the most part we use these experiences to satisfy our curiosity and need for sensation. It seldom happens that we set out with the intention of placing what we experience in our waking daily life in the service of our development. We are able to undergo development because something within us is continually asleep when we are awake during the day. I am not referring to times when people drop off to sleep but when they are fully awake during the day; for it is then that something within them remains asleep. It is this factor that is responsible for the fact that we do not eternally remain a child but are able to evolve.

What we are conscious of through our astral body is the ordinary state of wakefulness. The effect of this state is, however, that we are too strongly awake. We give ourselves up too strongly to the outer world in our ordinary waking state, we become completely absorbed in it. Why is this? It is because waking consciousness is strongly under the influence and sovereignty of Ahriman. Waking consciousness = Ahriman.

It is quite different in the case of sleep consciousness. Here we are too little awake; and we are over-engaged in our own development, in ourselves. We are totally engrossed in ourselves and to such an extent that all consciousness is extinguished. In sleep consciousness Lucifer has the upper hand. Sleep consciousness = Lucifer.

Thus our relationship with our astral body is such that when we are awake Ahriman has the upper hand over Lucifer, whereas when we are asleep Lucifer has the upper hand over Ahriman. They are in equilibrium only when we are dreaming; for then they are fighting it out with one another and maintain a balance between their forces. The ideas that are evoked by Ahriman in day consciousness and which he causes to harden and crystallize are then dissolved through Lucifer's influence and made to disappear. Everything is transformed into pictures when Ahriman is not rigidifying them into fixed notions, and they become flexible and mobile. Thus in the same way that in a pair of scales a state of equilibrium is achieved through the scales having equal weights on either side, with the result that what we have is not a state of rest but a state of balance, so also in human life we arrive in these circumstances not at a state of rest but at one of equilibrium. And the two forces that keep the balance, each one of which at any particular time weighs heavier, are Lucifer and Ahriman. In waking consciousness Ahriman's side sinks lower, in sleep consciousness Lucifer's side. Only in the intermediate state, when we are dreaming, the scales rock to and fro, not in a state of rest but delicately poised.

There is, moreover, evidence of the effective presence in the world of Lucifer and Ahriman when we come to consider higher aspects of human life. Two notions or concepts play a large part in human life. One of these is the concept of duty, or—if understood from a religious point of view—that of commandments. (We do also speak of duty in terms of a commandment.) The other notion is that of rights.

If you consider how the concepts of duty and rights—the right that a person has to one thing or another—play a part in human life, you will soon become aware that duty and rights are polar opposites, and that people's inclinations are such that they are sometimes directed more towards duty and at other times more towards rights. As you can see, we live at a time when there is a tendency to speak more about one's rights than about one's duties. All possible spheres of life make their claims. Thus, for example, we speak of workers' rights, the rights of women and so on.

Duty is the opposite concept to that of rights. Our age will be superseded by one where, because of the influence of the spiritual world-conception emanating from anthroposophy, duties will come to play a larger part. And in the future—and I mean a fairly distant future—there will be movements where there will be less and less emphasis on the demand for rights and far more upon duty. People will then be more inclined to ask: what is my duty as a woman or as a man in this or that situation? Thus an epoch where there will be an emphasis upon duty will supersede the epoch where the demand for rights holds sway.

As already stated, rights and duty play their part in human life as polar-opposite concepts. Now one can make the observation that when a person inwardly ponders questions of duty, he looks outside himself. Kant has brought this to expression by portraying duty as a sublime goddess to whom man aspires: 'Duty, you great and exalted name, you do not court popularity or curry favours but demand subjection . . .'[52] Man beholds duty as it were raying down its light from regions of the spiritual world. He experiences duty in a religious sense as an impulse deriving from the beings of the higher hierarchies; and when he submits himself to duty he goes out of himself as he feels this sense of duty, an aspiration which leads him to reach out beyond his ordinary self.

But this reaching out beyond his ordinary self, this aspiration towards spiritualization, would lead man into a situation where he would lose the ground from under his feet were he to give himself up wholly to this tendency. He would lose his sense of gravity if he were always only wanting to go out from himself. He must therefore try, in submitting himself to duty, to discover some means within himself of maintaining his sense of gravity. Schiller had a beautiful way of expressing this when he said that man has the most appropriate relationship to duty when he learns at the same time to love duty.[53]

There is much to be said for this idea. When someone speaks of learning to love duty, he is no longer merely submitting himself to it but he rises up out of himself and takes with him the love with which he otherwise loves only himself. He extracts the love that lives in his body and was egotism and loves duty. So long as it is self-love, it is a luciferic force; but when a person takes this self-love out of himself and loves duty in the way that he otherwise loves only himself he redeems Lucifer, he draws him out into the realm of duty and, so to speak, gives Lucifer a justified existence in the enactment and a feeling for the impulse of duty.

If, on the other hand, he is unable to do this, if he cannot draw forth love from himself and offer it to duty, he continues only to love himself. If he is unable to love duty, he is obliged to submit himself to it and become its slave; and although he is devoted to doing his duty, his obedience to it makes him dried up and hardened, he becomes cold and uninspired. He develops an ahrimanic hardness, despite following the commands of duty.

Ahriman ----> Duty <---- Lucifer

You see how duty stands in the middle between these two beings. If we submit ourselves to it, it destroys our freedom. We become the slaves of duty, because Ahriman from the one side approaches duty with his own impulses. But if we ourselves offer up to duty the power of our self-love as a sacrifice, thus bringing to it a luciferic warmth in the form of love, the consequence will be that, by establishing a state of balance between Lucifer and Ahriman, we find an appropriate relationship to duty. Thus through a moral deed we achieve a state of equilibrium between Lucifer and Ahriman. Ahriman from his spiritual domain causes us to have to submit to duty, with the result that it takes away our freedom. But then out of our own organism we bring him love, we bring him ourselves; and in this way we establish the right relationship to duty through the battle between Lucifer and Ahriman. Thus we are in a certain sense also the redeemers of Lucifer. When we begin to be able to love the tasks that constitute our duty, the moment has arrived when we contribute to the redemption of the luciferic powers, when we lead forth the luciferic forces—which are otherwise under the enchantment of our self-love—for the battle with Ahriman. In this way we redeem Lucifer from his spell of self-love; we set him free when we learn to love our duty.

In his letters *On the Aesthetic Education of Man*,[54] Schiller has posed the same question: How does one go beyond enslavement to duty to a love of duty? He did not mention Lucifer and Ahriman, because he did not think about this matter in cosmic terms. Nevertheless, these wonderful letters of Schiller on the aesthetic education of man are directly translatable into spiritual science.

With rights, on the other hand, in so far as we assert them, we find an immediate link with Lucifer. A human individual does not need to love his rights, for he does so anyway and it is perfectly natural that he should. There is a natural connection between Lucifer and rights in the feeling realm, in one's feeling about rights. Wherever rights are being asserted, Lucifer is present. Sometimes it is possible to see with absolute clarity how when some right or other is being propagated Lucifer's power is being strongly invoked. Here it is a matter of creating a counter-balance, so that we as it were call upon Ahriman to form an opposite pole to Lucifer, who is aligned with the right in question. We can achieve this by cultivating the opposite pole to love. Love is inner fire; its opposite is calmness or composure, the acceptance of what comes to us through world karma, the understanding of what is happening in the world—thus calmness through understanding. As soon as we approach our rights with a calmness borne of understanding, we summon Ahriman into the situation. It is harder to recognize him here. We release him from his purely outward existence, we invite him into ourselves and warm him through the love that is associated with rights. Composure has the coldness of Ahriman. By understanding what is in the world, we connect our warm, understanding love with the coldness outside in the world. Then we redeem Ahriman when we have a relationship of understanding towards what has happened, when we do not merely demand our rights out of self-love but understand what is going on in the world.

This is the eternal battle between Lucifer and Ahriman in the world. On the one hand man learns in a conservative way to understand circumstances as they are; he learns to understand them as they have arisen out of cosmic, karmic necessity. And the other aspect is that he feels in his heart the urge to make new conditions possible, the revolutionary stream. Lucifer lives in the revolutionary stream, Ahriman in the conservative stream; and in our life of rights we stand between these two opposite poles.

Thus we see how rights and duty represent a state of equilibrium between Lucifer and Ahriman. We only learn to understand things such as this, how the human physical body, etheric body and astral body function in our lives, how duty and rights manifest themselves in the relevant aspect of our lives and how all these things relate to the world around us when we learn to recognize the involvement of spiritual powers, and above all those spiritual powers that bring about the state of balance.

Just as we are able to observe what lives in the world as it is under the influence of the spiritual powers that bring about balance, so does our moral life represent a confluence of polar opposites. Moreover, the whole realm of moral, ethical life, with its poles of rights and duty, only becomes understandable when the interventions of Ahriman and Lucifer are taken into account. Similarly, the historical lives of human beings and historical events in general take their course in such a way that revolutionary and warlike—that is, luciferic—movements alternate with conservative and peaceful—that is, ahrimanic—movements. What we see is a constant balancing interplay between luciferic and ahrimanic forces. We cannot understand the world unless we view it in terms of opposites. What comes towards us in the world is presented to us in opposites, in dualistic terms. In this connection, Manichaeism[55]—if rightly understood and which has a dualistic quality—is fully justified. How Manichaeism has its rightful place also within spiritual monism is something that we shall have opportunities to speak about further in the future.

I have endeavoured to show you in these lectures how the world is the result of balancing influences. This is especially evident in artistic life. On this basis, we shall in subsequent lectures consider the arts and their development in the world and the part that various spiritual powers have played in the evolution of the artistic life of humanity.[56]

OLAF ÅSTESON[57]

Address, New Year Festival

Hanover, 1 January 1912

The Dream Song of Olaf Åsteson[58]

The so-called Dream Song, which will be recited shortly, needs to be prefaced by a few preliminary remarks.

A few days ago I mentioned this Dream Song in a Christmas lecture that I gave here.[59] I was able to say on that occasion that the fixing of the Christmas festival in the course of the year is not some kind of intellectual construct but that it has arisen from quite specific inner processes which can occur in the human soul when, as the highest fruit of its inner strivings, it attains to clairvoyant visions either through certain naturally available forces or through trained seership. We can gain a clear understanding of what the human soul may actually experience in such a situation if we consider the following thoughts.

Everything that finds expression in the sprouting and blossoming of plants, all that the light and warmth of the Sun conjure forth in spring and bring to full maturity through the summer, all this is fading into a wintry sleep, a wintry darkness at the time appointed for the Christmas festival by the historical consciousness of mankind. The time when the Christmas festival takes place is like a period of sleep, of darkness for the beings of nature. The situation with regard to the human soul is the opposite of what it is for outer nature.

Whereas the beings of nature descend into the darkness and the human soul accompanies them into this domain where the light of the Sun is obscured, it becomes lighter in the human soul or at any rate it can become so. It is possible for the soul, either quite naturally through a certain inherited form of clairvoyance to which I have often referred or by means of trained seership, to penetrate into the full light of the spiritual world where the mysteries of the spirit that lie hidden behind the outward phenomena of the senses may be revealed to it. And just as this descent of the plant world around the time of nature's wintry path is in accordance with a regular law, so does a similar law also underlie the spiritual blossoming of human beings, with the result that this inner radiance coincides with the darkness of the natural world at the time appointed for the Christmas festival.

Now it might appear that such things are being said purely out of a modern faculty of trained clairvoyance or, as our opponents might say, out of sheer fantasy. On the other hand, what human beings and popular cultures actually experience outwardly represents a fully valid, living proof of what is being said. I therefore found it extremely interesting that, having spoken for many years within our movement about this Christmas quality of seership—when the soul is most deeply immersed in clairvoyance—which leads us to an understanding of the true significance of the Christ, I was made acquainted with a remarkable vision living amongst our dear friends in Norway, where I was at the time giving a cycle of lectures.[60] Indeed, anyone who is familiar with such things will say at once that it is reminiscent of many similar visions that have always lived amongst Germanic peoples and of what many people have seen clairvoyantly during the 13 nights from Christmas Eve until the Feast of Epiphany on 6 January.

At such a time the human soul can behold the spiritual world, where it sees what its own destiny will be in a disembodied state when it is passing through Kamaloka; and it then becomes clear to the soul how a relationship is established between the higher spiritual worlds and the deeds of human beings here on the Earth. It is, moreover, interesting that the being who is the subject of this Dream

Song and to whom these visions in this northern region are ascribed is a person who bears the name Olaf Åsteson. According to the legend, in the course of these 13 nights he underwent in a kind of clairvoyant experience what people in the north are able to experience in their particular way as a vision. He experienced initially how human deeds are metamorphosed when someone has passed through the gate of death; but he also experienced how the Christ Being becomes involved with the journey of the disembodied soul and how Christ Jesus in His office as judge, who appears beside the old judge of the world, the so-called countenance of Jehovah, the Archangel Michael, has His part to play in the Nordic understanding of life after death. Thus the penetration of Christianity into the northern lands can be discerned alongside everything else that appears to Olaf Åsteson's clairvoyant consciousness, and everything becomes clear to him at the time of the festival of Jesus's birth during the 13 nights, through which he slept.

To what consciousness does this become clear? Now it is remarkable that this is indicated to us already in the name, which evidently in the north originally signified a human consciousness that is inherited from the ancestors. Olaf is rightly called Olaf when the ancient clairvoyant consciousness of his ancestors reawakens within him. 'The one who inherits his consciousness, his inner being, from his ancestors'—this is what is contained in the name Olaf; and Åste means love, the love that is transmitted in the blood from generation to generation. This son of love, Åsteson, is Olaf, the consciousness that has from the time of the old clairvoyance been transmitted from generation to generation as the ancestral heritage in a resurrected form. Olaf, who is born with this clairvoyant consciousness, recognizes the destiny of the human soul, while at the same time beholding the intervention of that Being whose entry into earthly existence we celebrate in the festival of the birth of Jesus.

It is remarkable that, whereas there is no doubt that such visions were widely experienced, especially in Germanic countries, this Dream Song seems to have been forgotten. For in 1850 a clergyman named Lanstad[61] began to collect folk songs in Telemark, a lonely mountain valley where few people were living at that time; and among the many other folk songs he found still vitally alive in the folk-memory—how long or from what time he did not know—the song of Olaf Åsteson, who during the 13 nights has seen the destiny of the human soul after it has passed through the gate of death and the entry of Christ Jesus into world history. He did not know when this song of initiation had emerged into the culture of these people, for it was living amongst them and was constantly being recited in association with a particular musical mood. The few people living in that lonely valley took great delight in it; and then it came to Landstad's attention, speaking to him of the secrets that it imparted from the very soul of the people about initiation in olden times. Thus it survived until Landstad discovered it still living in the folk-memory.

Of course, many people believe that the Dream Song is about Saint Olaf,[62] who introduced Christianity in AD 1030 and whose mother was called Åste, or love. This is the case with much that is both historical and spiritual in origin.

Moreover, it is interesting that this Dream Song spread rapidly amongst large numbers of Nordic peoples and lives in the hearts of the people of Norway. Indeed, there is a powerful movement in Norway towards bringing ancient times to life in a renewed way, including rekindling interest in the old northern language, which has an affinity to ancient Germanic languages, as distinct from the more recent Danish language. Now this song is in a language which is reminiscent of the oldest language still surviving in that region, and it speaks directly to the hearts of those who have a particular wish to revive their cultural past; and in the last 10 to 15 years it has not only touched their hearts but has also entered into their schools. Thus wherever people awaken to these old folk mysteries one finds them singing or reciting this Dream Song of Olaf Åsteson, who in the 13 nights from Christmas until 6 January was initiated as a result of natural forces into the sacred mysteries of mankind.

It is for these reasons that we would therefore like to present this Dream Song of Olaf Åsteson to you. Fräulein von Sivers[63] will recite it. I have made a provisional attempt to prepare a version that can be recited in German, now that Frau Lindholm[64] has helped me by rendering into German the distinctive language in which the song lives and continues to live as a kind of folk song. So now we shall hear it in this provisional form[65] that I have been able to give it in the course of these few days.

The Dream Song[66]

Hearken all, A song I have to sing,
The song of a wondrous youth.
I'll sing of Olaf Åsteson
Who slept so long a sleep.
Yea, Olaf Åsteson it was
Who slept a sleep so long, so deep.

He lay him down on Christmas Eve
And fell in a slumber deep,
He woke not till the thirteenth day
When folk to church did go.
Yea, Olaf Åsteson it was
Who slept a sleep so long, so deep.

He lay him down on Christmas Eve
And slept so soundly and so long,
He woke not till the thirteenth day
When little birds did spread their wings.
Yea, Olaf Åsteson it was
Who slept a sleep so long, so deep.

He woke not till on the thirteenth day
The Sun did shine upon the hills.
Then saddled he his nimble steed
And swiftly rode unto the church.
Yea, Olaf Åsteson it was
Who slept a sleep so long, so deep.

There the priest before the altar stood
The Word of God proclaiming.
Olaf sat by the church door
And told his many dreams.
Yea, Olaf Åsteson it was
Who slept a sleep so long, so deep.

All the folk, old and young, thereto
Lent eager ear and gave good heed;
Then did Olaf Åsteson
Relate to them his dream.
Yea, Olaf Åsteson it was
Who slept a sleep so long, so deep.

✳

I laid me down on Christmas Eve,
Deep sleep upon me fell;
And wakened not till the thirteenth day,
When folk to church did go.
The Moon shone brightly
And far ahead the ways did stretch.

Lo! I have been in cloud-wrapped heights
And deep in ocean depths;
And who so e'er will follow me
No laughter make glad his lips.
The Moon shone brightly
And far ahead the ways did stretch.

Lo! I have been in cloud-wrapped heights
And deep in miry sloughs;
And I have seen the blaze of hell
And one part seen of Heaven.
The Moon shone brightly
And far ahead the ways did stretch.

I fared forth o'er the Holy Stream
And over valleys deep,
The waters heard I, but saw them not
Where deep beneath Earth they run.
The Moon shone brightly
And far ahead the ways did stretch.

He did not neigh, my coal black steed,
My hound, he did not bark;
The bird of morning did not sing;
O'er all the selfsame wonder lay.
The Moon shone brightly
And far ahead the ways did stretch.

With sense enchanted forth I fared
Across the thorn clad heath.
My scarlet mantle was all torn,
And e'en the nails on my feet.
The Moon shone brightly
And far ahead the ways did stretch.

I came unto the Gjaller Bridge[67]
That hangs in the wind on high;
'Twas covered over with rich, red gold
And pointed nails in each bar.
The Moon shone brightly
And far ahead the ways did stretch.

The serpent stings, the hound he bites,[68]
The bull he bars the way;
Three creatures of the bridge are they,
Of fearful crooked mien are they.
The Moon shone brightly
And far ahead the ways did stretch.

The hound he bites, the serpent stings,
The bull sets to his horns;
They suffer none to cross the bridge
Who falsely have their fellows judged.
The Moon shone brightly
And far ahead the ways did stretch.

I wandered on across the bridge,
A narrow giddy path.
I had to wade into the mire
But far behind me now it lies.
The Moon shone brightly
And far ahead the ways did stretch.

I had to wade into the mire
My feet no bottom found;
And so I passed o'er the Gjaller Bridge,
The dust of death in my mouth.
The Moon shone brightly
And far ahead the ways did stretch.

*

So came I to those waters there
Where ice burned with flames of blue,
But God did put it in my heart
To turn me away therefrom.
The Moon shone bright
And far ahead the ways did stretch.

So went I on the winter way
That lay at my right hand;
And lo! I saw there Paradise,
The light spread o'er all that land.
The Moon shone bright
And far ahead the ways did stretch.

God's holy Mother there I saw,
No wonder could be more fair:
To Brooksvalin[69] now wend thy way
Where justice awaits man's soul.
The Moon shone bright
And far ahead the ways did stretch.

*

There was I in the other world
The space of many nights.
Only God alone can know
How deep was the suffering I saw.
In Brooksvalin
Where justice awaits man's soul.

Saw I first an evil man
A boy in his life had he slain.
The boy he bare within his arms
And walked in the earth to his knee.
In Brooksvalin
Where justice awaits man's soul.

Came I then on another man
Who wore a cloak of lead;
For in earthly life his soul
Was ever to avarice bound.
In Brooksvalin
Where justice awaits man's soul.

Then I came to men who wore
A raiment of fiery earth.
God grant grace to these poor souls
Who moved their neighbour's landmarks.
In Brooksvalin
Where justice awaits man's soul.

There came I to children two
Who stood in glowing coals.
God grant grace to their sinning souls
Who father and mother have cursed.
In Brooksvalin
Where justice awaits man's soul.

So came I to the house of shame
And witch wives stood therein.
Lo! They churned, they churned in red blood;
A heavy sore task it was.
In Brooksvalin
Where justice awaits man's soul.

Hot it is in the gulf of hell,
So hot no man could believe.
Over a pitchy cauldron they hung
And pounded a scoundrel's hide.
In Brooksvalin
Where justice awaits man's soul.

Lo! From the north in wild array
There came a horrid crew.
Grutte Graubart[70] rode before
With all his turbulent horde.
In Brooksvalin
Where justice awaits man's soul.

Yea, they came from out the north,
No blacker crew was e'er seen.
Grutte Graubart rode before;
He rode on a coal black steed.
In Brooksvalin
Where justice awaits man's soul.

Lo! From the south a glorious host
Came riding in holy calm.
At their head St Michael rode,
Who stands at Christ's right hand.
In Brooksvalin
Where justice awaits man's soul.

Yea, they came from out the south,
No nobler host was e'er seen.
At their head Michael of all souls
He rode on a snow white steed.
In Brooksvalin
Where justice awaits man's soul.

Came his host from out the south,
So great did it seem to me.
At their head Michael of all souls,
A horn he held in his hands.
In Brooksvalin
Where justice awaits man's soul.

Michael the guide of souls
He blew a blast on his horn.
Now must every soul come forth
Before the throne of justice.
In Brooksvalin
Where justice awaits man's soul.

Trembled then every sinning soul
Like an aspen leaf in the wind.
Not one soul was in that place
But sorely wept for his sins.
In Brooksvalin
Where justice awaits man's soul.

Michael, the guide of souls,
Then in the balance he weighed,[71]
Weighed the sins of all the souls
And Christ the Lord at his side.
In Brooksvalin
Where justice awaits man's soul.

✳

How blessed he who in Earth life
Unto the poor gives shoes.
He can indeed on the thorny heath
E'en walk barefoot without harm.
Thus speak the scales,
And truth gives tongue on judgement day.

How blessed he who in Earth life
Unto the poor gives bread.
He feareth not in spirit world
The fearful baying of the hound.
Thus speak the scales,
And truth gives tongue on judgement day.

How blessed he who in Earth life
Unto the poor gives corn.
He fears not on the Gjaller Bridge
To meet the bull's sharp horn.
Thus speak the scales,
And truth gives tongue on judgement day.

How blessed he who in Earth life
Unto the poor gives clothes.
He feareth not in spirit world
That frozen desert waste of ice.
Thus speak the scales,
And truth gives tongue on judgement day.

✳

Thus all the folk, old and young thereto
Lent eager ear and gave good heed.
There stands Olaf Åsteson,
Now has he told them all his dream.

O Olaf Åsteson, awake!
Awake! For thou hast slept so long.

ADDRESS, INTRODUCTION TO A LECTURE FOR MEMBERS[72]

BERLIN, 7 JANUARY 1913

Olaf Åsteson, the Awakening of the Earth Spirit

The time from Christmas until now is one of great importance and significance, also in an occult sense. It is referred to as the period of the 13 days; and the remarkable thing is that its importance is sensed by those people who have as regards their whole inner disposition still retained something of the old connection of the human soul with the spiritual world of which we have often spoken. As we know, so-called primitive people who live in the countryside or in a community that has been less affected by our modern civilization have retained more of the connection with the spiritual world that formerly existed in olden times than those who live in modern cities. For this reason we find so much in folk-poetry concerning experiences of the soul specifically during the time between Christmas and Three Kings Day, 6 January.

This is the time after the darkest point of the year and immediately after the winter solstice, when the Sun is again beginning its ascendant course and nature is most deeply immersed in itself and released and liberated from external influences; and when the human soul is likewise able to have experiences of a quite particular kind if it maintains its connection with the spiritual world. Those people who no longer possess the old clairvoyance but still retain an inner connection with the spiritual world feel a difference in the mysterious world of dreams at this time of year. What the soul can experience at such a time is highly meaningful, because if it is still receptive it has the greatest possibility of insight into the spiritual world. For someone who is wholly in tune with modern times, the course of the year is such that he no longer makes any particular distinction between the different seasons. Thus whereas a snowstorm may be raging outside and it is already dark at four o'clock and will be late before it grows light again, the city dweller has a similar experience to the summer months when the Sun unfolds its full strength. People have been sundered from the old connection with the cosmos, in which they lived when they were out in nature. But for those who have preserved a connection with nature, what happens at the time of the Christmas festival is not the same as events that occur at another time, for example at the height of summer. Whereas at midsummer the soul is most fully emancipated from its connection with the spiritual world, at the time when nature is most fully asleep it is connected to the greatest degree with the spiritual world and in former times experienced some remarkable things during this time.

Now there is a beautiful example of folk literature in the old Norwegian language which was recently rediscovered and, because of the exceptional degree of understanding displayed by the Norwegian people, has rapidly regained its popularity. It concerns a man named Olaf Åsteson, who still felt a connection with the spiritual world; and this poem beautifully describes what Olaf Åsteson experiences in the time between Christmas and Three Kings Day.

I made an initial attempt at the New Year Festival in Hanover in 1912[73] to present a German rendering of this Dream Song, and we can therefore experience it here as well. We shall now hear this song about Olaf Åsteson which tells of his experiences during the 13 nights.

[The recitation by Marie von Sivers now followed.]

The poem itself is old. But, as I have said, it has recently re-emerged as it were of its own accord amongst the Norwegian people and been very rapidly disseminated. The fact that something of this kind is being shared so widely is one sign among many others in the present time which demonstrates how great a longing there is to understand those mysteries which anthroposophy can disclose to us. That something of the kind that is being described here happens, or at any rate could happen a relatively short time ago, shows that this is no mere product of the imagination. This poem is by no means a work of fantasy but represents an actual reality, in that Olaf Åsteson is the representative of people of those northern regions who still had the possibility until approximately the mid-point of the Middle Ages of literally experiencing what is being articulated here.

When our Norwegian friends gave me this poem during a previous visit to Christiania[74] and wanted me to say something about it, this fact of general spiritual-scientific interest was uppermost in our minds. But what led to our wish to introduce this poem into our programme of studies was that it has many aspects which can be explored further, in that an anthroposophical understanding of it can enable one to have an ever deeper insight into what comes to light through this poem. Thus, for example, it was of immediate significance to me that Olaf—which is an old Norwegian name—has the surname Åsteson, or the son of Åste. From this I tried to discover something about the mother of this son. One can, of course, say all kinds of things—some of which might cause dissent—about the significance of the word 'Åst'; but it is not possible today to enter into all the questions that arise. Taking everything into consideration, the approximate meaning of Olaf Åsteson is that he is a son of that soul who descends from generation to generation and is connected with the blood that flows from one generation to another. Thus we have traced this name back to what we have so often spoken about in an anthroposophical context, that in former times the old clairvoyance was linked with the blood that flows through the generations. And so one might translate Olaf Åsteson as follows: Olaf who has been born from many generations and still bears the qualities of these many generations in his soul.

When we come to consider his experiences, it is of immediate interest to be aware of what the sleeping Olaf Åsteson lives through between Christmas and the ensuing 13 days, during which he does not wake up, that is, he is in a particular kind of psychic condition. If one lets the various verses that reflect the particular experiences in a directly accessible way make their impression on one's mind, one will be reminded of certain descriptions of the first stage of initiation, where it is indicated that the human individual is being led to the gate of death. It is shown throughout the poem that Olaf Åsteson is approaching the threshold of death. This is made particularly clear through the fact that he himself feels like a corpse, even to the point of feeling the earth between his teeth. And when we recall that when someone is undergoing initiation his ether body extends far beyond the confines of the skin and he becomes ever larger, so that he becomes part of the wide cosmic spaces, so likewise are we shown in this poem how Olaf Åsteson descends to the depths of the Earth and rises up to cloud-wrapped heights. All that a person has to undergo after death, for example in the sphere of the Moon, is similarly experienced by Olaf Åsteson. There is a poetic description of how the Moon shines brightly and how the way extends far into the distance. Then the abyss is described which has to be crossed in the world that lies between the human world and the world that leads out into the cosmic expanses. This heavenly bridge connects the human and cosmic worlds. Then our attention is drawn to the beings that find their expression in the constellations: the Bull, the Serpent. But for someone who can perceive the world in its spiritual aspect, the constellations are only the expression of what is spiritually present in the cosmic expanses. Then in the description of 'Brooksvalin' the world of Kamaloka is portrayed. We are shown how a kind of repayment or atonement takes place, how people experience in compensatory terms what they have not been able to achieve here on the Earth. But there is no need to interpret all the details of this poem; and indeed, this is wholly inappropriate for poems of this kind. But one should have the sense that these elements have arisen from a mood that is closely associated with what has lived far longer amidst such a people than amongst those peoples that inhabited the interior of the continent or have come in contact with the civilization of modern cities. Amongst the Norwegian people, whose language still has much that lies close to the threshold of occult mysteries, the possibility has long existed for souls to maintain a connection with what lives and weaves behind outward material phenomena.

You will recall my having explained that the cycle of the year has its counterpart in a spiritual course of events;[75] that in spring, when the plants put forth their shoots, when everything comes to life again and the days grow lighter, we have to recognize that the elemental and higher spirits connected with the Earth are engaged in what we might call a process of falling asleep. In spring, when the Earth is outwardly waking up, the Earth is from a spiritual point of view falling asleep; and when outer nature is fading and decaying, the spiritual nature of the Earth is awakening. Thus when around Christmas time outer nature is in a state of sleep, this is the time when the spiritual aspect of the Earth, which connects both the less significant elemental beings and also great, powerful beings with earthly existence, is most awake and active. Only from an outward perspective does it appear that we would have to associate spring with the awakening of the Earth and winter with its falling asleep. For occult observation it is the other way round. The spirit of the Earth, which consists of many spirits, is awake in the winter and asleep in the summer. Just as the organic and vegetable-like aspects of the human organism are most active during sleep (and extend their forces into the brain), whereas this purely organic activity is killed while we are awake, so is it with the Earth. When the Earth is most active, when everything has come into leaf and blossom and the Sun has reached its highest point around St John's Day, the spirit of the Earth is sleeping; and the fact that the Christmas festival, the festival of the awakening of the spirit, has been placed in the winter is not unconnected with these occult truths. The customs and traditions that have been handed down from former times harmonize in many respects with these occult insights.

Anyone who lives with an awareness of the spirits of the Earth does not only celebrate the St John's festival in the summer; for the

St John's festival in summer is in a certain sense a materialistic festival, celebrating what is being manifested through an outward materialistic revelation. But someone who has a connection with the spirit of the Earth, with what lives spiritually within the Earth, is, like Olaf Åsteson, most inwardly awake—that is, outwardly asleep—at Christmas time during the 13 days. This is also an occult fact, which for occultism has exactly the same significance as, for example, the fact of the position of the Sun has for ordinary materialistic science. Of course, materialistic science will take it for granted that in astronomy it describes the activity of the Sun in summer and winter in a purely outward way; and it would consider it sheer stupidity to put forward an idea which for the occultist is a fact, namely that the spiritual state of the Sun is at its most intense in winter and that therefore the conditions are then most favourable for someone who wants to develop an inner awareness of the spirit of the Earth and of everything of a spiritual nature. We may therefore conclude from this that anyone who is seeking an inner deepening of his soul can have the best experiences in the 13 days of the Christmas period, when inner experiences emerge without his even noticing them, although people today who are emancipated from outward processes can have occult experiences at any time. However, in so far as outer nature can nevertheless exert some influence, the time between Christmas and New Year is the most important.

So this poem reminds us in a completely natural way that much of what we have been able to speak about in connection with the time between death and a new birth was until relatively recently still directly accessible in certain regions of the Earth, and that many people have continued to be aware of it from direct experience.

ADDRESS, NEW YEAR'S FESTIVAL

DORNACH, 31 DECEMBER 1914

Cosmic New Year. The Waking of the Human Soul from the
Spiritual Sleep of the Age of Darkness

To begin our festive ending of the year, Frau Dr Steiner will recite the
beautiful Norwegian legend of Olaf Åsteson, who as Christmas
approached fell into a kind of sleep lasting for 13 days—the holy 13
days with which we have become familiar in a number of different
studies. During this sleep he had some important experiences; and
when awake he was able to recount them.

In the course of these studies I have made it apparent that spiritual
science can enable us to regain an understanding of treasures of
wisdom which in former ages were known to have been derived from
spiritual worlds. We shall continually encounter this ancient
knowledge of the spiritual worlds in one or another context, and we
will again and again be reminded that this ancient knowledge
derived from the fact that man was, by virtue of the way he was
organized in former times, able to have a relationship to the entire
universe and to all that goes on within it such that—to express it in
modern terms—the human microcosm was immersed in the laws, in
the happenings of the macrocosm, and that through being thus
immersed in the macrocosm he was able to have experiences about
matters of deep inner concern to him but which have to remain
hidden while he lives as a microcosm on the physical plane and has

access only to that knowledge which is available to the senses and to an intellect that is in bondage to them.

We know that only a materialistic view of the world can countenance the belief that man is as regards the cosmic order uniquely endowed with a capacity for thinking, feeling and will; whereas from the standpoint of a spiritual view of the world it has to be recognized that, just as there are beings below the human stage, there are also beings above the human stage of thinking, feeling and will. Human beings can acquire a relationship to these beings when they immerse themselves as microcosms in the macrocosm. However, we must speak of this macrocosm in such a way that it is not only a spatial macrocosm but that time is also of significance in the life of the macrocosm. Just as one must withdraw from all the impressions that can be made on one's senses from one's surroundings if one is seeking access to the depths of one's soul, just as one needs to create a degree of darkness by excluding sense-perceptions in order to kindle the light of the spirit, so must that spirit whom we may call the spirit of the Earth be shut off from the impressions of the rest of the cosmos. The outer cosmos must exert the smallest measure of influences upon the spirit of the Earth if it is to be able inwardly to concentrate its forces and capacities. In this way the mysteries that man needs to explore in conjunction with the Earth spirit as a result of the Earth having been separated as an earthly realm from the cosmos will be unveiled.

The time when the outer macrocosm has its greatest influence upon the Earth is that of the summer solstice, St John's. For this reason there are many accounts from former times of festive events and celebrations which remind us that such festivals took place at the height of summer when, by releasing the ego and merging with the life of the macrocosm, the soul surrenders itself in a state of intoxication to the impressions from the macrocosm.

In contrast, the descriptions that we find in legends and elsewhere of what it was formerly possible to experience when the macrocosm exerts the least influence upon the Earth remind us that the Earth spirit, when inwardly focused, is experiencing the mysteries of the soul-life of the Earth in the infinite expanses of the universe, and that when human beings give themselves up to this experience at the time when the least light and warmth is being transmitted from the macrocosm to the Earth they apprehend the holiest mysteries. Hence these days around the time of Christmas have always been regarded as sacred, because when man's organism still retained the capacity of sharing in the experience of the Earth when it was most concentrated he was able to live in companionship with the Earth spirit.

Olaf Åsteson, Olaf the son of Earth, experiences many mysteries of the universe during these 13 shortest days when he is transported into the macrocosm; and the northern legend that has recently been rediscovered from ancient records tells us of the experiences that Olaf Åsteson had between Christmas and New Year and until 6 January. We often have cause to remember this former way in which the microcosm participated in the macrocosm; and our studies will enable us to develop a closer association with phenomena of this nature. But first we shall hear the legend of Olaf the Earth son, who at this present time of the year experienced the mysteries of cosmic existence by living in companionship with the Earth spirit. So let us listen to these experiences.

[The recitation now followed.]

My dear friends, we have heard how Olaf Åsteson fell into a sleep that was to become for him a revelation of the mysteries of these worlds that are removed from the sensory world, from ordinary life on the physical plane. Through the legend we have received tidings of that ancient knowledge, those former insights into the spiritual worlds which we shall regain through the world-view of spiritual science.

It is often said that a feature of accounts of the human soul's entry into the spiritual world is that human beings are able to behold the spiritual world only when they experience the portal of death and then give themselves over to the elements. Thus the elements of earthly existence do not surround them as they do in ordinary life on the physical plane in the form of earth, water, air and fire but that they are lifted above this outward aspect, this sensory aspect of the elements and are immersed in the essential nature of these elements as beheld in their true nature, where beings are present within them that have a connection with the human soul.

We were able to sense that Olaf Åsteson experienced something of this state of being immersed in the elements when we heard how he arrives at the Gjaller Bridge, and how he crosses the bridge and explores the paths of the spiritual world that stretch far into the distance. This is a vivid description of the experience with the element of earth, of how he is immersed in it. The vividness of this description is such that he tells us that, like dead people lying in their graves, he feels earth in his mouth. There is then a clear reference to his encounter with the element of water and with everything that can be experienced in it, also in conjunction with its moral aspect. He then also refers to the encounter with the elements of fire and air.

All this is described in a wonderfully vivid way and focused upon the experience of the human soul's sharing in the mysteries of the spiritual world. The legend was discovered at a much later date; it was collected at the place where it was still living as an oral tradition. There is much about the legend in its present form that differs from how it was originally. The graphic description of the experiences in the realm of earth must doubtlessly have come first, then the experiences in the realm of water; and then the experiences in the realms of air and fire were probably far more differentiated than in the feeble echo that emerged after many centuries and is available to us today.

The conclusion, which as it is now is no longer reminiscent of the sublime language and superhuman overtones that characterized such folk legends, was without doubt likewise originally far more impressive and less sentimental than the present one, which is moving only on a human level; and the reason that it is moving is that it is associated with such deep mysteries of the macrocosm and human experience.

At such a time of year as the present, if we have a right under-standing of the seasons, there is much reason to remind ourselves that mankind was formerly in possession of a knowledge—albeit one that was far more hazy and nebulous—that has been lost and which must be rediscovered. We may therefore ask ourselves whether, in view of our recognition that it is of crucial importance for humanity that such knowledge is again made available, we should not regard it as one of our most urgent tasks to do everything we can to imbue the culture of modern times with this knowledge.

Much will be necessary if the change that has been indicated in the whole way in which people feel about their view of the world can come about. One thing will be particularly necessary, although this is one among many others; it is only possible to consider one at a time. It will be particularly important that our spiritual-scientific conception of the world can enable human souls to develop reverence and devotion for what was known in traditional ways in ancient times about the great mysteries of existence. There will be a real need to realize that in our materialistic times people have neglected to develop this reverence and devotion in their souls.

It is important that people become aware of the barren and empty nature of this materialistic age, and of the arrogance that has been displayed in the early centuries of the fifth post-Atlantean cultural period towards the revelations of ancient religions and esoteric traditions, which when approached with the necessary reverence enable one to sense the deep, deep wisdom that resides within them. How lacking in reverence is actually even our attitude today towards the Bible! Even if I disregard the appalling kind of modern research which totally mangles the whole of the Bible, there is still the dry and vacuous knowledge acquired through the senses and ordinary intellectual powers, and the inability to muster any feeling for the immense grandeur of human perception that we find in a number of passages. I should like to refer to a passage from the Book of Exodus, chapter 33, verse 18:

> And Moses said to God: 'I beseech thee, show me thy glory.'
> And Yahweh said: 'I will make all my goodness pass before you, and I will proclaim the name of Yahweh before you; and

will be gracious to whom I will be gracious, and will show
mercy on whom I will show mercy.'

But then Yahweh said: 'You cannot see my face; for no man
shall see me, and live.'

And Yahweh said: 'Behold, there is a place beside me; stand
upon a rock, and when my glory passes by I shall put you in a
cleft of the rock and will cover you with my hand while I pass
by. And when I take away my hand you shall see my back, but
my face will not be seen.'

If you take into account much that we have been able to embrace
within our hearts and souls in the previous years of our spiritual-
scientific endeavours and then approach this passage, you can have
the feeling that infinite wisdom comes to expression from it and that
the ears of people in the materialistic age are so deaf that they can
hear absolutely nothing of the infinitely deep wisdom that can be
discerned in this passage. I should like at this point to take the
opportunity to draw your attention to a booklet that has appeared
under the title *Worte Mosis* ('Words of Moses') and published by
Bruns Verlag, Minden, Westphalia, because the translations that it
contains from the five Books of Moses are better than in other editions. Dr Hugo Bergmann,[76] the editor of this little book, has taken
a lot of trouble over his interpretations.

I have often emphasized that if we want to gain insight into the
spiritual worlds we will need to acquire a completely different way of
relating to the world than the one that we have to the sense-world.
We have this world of the senses around us; we behold it and see it in
its forms and colours, and hear its sounds. It is a reality which we
confront; it influences us, we perceive it and we think about it. That
is how we relate to the sense-world. We are passive; its influence
works right into our souls. We think about the sense-world, we form
mental images of it.

A completely different relationship applies when we are involved
with the spiritual world. This is one reason why it is difficult to form
a true picture of what a person experiences when he enters the

spiritual world. I have endeavoured to characterize some of these difficulties in a little book entitled *The Threshold of the Spiritual World*. We form mental pictures of the sense-world, we think about it. If we accomplish everything that we need to do if we want to follow the path of initiation, a situation arises that we can characterize by saying that we are related to the beings of the higher hierarchies in the same way as the things around us are related to us: these higher hierarchies form mental images of us, they think us. We think the objects around us—the minerals, plants and animals; they become our thoughts. We in turn are the ideas, thoughts and perceptions of the spirits of the higher hierarchies; we become the thoughts of the Angeloi, Archangeloi, Archai and so on. We are apprehended by them, just as we ourselves apprehend plants, animals and human beings. We should, indeed, feel a sense of protection through being able to say that the beings of the higher hierarchies think us, they form conceptions of us. These higher hierarchic beings take hold of us with their souls. Thus we can visualize that when Olaf Åsteson went to sleep before the church door, he became a mental image of the spirits of the higher hierarchies; and while he slept the beings of the higher hierarchies experienced what the beings of the Earth spirit— which is for us a plurality—experience. And when Olaf Åsteson descends once more to the physical world, he recalls what the spirits of the higher hierarchies experienced within him.

Let us imagine that we are embarking upon the path of initiation. How can we relate to the spiritual worlds, which consist of a number of spiritual beings of the higher hierarchies in whose midst we wish to be? How can we relate to them? We can address them and say: 'How can we reach out to you, how do you reveal yourselves to us?' And then, when we have begun to understand the different kind of relationship that the human soul has to the higher worlds, these words will come sounding forth to us from the spiritual worlds:

'You cannot perceive the spiritual world in the way that you perceive the sense-world, which appears to you and impresses itself on your senses. We must form a conception of you, and you must feel yourself in us. Your feeling of yourself must be of a similar nature to what the thought that you think in the sense-world would experience were it able to experience itself in you. You must surrender yourself to the spiritual world, whereupon all the beings of the higher hierarchies who are able to manifest themselves to you will enter into you. This will then stream into your soul and live within it as a bearer of grace, in the same way that you live in your thoughts when you think about the world of the senses. If the spiritual world wants to pardon or show mercy to you, it seeks to fill you with its love! The fact of the matter is that you should not imagine that you can approach spiritual beings as you would the world of the senses. Just as Moses had to creep into a cleft of the rock, so must you make your way into the hollow of the spiritual world. You have to put yourself there. Just as a thought lives within you, so must you seek to engage with spiritual beings. You yourself must live as a cosmic thought in the macrocosm. What you experience in this way is not something that you can experience for yourself during your earthly life between birth and death; this can happen only after death, when you are dead. No one can experience the spiritual world in this way before he has died, but the spiritual world can draw near to you, bless you and fill you with its love. And then, if once you have been in the spiritual world—or while you are in it—you develop your earthly consciousness, it will be illumined by the spiritual world in its essential reality.'

In the same way that a human being confronts an object that is external to himself, and that object is engraved upon his consciousness and is then inside it, so is man as regards his soul-being within the cleft or hollow of the spiritual world [drawings 1 and 2]. The spiritual world passes through him. Here the human individual is confronting the phenomena. When he enters the spiritual world the beings of the higher hierarchies are behind him. He cannot now see their face, just as thoughts do not behold our countenance when they are within us. The face is in front; thoughts are behind, they do not see the countenance. The whole mystery of initiation resides in the words that Yahweh speaks to Moses.

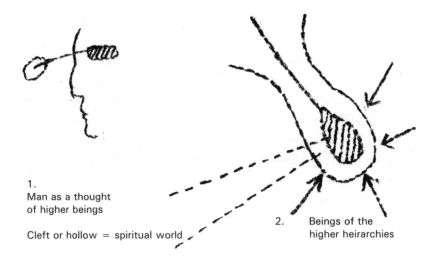

1.
Man as a thought
of higher beings

Cleft or hollow = spiritual world

2.   Beings of the
     higher heirarchies

And Moses said to God: 'I beseech thee, show me thy glory.'

And Yahweh said: 'I will make all my goodness pass before you, and I will proclaim the name of Yahweh before you; and will be gracious to whom I will be gracious, and will show mercy on whom I will show mercy.'

But then Yahweh said: 'You cannot see my face, for no man shall see me, and live.'

(Initiation does indeed bring one to the portal of death.)

And Yahweh said: 'Behold, there is a place beside me; stand upon a rock, and when my glory passes by I shall put you in a cleft of the rock and will cover you with my hand while I pass by. And when I take away my hand you shall see my back, but my face will not be seen.'

It is the opposite of the way that one perceives the sense-world. One has to summon forth much of the effort that one has made in one's spiritual-scientific endeavours if one is to meet a revelation of this nature with the appropriate devotion and reverence. But then such a feeling of reverence towards these revelations will gradually grow within the human soul; and this reverence, this devotion, is one quality among many others that we need in order to bring about the change in mankind's spiritual culture of which we have been speaking.

The time when the impressions reaching the Earth from the macrocosm are at their lowest level, the time extending from Christmas until beyond New Year and roughly until 6 January, is highly suitable for remembering not only the purely objective aspects of spiritual knowledge but also the feelings that will necessarily arise within us when we embrace spiritual science. We are therefore in a very real way involved once more with the spirit of the Earth, with whom we form a totality and the old clairvoyant knowledge is also linked, as we know from this legend of Olaf Åsteson. In the materialistic age mankind has in many ways lost this reverence and devotion for spiritual life. It is of prime importance to ensure that this reverence and this devotion are recovered, for only through this will we be able to develop the frame of mind that can lead us towards the new spiritual science in the right way. At present the mood with which spiritual science is approached is still similar to the way that one approaches ordinary science. In this respect a thorough trans-formation is needed.

As a result of losing its insight into the spiritual world, mankind has also lost its right relationship to its own essential nature. The materialistic view of the world has given rise to chaotic feelings about world existence in general. These chaotic feelings about the world and about humanity were bound to arise in the time of materialism. We have only to conceive of a time—and this time is our own, the first centuries of the fifth post-Atlantean cultural period—when people no longer have any idea that man's being is of a threefold nature, that he has a body, a soul and a spirit.[77] For this is indeed the case. Thus what we must necessarily regard as the basic elements of spiritual-scientific knowledge, namely man's threefold nature as a being of body, soul and spirit, was something that has been altogether absent from people's consciousness from the first four centuries of the fifth post-Atlantean cultural era until our own time. Man has simply been man; and if anyone speaks about structures along the lines of body, soul and spirit, this is considered to be complete and utter nonsense.

One might think that matters of this kind are of significance only in the realm of knowledge. However, this is not so. They also have significance for the whole way that human beings involve themselves in life. In the fourth century of modern times or, as we would express it, of the fifth post-Atlantean cultural epoch, three mighty words came to prominence in which the people of this time understood, or at least endeavoured to understand, the very essence of human will in terms of earthly experience. These are deeply meaningful words, but they acquired their distinctive quality through the fact that they entered upon the stage of human history at a time when people knew nothing about the threefold nature of man. Humanity heard about liberty, equality and fraternity.[78]

It was a matter of profound necessity that these words sounded forth in the context of modern culture at a particular time. They can only really be understood if one understands what significance these words can have for human nature as it really is. So long as these three words are imbued with those chaotic feelings that are engendered by the notion that man is simply man, and that the threefold picture of his being is sheer nonsense, people will not be able to work constructively with the guidance which they offer. For the three words cannot be directly applied to one and the same level of human experience. This cannot be done. Some simple reflections which, probably because of their very simplicity, do not unveil to you the gravity that underlies them can indicate to you that, if applied to the same level of human life, the essential meaning underlying these three words can lead to serious conflict.

Let us consider to begin with the realm where we find fraternity in the most natural form: that of human blood relationship, the family, where we do not need to establish brotherly love because it is inborn; and then think how it warms the heart to see true, genuine fraternity within a family, where everything is connected in a brotherly way. But without wishing in the least to diminish the wonderful feeling that we can have of this degree of brotherly love, let us endeavour to see what can arise within the brotherly confines of the family precisely because of this quality. There may be a member of the family who does not feel happy within its justified brotherly domain and longs to escape from it, because he feels that he cannot develop inwardly amidst its fraternal bonds, that he must leave the family where he can live in such a brotherly way in order to develop his inner freedom. Thus we see that freedom, the free unfolding of the life of soul, can be in conflict with even the most well-intentioned kind of brotherliness.

Of course, someone who thinks in a superficial way may say that no proper brotherhood would fail to support a person's freedom. But people can say whatever comes into their head. Of course they will say that everything should be allowed for. I recently received a dissertation in which one of the theses being defended was that a triangle is a rectangle. One can, to be sure, defend such an argument; it is even possible to prove that a triangle is a rectangle! Thus one can also conclusively prove that brotherhood and freedom are compatible. But that is not the point. The issue here is that for freedom's sake brotherliness has had to be abandoned in many areas and will continue to be so. I could give numerous other examples of this.

If we wanted to gather up all the discrepancies between fraternity and equality, it would take us a very long time. Of course, one can in abstract terms imagine that everyone can be equal and show that fraternity and equality are mutually compatible. But if we are really serious about life we will not be interested in abstractions but in observing reality. The moment we come to be aware that man's being has a bodily aspect, which manifests itself on the physical plane, a soul aspect, which is enacted in the soul world, and a spiritual aspect that comes to expression in the spiritual world, we see the connection between the three weighty words that we have highlighted in their true perspective. Fraternity is the most important ideal for the physical world, as freedom is for the soul world. In so far as man dwells within the soul world it is appropriate to speak of the freedom of the soul, that is, of social conditions which fully guarantee this quality of inner freedom. And if we bear in mind that, in order that we may dwell in spirit land, each of us must aspire towards spiritual knowledge from our own individual standpoint, we would very soon come to see what would become of our spiritual conceptions if each of us were only interested in our own path and were to arrive at a completely different spiritual content.

As human beings we can find some degree of harmony in life only if we seek the spirit, each one for himself, and yet are ultimately able to arrive at the same spiritual content. We can speak of the equality of spiritual life. Fraternity has to do with the physical plane and with everything that is associated with the laws of the physical plane and affects the human soul from this physical plane. Freedom relates to everything that affects the human soul in the form of laws of the soul world; while equality has to do with everything that impinges upon the human soul through the laws of the spirit land.

Thus a cosmic New Year must dawn where there will be a Sun that radiates ever greater powers of warmth and light—a Sun that needs to bring light-filled warmth to much that has been living on in the age of darkness but has been veiled in obscurity. This is the distinctive aspect of our time, that much is striven for and expressed that is not understood.

However, this too can instil within us a mood of reverence and devotion towards the spiritual world; for whereas many people had an aspiration for fraternity, freedom and equality in the fourth century of the fifth post-Atlantean era and were uttering these words, even though they did not really understand them, it is now possible for us to understand them and to find an answer to the question: where did these words come from? The divine-spiritual cosmic rulership has implanted them in advance into the human soul when it did not as yet understand them, in order that key words of this nature might engender true cosmic knowledge within the soul. Even in phenomena of this kind we can observe the wise guidance inherent in world evolution. We can observe this guidance everywhere both in recent times and in the more distant past; and it becomes apparent to us that we often see only retrospectively that something that we did previously was actually wiser than we could have achieved with the wisdom that was at our disposal at the time. I drew attention to this at the beginning of my book *The Spiritual Guidance of the Individual and Humanity*.[79]

If you take account of the fact that certain seminal words enter the evolution of the world and of humanity which can only gradually be understood, you will probably become aware of an image which would be an appropriate way of characterizing the part of the fifth post-Atlantean cultural epoch which has now elapsed. It can in a certain respect be compared with the time of Advent, when the hours of daylight are becoming ever shorter. And now in our own time, when we are once again able to have some knowledge of the revelations of the spiritual world, evolution is entering a phase when we can have the idea that the days are growing longer and longer and we can speak of them in such a way that this present period can be viewed as comparable to the 13 days and to the time of increasing daylight.

But there is more to it than this. It is not right, not right at all, if we were to find only critical things to say about the materialistic period of the last four centuries. This modern age came into being through discoveries and inventions that are regarded as 'great' in the materialistic age, for example, sailing around the world, discovering countries that had been hitherto unknown and starting to colonize the Earth. This was the beginning of materialistic culture. Then the time gradually came when people almost became suffocated with materialistic culture. All of man's intellectual powers were devoted to understanding and taking hold of the material aspect of life; and as we have seen, the insights, visions and perceptions that had shed light upon the spiritual world from sources of ancient knowledge increasingly faded into oblivion.

And yet it would be wrong merely to denigrate the materialistic age. It would be greatly preferable to think of things this way: that in its waking part the human soul has been thinking and pondering in a materialistic way and has given rise to a science and a culture out of these materialistic thoughts, but that the human soul is a totality. One could say that one part of the human soul established this materialistic culture. This part had formerly been inactive, human beings knew nothing of outward science, they knew nothing of outer, material life; for at that time the spiritual part was more awake. [A drawing was made.] In the last four centuries the part of the soul that brought materialistic culture into being was awake, while the other part was asleep. But it is also true to say that the forces that mankind is now developing in order that a resurgence to spirituality may take place among us were implanted during the age of materialistic culture in the soul-members that were asleep. During these times mankind was indeed an Olaf Åsteson as regards spiritual knowledge. This was indeed so. And yet humanity has still not woken up! It is the task of spiritual science to awaken it.

The time must come when both young and old hear the words that are spoken out of the part of the human soul that has been asleep in the age of darkness. The human soul has been asleep for a long time, but the spirits of the world will approach it and call out to it: 'O Olaf Åsteson, awake!' We must prepare ourselves in the right way so that it does not happen that we are confronted by the call, 'O Olaf Åsteson, awake!', and do not have ears to hear it. The reason why we study spiritual science is to enable us to have ears to hear when the call to be spiritually awake rings out in the course of man's evolutionary journey.

It is good if we sometimes call to mind that man is a microcosm and that there are many experiences that we can have as human beings when we open ourselves up to the macrocosm. As we have seen, this present season is favourable for such an endeavour. Let us try to make this New Year's Eve a symbol for the New Year's Eve which is a necessary part of human evolution, when the new era in which an ever greater measure of light, soul light, vision and knowledge of everything that abides in the spiritual domain and can stream and flow from thence to the human soul will begin to approach. Let us bring the microcosm of our experience on this New Year's Eve into connection with the macrocosm of human experience throughout the Earth; and we will then be able to sense something of the dawning of the great, new cosmic day in the fifth post-Atlantean era, at whose beginning we now stand and whose eve we wish worthily to celebrate.

ADDRESS FOR A RECITATION OF THE DREAM SONG OF OLAF ÅSTESON

(UNDATED MANUSCRIPT)[80]

We are going to hear a rendering of a remarkable folk-poem. It concerns the young Olaf Åsteson, who lives in the legend deriving from the Norwegian people. A dream experienced by this Olaf Åsteson is related in a poetic form that well reflects its folk origins: a dream which, according to the legend, tells that he had a long sleep of 13 days and nights, those 13 days and nights that lie between Christmas Eve and Three Kings Day, 6 January. These 13 days play a part in many folk traditions. In order to understand what is expressed in such traditions, one needs to visualize that until a relatively short time ago people living in rural areas and mountainous regions felt an intimate connection with the flow of natural rhythms. They felt differently when the plants in spring sprouted forth from the Earth to when in autumn there was an expanse of bare soil; their feeling was different again when the Sun spread its fiery warmth through the heavens at St John's Tide, and again different when the snow-laden clouds hid the Sun's rays from view in December. In summer the soul lived with nature; in winter it withdrew into itself, it lived within itself. This withdrawal of the soul into itself was of a particularly intimate nature towards Christmas time, when the nights are longest. At such times the soul had the experience of withdrawing completely from the outside world as in sleep, when the eyes no longer see and the ears no longer hear. A brooding quality

descended upon the soul as it was immersed in its inner pre-
occupations, which in people who were especially disposed for this
took on the character of a dream. Many souls then experienced their
immersion in the spiritual world in a particularly vivid way. Everything that they felt about guilt and sin, about the hopes and cares of
their lives, welled up before them. And just as dreams take on
particular forms as morning approaches and the first rays of the Sun
light up the sleeping face of the dreamer, so does the soul's brooding
and dreaming acquire a particular form when from Christmas
onwards the Sun begins to appear earlier in the heavens, when the
approach of the new morning of nature is sensed. Anyone who has
ever lived with people from rural or mountainous areas will know the
dream experiences initiated by the Folk-soul in other worlds which
feature at such a time.

At present there are no longer many such experiences. They disappear when locomotives and factory chimneys begin to invade the
countryside. In many regions it is the case that even the legends of
ancient dream worlds have already vanished from the memory. In
areas which have acquired less of the modern culture of industry and
commerce, such as certain parts of Norway, beautiful parts of the
world of legends have been preserved, as we find in our song of Olaf
Åsteson. It has an ancient origin, but it lived until recently amongst
the Norwegian people and is being rapidly disseminated, so that
many people are aware of it again after it had long disappeared from
view.

It tells of a long dream that Olaf Åsteson dreams, and in which he
experiences the destiny of souls after death. This has its basis in the
idea that the soul journeys after death into the world of the stars, that
for example it enters regions lying in the neighbourhood of the
constellations of the Bull, the heavenly Serpent and the Dog, and
comes to the spiritual region of the Moon. The soul enters these
worlds by crossing the Gjaller Bridge, which connects the earthly
with the spiritual world. In many folk legends this bridge is represented by the rainbow. One part of this spiritual world is Brooksvalin, where the deeds of human souls are weighed and the

appropriate measure is allotted for their atonement. The whole way in which the song portrays the experience is indicative of the time when it was being shaped by the folk poem. The ideas of life after death are not as yet wholly Christian; they to some extent bear the mark of having been formed during the old pagan era. Nevertheless, the time when Olaf experiences his dream is imagined in Christian times. This is made clear not only because he relates his dream by the church door but also because the Christian notions of Michael and Christ are found interposed amongst the pagan images of the Gjaller Bridge and Brooksvalin. Indeed, in Christ's approach from the south one can find a direct echo of the arrival from the south of Christianity in Norway. We are probably dealing here with a folk poem that is between eight and nine hundred years old, since it was around this time that Christianity reached Norway.

In presenting this folk poem our intention is that your spiritual vision is directed towards the life of the Folk-soul, who through such a legend as that of Olaf Åsteson shows that it was conscious of its connection with the spiritual world, who inwardly experienced pictures of this connection which gave it the certainty that the spiritual world exists. For if someone were to have approached Olaf Åsteson and said to him that there is no such thing as the spiritual world and that scientists have proved this, Olaf Åsteson would have looked at him with a gravely sympathetic eye and would then have probably smiled at him compassionately and said: there are more things in heaven and Earth than you will ever dream of with all your academic studies.

THE NATIONAL CHARACTER OF THE
RUSSIAN PEOPLE

Address for Russians Attending the Lecture Cycle *Spiritual Beings in the Heavenly Bodies and in the Kingdoms of Nature*[81]

Helsinki, 11 April 1912

As we try to enter more and more deeply into theosophical life and knowledge, we often feel the need to ask ourselves: why do we have such a wish to find theosophical ideas in the intellectual life of our time? Such a question comes to our mind quite naturally and effortlessly, and the word that then clarifies, and more than clarifies, our feelings in this regard is the word responsibility.

Responsibility! This word is more than adequate to exclude any thought from our mind that suggests that we are involved with theosophy out of some kind of need to satisfy a personal longing. If we then try to understand, even without formulating our thoughts very clearly, what this word responsibility signifies for us in relation to the spiritual impulse of theosophy, we will come to see ever more clearly that we owe it to present-day humanity and our best efforts to serve it to concern ourselves with theosophy. We should not study theosophy purely for our own pleasure or in order to satisfy some kind of personal longing by doing so, but on the contrary we must feel that it is something that present-day humanity needs if the process of human evolutionary development is to go forward. We need to keep firmly in mind that without theosophy (or whatever we may like to call it), without that spiritual life that we envisage, earthly humanity will be faced with a desolate future, a truly desolate future. I say this for the simple reason that all the spiritual impulses of the past that have been given to mankind are exhausted, have gradually fulfilled their potential and are unable to bring new seeds for human evolution. If only the old impulses were to continue to have an influence, the future prospect would inevitably be one where to an unprecedented degree technology of a purely external kind will not only overpower and outwardly overwhelm human beings but will paralyse them and take them over even to the point of utter destruction, because it will drive from the human soul everything of a religious, scientific, philosophical and artistic nature and also any kind of higher moral feeling. People will become something like living automatons if new spiritual impulses are unable to take hold. Thus when we think of theosophy, we must feel that we have been led by our karma to have some awareness of mankind's need for new impulses.

With this in mind we may ask ourselves what each one of us, with our particular questions and abilities, can do out of this overall sense of responsibility. In order to answer this deeply felt question, it may perhaps be particularly instructive for you, my dear friends, to consider the way in which theosophy came into the world in recent times and how it has developed over the course of the last few decades until now. We should never forget that there is something of the nature of a cultural miracle about the way that the word theosophy came to prominence amidst the modern age. This spiritual miracle is connected with a personality who is strongly linked to you, my dear friends, in that she did in a certain sense have her spiritual roots from among your own people. I am referring to Helena Petrovna Blavatsky.[82] No one in Western Europe would dispute the thought that the body in which the individuality who was in this incarnation called Helena Petrovna Blavatsky was dwelling could only have derived from Eastern Europe and specifically from Russia; for she had all the Russian characteristics. But she was taken away from you through circumstances of a quite particular kind, in that the particular karmic conditions of the present time led her to the West. Let us consider for a moment what kind of extraordinary cultural miracle she represented.

In many ways Helena Petrovna Blavatsky was a figure who throughout her life remained like a child, indeed like a real child. Never at any point did she learn to think logically, nor did she learn to keep her passions, desires and longings under the least degree of restraint (and at any time they were prone to extreme degrees of excess); and she had very little scientific training of any kind. Through this personality—and it was perhaps inevitable that it was through the medium of a personality who was chaotic, confused as well as colourful—a comprehensive body of the most sublime eternal wisdom appertaining to humanity was revealed to the world. Anyone who is well-versed in these matters will find in Helena Petrovna Blavatsky's works elements of wisdom, truth and knowledge which were completely incomprehensible to the intellect and soul of Blavatsky herself. If one considers the facts without prejudice, it is absolutely clear that—as regards everything she wrote—Helena Petrovna Blavatsky's intellectual faculties were merely the means whereby great and significant spiritual powers were able to communicate with mankind. It is equally clear that no one in Western Europe could have been the recipient of these impressions in the way that they needed to be received at the beginning of the last third of the nineteenth century. It needed the quite particular nature of Helena Petrovna Blavatsky, which was on the one hand selfless, almost devoid of self, and on the other hand thoroughly self-centred and egotistic, in order that what indeed occurred could be brought about by higher spiritual powers. The selfless part of her nature was necessary because a Western European mind would have transformed what had been revealed to it into its own thought-forms, its own intellectual substance; while the self-centred aspect was also necessary, because amidst the crudely materialistic Western European way of life there was no alternative but to clothe the tender hands whose task it was to nurture and cultivate the occultism of the modern age with iron fists forged from such an extreme temperament. It is a remarkable phenomenon. But, my dear friends, Helena Petrovna Blavatsky made her way to the West, she went to that part of the civilized world which, with the exception of America, is as regards its whole particular nature, structure and configuration the most thoroughly materialistic area of our present time and which in its language and its thinking lives to an extreme degree in materialistic thoughts and feelings. It would take me too long to explain which power it was that led Helena Petrovna Blavatsky to England. And so we see that the wealth of occultism that came so miraculously to expression through a medium (and I am not implying any spiritistic connotations) was directed initially towards the West of Europe.

Within this Western European context the destiny of this occultism was sealed in a certain direction, for with the founding of the theosophical movement in this materialistic European West a significant karmic obligation also came to fulfilment. Western Europe has a considerable karmic debt; and it cannot penetrate the mysteries without this karmic debt becoming apparent in some way or other. Whenever occultism becomes part of a situation, karma is immediately intensified; and forces are brought to the surface which otherwise remain hidden. What I now have to say is said in order to describe the actual situation and is not intended as a criticism. In the course of carrying out something that was a historical necessity, the European West committed innumerable injustices against the bearers of the spiritual culture of olden times, the bearers of the ancient occult mysteries, as a result of which these spiritual forces have become ossified and have ceased to be available, although they live on in the depths of the soul. This is indeed the case in India and South Asia. As soon as occult impulses came to Western Europe, a reaction immediately began to manifest itself against the spiritual forces active in the depths of Indian culture; and it became impossible—it had already become so in Blavatsky's time—to sustain what certain spiritual powers had intended to be the spiritual movements necessary for our time. This simply became impossible. The intention had been to give mankind a wealth of occult teachings which could be suitable for all people, for all hearts, teachings to which each and everyone could respond. But since it had become necessary to transplant the impulse to Western Europe, an egotistical reaction came about. Those spiritual powers that wanted to give the world a new impulse irrespective of any kind of human differentiations were thrust into the background; and India, whose occultism had initially been suppressed, took karmic revenge by pervading at its first opportunity the occultism that had appeared in the West with its own national egotistic occultism. This occurred during Helena Petrovna Blavatsky's lifetime. It was already happening when she was formulating the great truths and wisdom contained in her book *The Secret Doctrine*. Her first work, *Isis Unveiled*, demonstrates the chaotic, illogical, passionate and confused nature of her being, but throughout the book there is the indication that powers wanting to guide her towards a universally human purpose were watching over her. *The Secret Doctrine*, in addition to its undisputed elements of greatness, is pervaded throughout by particular human interests emanating from certain occult centres, which do not have universal human interests in view but more parochial interests. Modern Tibetan, Indian and also Egyptian initiations are invariably focused on more parochial concerns and wish merely to take revenge on the Western world for suppressing Eastern occultism and for the fact that the West conquered the East through materialistic means. It did conquer the East through factors of this nature, but only in so far as Christianity was received into the truly progressive stream of human evolution. Christianity did not reach the East from Asia, nor did it emanate from Asia to the south; the direction of its movement was towards the west.

Now, my dear theosophical friends, you may well say that this is all fine. The West went on to accept Christianity, and since Christianity is a stage in the advancement of mankind it is only natural that the West should have been victorious over the East. If only this were so! If this is how things really were, the consequences would indeed follow. But it is not. Christianity, which has come into the world after hundreds and thousands of years of preparation, has never yet prevailed anywhere on the Earth; and anyone who believes that he could in any real sense represent the Christ principle and the Christ impulse in our present time would have succumbed to indescribable arrogance. What is it that has really happened? Simply that the peoples of the West have embraced certain purely external features of Christianity, taken possession of Christ's name and clothed their old cultures that were indigenous before Christianity came to Europe—warlike cultures that have been transformed into modern industrialism—with Christ's name. Does Christ truly reign in Christian Europe? No one who belongs to an occult movement would ever accept that Christ rules over Christian Europe. Rather would he say that you speak of 'Christ', but you are really referring to what the ancient populations of Central Europe meant when they spoke of their god Saxnot. The symbol of the crucifix hovers over the peoples of Europe; but in a certain sense what really rules over them are the traditions of the god Saxnot, whose symbol is the erstwhile short Saxon sword which embodied the expansion of material interests, for that was the particular calling of the European tribes. This preoccupation therefore also gave rise to the noblest flowering of materialistic culture: chivalry. In no other culture is there anything resembling the chivalry of Western culture. It would not occur to anyone to compare the heroes of the Trojan War with medieval knights. So Christ is not much in evidence in people's lives; they merely speak about him. Thus when Westerners speak about Christ, Eastern peoples feel that they—the Eastern peoples—know far more about the spiritual understanding of the world and about the mysteries of existence. The Eastern peoples are well aware of this.

It is not difficult to see that the Eastern peoples are well able to appreciate their superiority in a spiritual respect. What do most Western people do today when mysteries of existence are being revealed? Well, we sit together in very small groups when we speak of the all-prevailing spiritual powers and mysteries which surround us everywhere, as we did yesterday evening. As far as ordinary Western Europeans are concerned, this is sheer folly or madness, for they are still unable to understand Paul's words to the effect that what is wisdom to God is often foolishness to human beings, and what people regard as foolish is regarded as wisdom by God.[83] And only those whose minds have been infected by Western Europeans in the East would dream of quibbling in the least about the deep truths concerning the spiritual mysteries of the cosmos that I have been trying to reveal here were they to hear them, for to those involved with the spiritual life of the East such things as I was saying yesterday, for example, would be regarded as self-evident. So we should not be surprised that, when they are assailed by Europeans, these Eastern peoples experience this as if they were being attacked by a herd of wild animals and defend themselves accordingly, while not feeling offended by behaviour which they regard as the fruit of an inferior attitude. For the reasons that I have indicated (whether or not they are justified is of no relevance at this point) and from the traditional Eastern point of view, we Westerners are regarded by adherents of Brahmanism, for example, as beings who are quite obviously inferior.

If we turn from Brahmanism and consider, for instance, the cultures of Central Asia, of Tibet and China, cultures which will in the near future have a significance for the world that would seem inconceivable to people today, even though—if we develop an awareness of this situation and realize that the souls of many of Zarathustra's pupils are even now incarnated in these cultures—it will not be long before this happens, we will need to take these matters very seriously. We shall also be able to see that, in everything that Helena Petrovna Blavatsky communicated, occultists from India, Tibet and Egypt were endeavouring to impart their own heritage of wisdom through her soul, although as regards its essential nature this wisdom belongs to a previous era of human evolution. Indeed, we must recognize this outdated nature of the oriental wisdom in Blavatsky's teachings. We should, moreover, not deny the significance of the fact that, were Chinese culture to break its fetters and flood the Western world, it would bring with it a spirituality that in many respects is the unadulterated successor of ancient Atlantis. The effect of this would be equivalent to something that had been held back and has the capacity to spread throughout the world being released; and on a small scale this is what the old culture of India has taken the opportunity to do.

As a result, my dear theosophical friends, there was an initial instance of the application of a principle that is of significance for any occultist; and this meant that the theosophical movement was no longer a suitable instrument for the further evolution of European culture. Every occultist is familiar with this principle, which states that no special interest of whatever kind should ever be allowed to override the general interests of mankind either amongst the guiding powers of occultism or on the part of anyone active in an occult movement. It is impossible to be effective in the occult realm if a particular interest outweighs the universal interest of humanity as a whole. The moment that a parochial interest enters the occult domain in place of universally human interests, the way lies open for genuine errors to occur. It was therefore possible at that time for all sorts of errors to enter the theosophical movement. Because of the way that England and India are related on a karmic level, the opportunity arose for those sublime powers that were present at the outset of the theosophical movement to be falsely impersonated; for it is quite normal in occultism that powers bent on pursuing their own special interests take on the form of those who have previously given the true impulses. Thus from a certain time in the unfolding of the theosophical movement it became completely impossible simply to accept everything that was going on within it, and it was karmically decreed that it became ever less possible to do so. As a result, when we were called upon to join forces with the theosophical movement there was nothing for it but to return to its original sources, which, as we can clearly state, are of a universally human nature and not serving any particular interest. You may therefore have seen that we try in Central Europe to approach the occult sources in such a way that you will not find anything associated with any special interest in what you encounter. If you compare whatever in Central Europe is tinged with special interests with what you know of the theosophy that we pursue here, these two elements are mutually incompatible. Apart from the fact that my books are written in German (and they have to be written in a language of some kind), you will find nothing distinctively German in this theosophy, nothing that is in some way connected with the outward traditions of Central Europe. Whenever there is a tendency to connect theosophy with interests of a parochial nature, you immediately arrive at an impossible situation.

It has been the particular task of Central Europe to free theosophy from the specialized characteristics that it has received in the European West. It was our mission to release it from all trace of such interests. And the further you delve into such matters, you will find that I was myself in a position to separate everything that I was enabled to bring of a theosophical nature from any sort of parochial interest. There is, my dear theosophical friends, something symbolic about the fact that I needed only to allow myself to be guided by what lived as a direct impulse in my present incarnation (and I trust that I shall not be misunderstood, as I am merely stating what actually occurred), in that those people who were the physical bearers of the blood that represents my line of descent originated from the German part of Austria; and I could not be born there. I was actually born in a Slavic region, which was completely alien to the whole environment from which my ancestors came. Thus from the very beginning of my present incarnation (and I am merely offering a characteristic example) it was symbolically impressed upon me that in Central Europe our task was to extricate theosophy from any kind of special interest, so that in Central Europe it may indeed appear before us as a goddess, as a divine being who has been set free from human qualities and who has on an ongoing basis just as much to do with people living in one place as with those living somewhere else.

This ideal of ours, my dear theosophical friends, will—for all its apparent simplicity—need to be in the forefront of our minds, since it is more difficult to implement it than to talk about it. It must stand before us as our ideal of truth and sincerity, unalloyed divine truth. If we make efforts of this kind, we may perhaps—not for ourselves but on behalf of that impersonal quality that Central

Europe can contribute to the whole mission of Europe—find the path whereby this divine theosophy can find its way to the East. And if I now go on to describe how theosophy has taken hold in the West, is being transmitted through Europe and now needs to come to the East, I should like once again to give strong emphasis to the word responsibility, to having a real sense of responsibility. The cultures in the world evolve in such a way that one culture develops with another as though within a spiritual sheath. One culture forms a connection with another. Because theosophy in Central Europe had to be so impersonal, its spiritual character has come to be one that is devoid of attachment to any special interests. As a result, my dear theosophical friends, there is something aloof about this theosophy, an aloofness that comes from being untouched by such interests; and so it will not appeal to those who cannot open their hearts to something that does not serve some kind of particular interest.

However, the spiritual quality that is possessed by this theosophy can indeed be found by souls who thirst and long for it. And at this point I may say, my dear theosophical friends, that I have from the spiritual world itself become acquainted with a soul that has a great longing for the spirit that comes to expression through theosophy. I came to know this soul in the purely spiritual world. If we ascend in the sequence of the hierarchies to the individual Folk-spirits and speak amongst the various Folk-spirits of the Folk-souls, amidst the Folk-souls who are, so to speak, still young and who must evolve further we find the Russian Folk-soul. I know that this Russian Folk-soul longs for the spirit that finds expression in theosophy. It longs for it with all the forces which it can muster. I have been speaking here of a sense of responsibility because you, my dear theosophical friends, are children of this Russian Folk-soul. It exerts its power and influence within you and you have a responsibility towards it. This responsibility is something that you must learn! Do not take it amiss if I say that this Russian Folk-soul has frequently had occasion to tell me many, many things. The most tragic of these communications was what the Russian Folk-soul was able to tell me around the year 1900. It appeared in a particularly tragic light at that time because what I was able to see then was something that I could rightly interpret only long afterwards, namely that this Russian Folk-soul is understood today to a very limited degree. In Western Europe we have learnt a great deal from Russia, and there is much that has made an enormous impression upon us. We have become familiar with the great impulses of Tolstoy, the deep psychological insights of Dostoevsky and latterly the figure of Solovyov, a man who—if we become aware of what he is really saying—always gives us the impression that what he writes is who he is. And we see his writings in their true light only if we sense that the Russian Folk-soul is standing behind him. Moreover, the Russian Folk-soul has far more to say than Solovyov himself manages to say, for there is in this far too much of what has been assimilated from Western Europe.

Think, my dear friends, of this word responsibility, and call to mind that you have this task of making yourselves worthy of the Russian Folk-soul and that you need to recognize its longing for impersonal theosophy. When you have come to recognize theosophy in what lives in your innermost impulses, you will have all sorts of questions which can only arise from within a Russian soul—questions that address the spiritual questions of theosophy.

I have experienced so much in the way of noble, lofty and beautiful feelings that have come towards me from Eastern Europe, so much true human love and goodness, compassion and overflowing feelings as can be attributed only to a delicate and intimate observation of what lives in the world and an intensely personal relationship with the ruling powers of existence. Out of such deeply intimate, beautiful and noble feelings, many questions have been put to me by those belonging to the Russian people—questions which *must* be asked, because unless they are answered mankind will not be able to go on living in the future. Questions that can only come from Eastern Europe have hitherto been posed to me only by the Russian Folk-soul on higher planes. I often felt obliged to think that the children of this Folk-soul still have a long way to go before they understand their Folk-soul, before they understand what this Folk-soul really longs for and how much still separates them from it. Do not, therefore, hold back from seeking the path to your Folk-soul; for you will find it if that is what you really want. It is from your Folk-soul that you will discover those questions which must be answered if mankind is to have a future. But do not be afraid of reaching beyond personal interests, for you need to be mindful of the great responsibility that you have towards the Russian Folk-soul; for in future the Folk-souls will need the human beings who are their children to attain their objectives. And do not forget one thing. That power which can support a person at the highest level and can lead him to the most beautiful and most radiant heights of the world is most exposed to the danger of falling prey to errors. What you need to do, my dear theosophical friends, is to imbue the spiritual domain with soul. You can do this because the Russian Folk-soul has infinite depths and possibilities for the future. But it is necessary that you are conscious that the soul element that is able to raise itself to the spirit and in this way to pervade it exposes you to the great danger of losing yourself in purely personal factors and of being confined by them. The fact is that individual, personal factors are reinforced when nourished by concerns of the soul.

You will not be confronted by the obstacles that so frequently manifest themselves in Western and Central Europe. You have little inclination towards scepticism, which affects you only through Western influences. You will develop a certain feeling for distinguishing truth from untruth and dishonesty in the realm of occultism, where truth and charlatanism are so closely entangled with one another. Scepticism and cynicism do not pose any danger to you. Your danger will be that the powerful soul-qualities of your personalities have a tendency to surround you with astral clouds which prevent you from reaching through to the objectively spiritual domain. Your fire and your warmth are well able to envelop you with a cloudlike aura which prevents the spirit from gaining access to you; your very enthusiasm for the spirit hinders it from finding its way to you. But bear in mind that you have the great advantage—and I mean this in the ideal, spiritual sense—of having the legitimate special interest that it is your destiny (that is, it is the destiny of your

Folk-soul) to be able to receive theosophy, which people in Central Europe had to embrace as a divine power elevated above all human concerns, as a special interest of the Russian people in the way that no other people can receive it, as something that you can cherish and cultivate as your very own. For through your destiny you are well adapted to inspire the spirit with *soul*. This has often been said in our circles, but it is up to you to take the first possible opportunity not only to develop feeling and will but also in a quite particular way to cultivate energy and persistence, and—to speak in practical terms— to say less about how theosophy should be in the West and how it should be in Russia and elsewhere and what is good in one situation or another but, rather, resolve to unite yourselves with theosophy with all your heart and soul. The rest will follow from this; it will surely follow.

This is, my dear friends, something of what I wanted to say to you; and I wanted to say it because whenever I am asked to speak I am aware of the sense of responsibility that we people of our time have towards theosophy. In the West people should have the feeling that they are committing a sin against humanity if they are able to receive something of theosophy and do not want it, reject it—a sin against humanity! It is sometimes very difficult to understand, for one must have an almost transcendental sense of duty, my dear friends, if one is to have such a feeling of responsibility towards mankind. Your Folk-soul tells you that it entrusts you with this obligation; it has already taken on this obligation towards mankind on your behalf. You need only to find your way to it. You need only to allow your thoughts, feelings and will-impulses to speak, and if you have this feeling of responsibility towards the Folk-soul you will at the same time be fulfilling this obligation towards mankind. It is for this reason that you are placed geographically between Western Europe, which *must* embrace theosophy but for which it cannot be a personal matter to the degree that it is for you, and the Asiatic East, which has had occultism and spiritual culture since ancient times. You would per-haps never manage to fulfil your task in relation to the spiritual culture of mankind in this difficult situation in which you have been placed if you had to think only of your obligation towards humanity. For the temptations become absolutely enormous if you bear in mind that you have, on the one side, the European West, which has caused many of the children of your Folk-soul to be untrue to themselves. Indeed, we may have the feeling that a large part of what has been written by Russians and then brought to us in the West has nothing to do with the Russian Folk-soul but is a reflection of all manner of Western phenomena. The second temptation will come from the East, when the power of its spiritual culture emerges. It will then be your duty to know that, for all the greatness of this spiritual culture of the East, people in our present age have to say to themselves: our task is not to bring the past into the future but, rather, new impulses; we should not simply embrace any kind of spiritual impulse emanating from the East but cultivate what the West can itself bring forth from spiritual sources.

If you fulfil your obligations towards your Folk-soul, the time will come when Europe will begin to understand the essential nature of the Christ impulse within the spiritual evolution of mankind. It would be my wish, my dear friends, that through everything that I have sought to say with and through these words, and above all through whatever in these words you are able to transform into impulses of your own, you will endeavour not merely to feel that theosophy is something of great significance but above all else take theosophy into your deeds and the will-impulses of your souls and direct your lives and actions accordingly.

ADDRESS FOR RUSSIANS ATTENDING THE LECTURE CYCLE *THE OCCULT FOUNDATIONS OF THE BHAGAVAD GITA*[84]

HELSINKI, 5 JUNE 1913

When we were gathered here last year, those who were present together with our Russian friends carried in their hearts as an unfolding bud, as it were, the awareness of something that has been developing over the course of the past year and should live ever more strongly in your hearts, namely that theosophy—or, as we also call it, anthroposophy—is not something that people should imbibe as another form of knowledge or belief-system but that it should in a certain sense take hold of the whole soul of each individual and, indeed, the soul of the whole of humanity in our time. This awareness needs gradually to develop, and we should not think or—what is more to the point—delude ourselves that it will be easy to arrive at its full significance and potential. Only very gradually and slowly will we manage to achieve a real experience of the significance of the theosophical impulse.

Such a truth may seem to be a matter of stating the obvious, but this is an instance where something that may appear quite trivial must be regarded with the utmost seriousness. Let us consider one particular aspect of the wealth of insights that arise from this way of looking at things. Thus it is, for example, nearly two thousand years since the Christ impulse came down from higher worlds to earthly life; and it is a fact that the Gospels are one of the most widely distributed texts in the world and, moreover, that for many, many centuries millions of human souls have believed that they have a right relationship to Christ. And yet it is equally true that anyone who is truly honest and is not immodestly ascribing to himself an understanding that he does not really possess has to struggle in our time with the question: what in actual terms is the Christ impulse? All that such a person can hope for is to gain an understanding of the Christ impulse through new revelations from the spiritual world! To give a specific instance of this problem, I can relate that last year together with some friends I attended an Easter service of the Russian Orthodox Church.[85] Immediately afterwards I tried to give expression to what I had experienced by putting it into words, so as to give you food for thought. What flowed forth from the service was a consciousness of the dead Christ, whereas the message that needs to flow to humanity for its salvation both in our time and the future is of the eternally living Christ. And yet, when I thought about what lay at the background to that service, a different picture arose in my mind of what the individuals who did not measure up to the demands of this service were actually engaged in there. Thus I saw in the background of the service a tableau of ancient holy mysteries which have evolved into what lives outwardly in the forms of this religious service; and although many people feel this in their hearts, the very people who ought to be, or consider themselves to be, the best qualified interpreters of these mysteries for our present time have the least understanding of them.

Try to ponder the thought that such examples engender ever more deeply, that theosophy proceeds from each individual heart and that through theosophy or anthroposophy something completely new needs to flow into human evolution. Try to engrave into your hearts the truth that the signs of the time are such that, at any rate in the quiet intimacy of our own hearts, we can never make any kind of compromise with what is around us. A new plant cannot simply arise out of an existing one but can emerge only if the old plant dies, making it possible for a new plant to be formed out of one single point, namely the seed. Thus theosophy is, my dear friends, something that must develop in our hearts and souls as a completely new seed; and out of everything of which the old plant of humanity consists it must retain only that which is universal, which we behold when we contemplate the Mystery of Golgotha. The leaves and trunk of the ancient culture of humanity will have to fall; the blossom, the Mystery of Golgotha, will have to remain as a memory of the seed which is to be developed through theosophy. And this seed, my dear friends, will need to be the bearer of the consciousness of bringing this blossom to its full maturity in ever renewed ways. The Christ impulse will then live in many forms over the course of human evolution and yet ever be the same, just as every new flower bears within itself the power and beauty of the old flower. But at the same time it will be what it seeks to be in its innermost essence, something that arises in ever renewed ways, an ever renewed understanding of what was given as a new beginning of human evolution when the blood flowed from the wounds of Him who took on human form in order to experience death amongst mankind.

My dear friends! All the worlds that we can traverse from our physical world through the higher worlds always have something in common. It is true that when we enter a higher world we constantly find new things, but nevertheless there is always a feature that is shared with the one before it. When we come to know the higher worlds, there is one thing that can exist only as a physical phenomenon which is not to be found there. The Gods of the higher worlds can experience many things, but the one experience that they cannot have is that of death; for death does not exist in the supersensible worlds. The beings in the supersensible worlds undergo transformation, they pass from one form into another; but one cannot die in the supersensible world. The physical phenomenon of death can only exist as a physical phenomenon. And among all the Gods and spirits, the only one who, in order to share the destiny of mankind, has descended into the world of human beings has been the Christ, who united Himself with mankind not only through His life but through His death, from whence new life-forces have streamed forth. Contemplation of the death on Golgotha must become the germinal point for ever new life-forces, for what a God has willed to accomplish for humanity by means of an ultimate sacrifice is concentrated at one single point of human evolution in this death. If you try to ponder this thought and let it become a living meditation, you will see that it can become the source of the strongest life-forces for every human soul. Thus there is no more sublime picture than the Cross erected on Golgotha.

My dear friends! An infinite amount is connected with an imagination such as that of the Cross on Golgotha for the whole of mankind. This symbol, which was at the same time an actual reality, has been in existence for well-nigh 2000 years, and we must increasingly learn to understand it over the future course of human evolution. These are simple, primitive thoughts, but their purpose is not to lead us into metaphysical speculations but to engender feelings that can make us capable of approaching human evolution as a whole in the right way.

You are aware, my dear friends, that human evolution is differentiated into distinct elements, which take the form of individual nations and peoples. Each people has a quite particular basic character, which arises from the fact that it has as its leader one of those spirits whom we collectively designate as the hierarchy of the Archangels. These Archangels are the highest representatives of the various peoples. A spiritual outlook on the world must enable the human soul to establish in future an ever closer connection as an individual soul with the ruling Folk-soul from the rank of the Archangels; and only if we come to understand what this Folk-soul is willing on our behalf (if this Folk-soul has an intention that it wants to develop for the future) are we able to collaborate with it in an appropriate way in the spiritual evolution of mankind. In this respect we need to make a firm distinction between the Western European Folk-souls and the East-European, Russian Folk-soul.

I am not now speaking of the outward aspect of Russian culture, of what exists as Russian national culture on the outward physical plane. I am speaking of your Folk-soul who is indeed present in the spiritual world, awaiting its future task full of expectation, hope and confidence. If one compares this Folk-soul with Western European Folk-souls, one has the impression of a youthful, aspirational being on the one hand and old, sterile beings on the other. Central European culture has a mediating function between Western and Eastern Europe which is fundamentally misunderstood if one equates it with the other cultures. This culture of Central Europe has the quite distinctive task of acting as a herald of past ages for later times. Just think, my dear friends, how the whole European culture of the Western world came into being. The advanced posts of the oriental peoples had extended to ancient India and had developed a great, all-pervasive culture there, as we encounter it in ancient Indian culture from the time of the *Bhagavad Gita*. These peoples had migrated to Southern Asia. Whereas wise teachers such as the Rishis and Zara-thustra taught amongst them, the peoples who resided in the wide expanses of the European countries, and also in your country, were through the wisdom of world evolution left behind in primitive conditions. In Asia there was a blossoming of far-reaching thoughts in the Sankhya and Vedanta philosophies, while these European peoples had simple, primitive cultures. Why? Because any advance in cultural development is predicated on everything that arises subse-quently as a new impulse being first received by people in a primitive state of development. The peoples of the East, who had risen to a certain height of intellectual development, could never understand the Christ impulse, for example; it was beyond the bounds of pos-sibility for them to understand it.

The peoples of Western culture had not yet come to the point of embracing the spiritual domain in an intellectual way; that which lives as a power radiating from the heart to the head had not in them extended to the head. In India everything was a culture of the head, whereas among the European peoples everything was still con-centrated in the heart in primitive feelings of primordial strength. It was only possible for such peoples gradually to assimilate the Mys-tery of Golgotha into their feelings because they had not gone beyond the soul-qualities of the heart. Thus because European culture had a fresh, primal energy through having remained behind (and fresh, primal energies are more closely related to divine forces), it was the culture that was ready to receive the Christ impulse. So in the Western world two streams flowed together which, for anyone who has any feeling for such matters, are sharply to be distinguished from one another. There is a marked difference, for example, between the underlying tone of Fichte, the Central European philosopher, and the underlying tone of Spinoza, who was also a European philosopher. It can happen in human evolution that what belongs to the general culture of the time can be borne by the same individuality; for as some of our friends may know, the individuality of Spinoza reappears in Fichte. But as an individual personality of the eighteenth and nineteenth centuries, Fichte was imbued with the whole power of the Christ impulse, while Spinoza—who was the same individuality—stands in the other stream and has no connection with this impulse.

There is, however, much that needs to enter European culture which is not yet present; and there must be an interaction between what has in a certain sense become old and what is youthful and full of hopeful anticipation. The Russian Folk-soul, this being from the rank of the Archangels, is young and full of hope, its task lies before it. It will be the task of Russian theosophists to find the bridge from the individual soul to the Folk-soul, to learn to understand what the Folk-soul is wanting of them. You will find, my dear friends, that it will—given certain preconditions—be easy for you to bring the Christ impulse to life within your hearts because of what lives within your souls. But on the other hand you will also have to face the experience that, because you have a certain inner proclivity for enlivening the Christ impulse, you will be exposed to great difficulties. You will have to experience to a high degree the profound truth that you will have to draw upon your inner resources and bring theosophy to life within your own hearts; for since theosophy is a message for our time it will not make any compromises with other world-conceptions. It therefore addresses other outlooks in a clear-cut way, in stern words which have been heard before in the course of evolution. Those who want to find theosophy amidst cultures that have hitherto had an outward, materialistic character—and that is true of all cultures of the present, or at any rate virtually so—and seek to make a compromise with them will hear resounding in all sternness the words of Christ Jesus: 'Let the dead bury their dead. Follow me!'[86] What is meant by 'the dead' here are the various cultures inclining towards materialism; they are well able to run themselves into the grave. 'Let the dead bury their dead!' But human souls should be guided by their understanding of the spiritual impulse that pervades the world in the form of the Christ impulse. So if you direct your enquiries towards old traditions and practices, you will, my dear friends, not find anything that leads you to theosophy. It is good to explore these old traditions in order to show how the divine world lives in them, but a person comes to theosophy today because his soul is not old and senile but is like yours—fresh and direct, encountering theosophy in the way that you do, uninfluenced by any traditions. The theosophical impulse requires from your souls not only cognitive power but living energy.

My dear friends! Many of you, perhaps most or even all of you, feel within yourselves—even though you may express it differently—the grief and sorrow of being temporarily separated from your Folk-soul. Many of you feel, even if your beliefs are otherwise—and again this may apply to most or perhaps all of you—that you need a new stimulus for your will and energies. Begin—or indeed resolve—to see, my dear friends, that what you experience so deeply as the sorrow of will and motivating forces that often seem so inadequate is the virginal quality of your will; make a resolve to view this as a will that has remained untapped and which is waiting to be stirred into action by the theosophical impulse! Let the theosophical impulse become a force of will within you! Try to transform sorrow into strength, your weakness of will into a theosophy that is a living power within you, and you will really be able to embark upon a theosophical life. Try to find a way of reinvigorating what is still weak in you and is not fully present. You will then become the best representatives of theosophy. And bear in mind that the souls which are now dwelling in your bodies are not destined only to reincarnate in Eastern Europe. They are destined to be spread throughout the Earth in their next incarnations. And as you prepare for your new incarnation in the course of your life between life and death and a new birth, some words will be addressed to you. To some of you it will be said: 'You have fulfilled your task, you can take what you have received on Earth—which could have been received only on Eastern European soil—into the world.' To the others it will be said: 'You cannot.'

My dear friends, regard what you now feel for theosophy as an instinct for what I have just been saying, as a vague feeling that you have for what constitutes your task. If you think of it in such a way that it can give you strength that flows from your ego into your thinking, feeling and will, from there into your life and from there into your blood, you will be interpreting this instinct out of which you are now hastening towards theosophy in the right way.

You are now assembled together here. Despite the great difficulties that exist in your country, you have managed to come together without impediment. Make use of this opportunity to foster a strong inner concord so that each and every one of you can form a bridge to the Folk-soul. It cannot be my task, my dear friends, to speak in detail about which services should be rendered to this Folk-soul; but I can speak to you about something else, and I should like that you transform into a feeling what I am obliged to express in words. You are in a particular situation, my dear friends. You are in a certain sense in an opposite situation to a people who are dominating the Earth for a brief period of increasing splendour. I am referring to the North American people. Consider, my dear friends, that these North American people, who are your opposites, began gradually to advance westwards at the time when the age of materialism had begun in Europe, and they developed it further. You need to bear in mind that the roots of Americanism lie in materialism, and that the people who colonized America undertook this armed with the ideas of civilized Europe several centuries ago. What did these people do?

They did what uneducated people otherwise do when they clear ancient forests, prepare the land area by area and bring the soil into cultivation but with the materialistic ideas of modern science and modern social organization. Everything arose out of materialism. Let us consider one of their most important writers, a man whom, moreover, the Americans have chosen as their leader, Woodrow Wilson.[87] Wilson is certainly a significant writer who has made some brilliant studies of social affairs; but if we really look at his concepts and ideas and everything that he stands for as the representative of the American people, what do we find? A house of cards. If a single breath from the spiritual worlds were to blow upon this house of cards, it would collapse and the whole culture that it typifies would fall with it. Every detail that has gone into the making of American culture can be found in ordinary history books, in the culture of the preceding centuries. Everything is openly there to see; and everything that we find is man-made.

If you ask yourselves where your national character, your spiritual life, comes from and what is the source of the best qualities that you cherish in your souls, you will not find it on the Earth. It cannot be found in this way, for it originates in the spiritual world itself. This is no house of cards but a living organism! We should never regard such things as a justification for arrogance but, rather, as a reason for humility and modesty; for we should not be deriving from this a brazen self-consciousness but a true sense of responsibility.

My dear friends! I was speaking yesterday about freedom. A lot of water will have to flow under the bridges of Europe before a certain number of people fully understand what is meant by a freedom of this nature. What is freedom? Looking at this from the point of view of the extreme West, what is freedom to an American? It is what makes his life as comfortable as possible. He refers to freedom as that which needs to be incorporated into the social order so that every individual has the best chance to get on in the world. Our idea of freedom, says Woodrow Wilson,[88] is different from that of Europeans, because we think of it in practical terms. This is what an American himself says about it. A knife is used to cut with and a fork to eat with, because that is the practical thing to do. Americans espouse freedom because of its practical advantages, because it offers the best way of achieving what is agreeable to them. For Americans, freedom is a utility product, it brings them benefits. My dear friends! For Western Europeans freedom has been something very different, it has been a high ideal, something that they have looked up to. It is worthy of being spoken of in poetic terms. For a European it is a 'high and glorious goddess',[89] for an American it is a useful cow which provides him with milk and butter. I am not advancing this view myself; it is put forward by the man who will be responsible for leading the United States of America. It is not my task to express an opinion of my own but merely to be the interpreter of what lives in the spiritual world. The American version of freedom has been characterized here by an outstanding representative of the American people. Whereas if we take into account all that heroic spirits in Europe have achieved in order to describe this divine freedom as a high, majestic goddess, this amounts to saying that all our enthusiasm, thoughts and feelings go out towards the ideal of freedom that lived within these Europeans.

But you need to understand, my dear friends, that freedom must become something quite different again for those who share in a spiritual view of the world. You would be seriously mistaken if you did not realize that everything must be fashioned anew. We are faced with the challenge that freedom must become altogether different from the high ideal that the best human minds have hitherto cherished. For we know that as human beings we shall shortly be granted access to a divine spring, that we will be enabled to drink water of the spirit and that this water will live in our souls, and that we shall have to ensoul freedom—just as we incorporate our soul in our body. Thus on the one hand freedom is a practical tool for outward life and, on the other, a lofty spiritual ideal; but freedom needs to be a quality that is enshrined within the soul and is higher than the soul and, moreover, to the same degree as the soul is higher than the body. We shall learn to ensoul freedom, which will be no small thing to learn; and then we will be able to go forwards in accordance with the wishes of the eternal, spiritual powers for human evolution through their having enabled theosophy to flow into your souls.

It has been my wish, my dear friends, to share with you some simple words directed not to your intellect but to your hearts, since you have found it possible to devote yourselves to theosophy also outwardly within your country. So let us take the opportunity to make ourselves aware at this moment of the lofty task that has been given to us through a spiritual conception of the world. My dear friends, this consciousness will—if we are able to dwell within it— enable something to radiate forth from the quiet work in theosophical branches which will have a healing influence for the whole country; for we will only begin to understand spiritual life once we know that it is not only what we can do outwardly for the spreading of theosophy that actually contributes towards this aim, but that when we work together as well as we can to achieve an understanding of theosophy the effects of our spiritual endeavours stream forth imperceptibly. And just as we well know that a town where there is a theosophical lodge is—even if only a few people have been engaged in theosophical activity there—after 30 years quite a different place from one where there is no theosophical lodge, your country will become altogether different if you have an inner understanding of what theosophy can give you. I am not speaking to you as a Western European or as someone belonging to this or that nation. I know that that is not the case. But perhaps it is just for this reason that I am able to say to you that salvation will come to Russia, but this salvation is not something to be sought on a false path. Nor am I saying this because I love theosophy; I am saying this because the whole of human evolution can assure us that this is true. There is a path of salvation for Russia and it lies through theosophy. For other regions of the Earth theosophy will be highly beneficial and a means of real progress. For Russia theosophy will be the only salvation, something that is essential in order that this Folk-soul is not called upon to take on tasks in the world other than the one that is destined for it.

With these words I should like to inaugurate your newly founded branches, for I know that the holy significance of these words will be fully embraced within your hearts. It will then be possible for that connection to be established in your souls which is necessary for the salvation of your country: the connection of the Mystery of Golgotha with the human understanding of this mystery. Then the Spirit who must become the regenerator of your country will reign in your hearts, and your gatherings will radiate forth what your earthly region needs. With such thoughts as these and out of a sense of reverence for the guiding powers of human evolution I should like to call down every blessing for your work, the blessing of those powers which make it possible for the Mystery of Golgotha to flow into your hearts, so that this blessing continues to radiate from your souls and from your work into your country. And I know that this blessing is always present whenever we are worthy of it. So as we stand at the point of departure for our work, may the image of these thoughts hover over us as a new spiritual impulse which must stream into human evolution, just as the spiritual leaders of this impulse hover over the work that we seek to carry out in all sincerity. Then from this image will arise the awareness that we are doing what must be done for a limited region and, hence, also for the whole realm of human evolution; and so from this we know what we have to do. May in this sense the blessing of the wise leaders of the world and of humanity guide your work, may it arise powerfully within your souls as a source of light; for then this light will be able to radiate forth and you will be able to accomplish much that is essential for healing, for progress and for the true evolution of mankind.

QUESTION AND ANSWER SESSION

HELSINKI, 7 APRIL 1912[90]

Question: There are people in Finland who have begun to doubt about the future of Finland; and there are others who are full of enthusiasm for a future Finnish culture. Do you think that the Guardian Angel of Finland still has something to do in the world?

Rudolf Steiner: It is probably as well that where such questions are concerned it is a general rule among occultists not to answer them at any great length. It is wholly understandable that for an objective, open-minded judgement of many answers that we may be accorded from occult research, a high degree of impartiality is necessary which—if I may emphasize this—we do not always find in practical life. Hence it is necessary that I am unable even in this place to answer this question, which concerns the social life of our present time and the forces living within it, in any greater detail than any other practising occultist. What I am able to say regarding this question can be indicated in a few words along the lines of what I said when I was speaking about Folk-spirits in Christiania.[91] I said then that the Folk-spirits of certain territories of smaller nations have a far greater significance for the future of mankind than one would generally suppose in the wider world today. Populations which have in a certain sense played less of a part in recent times in the 'great concert' of European and world evolution have for the time being been allotted the task of conserving certain significant aspects of human

202 * OUR CONNECTION WITH THE ELEMENTAL WORLD

culture outside of the wider process of cultural development. Inasmuch as I have been able to concern myself with the cultural life of Finland, I can say that what I said in Christiania should be recognized as being true for Finland. I ask you not to regard this as something said to Finns by someone of German-speaking origin who has the intention of saying something that is agreeable to them. It will never happen that I say something in order to please anyone or a group of people; it is simply that, according to my conviction, that is, my research, it is true.

If—in so far as this is possible for an occultist—as a non-Finn one studies Finnish cultural development, one would have to say that as regards its spiritual evolution Finnish cultural life is among those cultures that will play a large part in the future cultural evolution of Europe. I say this quite objectively, irrespective of my nationality or the language that I speak. The most diverse Folk-spirits will have a contribution to make towards the future of the Earth; but everything that we may recognize as what is most characteristic of Finnish cultural life has something about it which should not be absent in a future world culture, if this world culture develops in the ways that our occult knowledge would have us believe. The course of world evolution is such that, as evolution advances, something that was already present in earlier cultural periods must at some later point be renewed or re-assimilated. For example, many things in our present, fifth post-Atlantean cultural period have been derived from the Egyptian age; in the sixth cultural period many things from the age of ancient Persia will re-emerge, and in the seventh from the ancient Indian culture. This ancient Indian culture, which lives on beneath the surface, will experience a mighty reawakening in the seventh post-Atlantean cultural period.

What is the case on a large scale with respect to these repetitions also takes place amidst those populations that become the living guardians of certain spiritual forces in the course of evolution. Thus I am convinced that in the Finnish culture some secret forces are concealed which are sensed today by the present population of Finland in connection with the renewal of the ancient sagas of the old culture of Finland, as I believe (and I say this quite explicitly), and that there is in all of this something of the greatest importance which is in many respects still hidden but which will emerge in its full significance (and more so than is the case at present) and will make an impact upon the future culture of mankind. I believe that there is some justification for repeating the assertion that Finnish culture will in future have something remarkably significant and light-filled about it. Again I must emphasize that what I have said represents my own conviction and is said, so I believe, out of my occult knowledge and not in order to flatter anyone. I would just as easily have said something unpleasant if it had been the truth.

Question: The *Kalevala* shows us that it is justified to speak of a past spiritual culture of Finland. A culture presupposes a higher influence. Hence one can perhaps speak of ancient Finnish mysteries. Do you know anything about the nature of these mysteries? Would you say something about them?

Rudolf Steiner: It is easily possible to understand that someone who knows the *Kalevala* only through a translation will inevitably over-look certain details which are highly important for the effect of such an epic poem. But this epic poem, the national poem of Finland, appears to someone who considers it in an occult light as something of such significance and so clearly arising out of occult antecedents that there would be some justification for recognizing its occult background, even if one cannot enter into the great beauties that can of course be discerned only in the language of the original poem.

What is distinctive about the *Kalevala* is that its occult foundations are immediately obvious. For me this was highly striking—I am saying this here, although it will be necessary to repeat some of these thoughts in my public lecture the day after tomorrow[92]—when I first encountered the three heroes of the great Finnish national epic who are so well known to you, Väinämöinen, Ilmarinen and Lemminkäinen. (Forgive me if I sometimes make mistakes in the pronunciation. It is quite understandable if one doesn't manage to pronounce such a difficult language as Finnish perfectly.) When one encounters these three heroes, as an occultist one immediately ceases to speak of ordinary heroes, as the word is often used in other national epics. It was striking for me to discover three quite distinct things behind these three principal heroes. As you know, in my book *Theosophy*[93] there is a description of the full extent of human soul-life in its three main aspects, which is in accordance with what is given in the oldest European mysteries and is fully in harmony and agreement with the Rosicrucian mysteries of modern times; and I call them the sentient soul, the intellectual or mind soul and consciousness soul. We should think of human evolution in such a way that these soul-members developed one after the other. Firstly the sentient soul developed in the three sheaths of the physical body, ether body and astral body. Later the intellectual or mind soul developed on its foundation; and the richest fruit of this evolution is the consciousness soul. We must imagine that behind everything that happens in the physical world (and therefore also behind man's participation in these forces) there are spiritual beings. Thus behind the physical world in which we human beings live we must envisage the spiritual bestowers and bearers of the forces of our sentient soul, our intellectual or mind soul and our consciousness soul. I cannot now enter into these details; but it became an absolute certainty to me that Väinämöinen can be recognized as the bearer, the giver, the bestower of man's sentient soul, so that everything that we refer to in European theosophy as the forces of the sentient soul must appear as a gift of the spiritual being who bears the name of Väinämöinen in the *Kalevala*. These things do not merely have a historical context; for in this historical dimension there is always a place for occult forces. That is not to say that behind these personalities there are not also historical heroes; but what lies *within* these heroes is something that we are obliged to recognize. The bestower of the consciousness soul is Lemminkäinen. Because he is the bestower of the consciousness soul, Lemminkäinen is in what might be called a Dionysian situation; for if one knows the mystery of the state of being dismembered amidst the world expanses,[94] it is remarkable to find in the *Kalevala* the incident of the dismembering of Lemminkäinen. Thus when we enter into these elements of the *Kalevala*, we find what we portray in theosophy with regard to soul-development, which itself derives from the oldest mysteries of Europe (and pre-eminently from the northern mysteries) but is also in accordance with the Rosicrucian and Grail mysteries, everywhere expressed in mighty pictures which, precisely because they have a pre-human or super-human aspect, expand into immense proportions. Thus even this purely *external* circumstance makes us aware of what lies behind this poem; for in its mighty pictures it reflects ancient, holy truths of the mysteries which have their origin in the deepest mysteries of the European North (although I cannot go into further detail here, it must be acknowledged that this is the ultimate source of what we find expressed in this poem). This is apparent, for example, from even a cursory study of the way that the creation of the world prior to the appearance of man is described in the first runes. This corresponds to everything that is contained in the European mysteries about the origin of the world, albeit expressed in majestic images. These are the embodiments of truths deriving from the mysteries, in the way that an earlier consciousness had received them. Additionally, it is also possible to verify from occult history, from the Akashic Record, the direct connection between these Finnish imaginations—I am now being careful to speak of the *imaginations* underlying the *Kalevala*—with the pictures that have been given in the old European mysteries about the marriage of heaven with the Earth.[95] Thus we encounter what we may recognize as an interaction between the upper and lower regions in the sense of the mysteries in the first rune.

Hiedurch wird freundschaftlich
eingeladen zu dem • • • • • •

welchen

Vortrags-
Cyclus ✿✿

Dr. Rudolf
Steiner

in Helsingfors

in der Zeit vom 3 bis zum
14 April 1912 halten wird • •

Anmeldungen und Wünsche bezüglich der
Unterkunft werden erbeten an Herrn Dr.
Edvard Selander, Hoplaks Helsingfors
(Sprechstunden vom 30 März an täglich
von 6—7 Uhr Boulevardstr. 7 Teos. Biblio-
tek). Karten für den Cyclus á Rmk 12 =
Fmk 15 daselbst zu haben • • • • • • • • •

Invitation to the lecture cycle given in Helsinki in 1912

✴ ✵ ✴ Programm

Vortrags-Cyclus

Die geistigen Wesenheiten
in den Himmelskörpern und
Naturreichen • • • • • • • •

in 10 Vorträgen, abgehalten im Saale des
schwed. Normallyceum.   8 Uhr abends

Zwei
öffentliche Vorträge im Solen-
nitets Saal der Universität:

1.   Dienstag d. 9 April 8 Uhr abends

Das Wesen nationaler Epen mit spe-
ziellem Hinweis auf Kalevala

Eintrittskarten á Rmk 1: 20 oder Fmk 1: 50

2.   Freitag d. 12 April 8 Uhr abends

Der Okkultismus und die
Initiation • • • •

Eintrittskarten á Rmk 1: 20 oder Fmk 1: 50

Theosophen in Finnland • • •

Anrufung des Maße soll nicht Phrase sein —
Ajax … mit Götterblut
Agamemnon — der … König:
Iris in … gestellt
Die Götter in der Gewalt der Menschen —

Grimm S. 298 —
    " S. 307
    " S. 327 aber
    " S. 330 Vielseitigkeit —

Tötung des …
360: Thetis' Doppeldasein
        395 Nibelungen   417

Notebook entries for the lecture of 9 April 1912

Von oben westel. Besetz der Erde –

W. — der in Principio befehlte Mensch, der alte Cultur. schafft.

Aino —: die vermenschlich geistige Cultur –

W. – Sampo schmieden:

Hm.

Lit. Kysteili – Saari = Insel.
zerstückung. | der Einzelgeist.

Wn – von Wipunen verschlungen.

Kul.: wie alles über das menschliche Maß
hinauswächst —

die Vorstellungen tauchen wie Erinnerungen
auf —

Griechen: die Menschen empfinden sich
gegenüber der Götterwelt — die Götter
sind da —

Mit.: die Menschen sind das; sie tragen in
sich das Göttererbe — sie entdecken es
in sich —

NOTES

Sources of the texts: The lecture in Helsinki of 9 April 1912 and the address for Russian listeners of 11 April 1912 are based on the notes of Georg Klenk, while the typewritten report of the address has some corrections in Rudolf Steiner's hand. There are some notebook entries made by Rudolf Steiner (notebook no. NB 565 from the archive) relating to the lecture of 9 April 1912. The authors of the notes of the lecture of 9 November 1914 in Dornach, the address of 1 January 1912 in Hanover and that of 5 June 1913 in Helsinki are unknown. Original shorthand reports by Franz Seiler exist for the lectures of 14, 15, 20, 21 and 22 November 1914 and also that of 31 December 1914, with the latter including some corrections by Rudolf Steiner. The basis for the text of the address of 7 January 1913 is a manuscript by Walter Vegelahn, while there is also an original shorthand report by Franz Seiler. The undated Address for a Recitation of the Dream Song of Olaf Åsteson is a handwritten manuscript by Rudolf Steiner (ref. NZ 5283–5285 in the archive). The report of the question and answer session probably derives from Georg Klenk. This fourth [German] edition of the volume (1993) has been revised and prepared for publication by Martina Sam, on the basis of previous editorial work by Edwin Froböse.

The drawings in the text have been compared and corrected in the light of the available records (the original blackboard drawings have not been preserved) and some new drawings added by Carlo Frigeri.

Previous publications in English: The three lectures of 20, 21 and 22 November 1914 were first published in English in 1948 by Rudolf Steiner Publishing Co. and reprinted under the title *The Balance in the World and Man* by the Steiner Book Centre, Inc., North Vancouver, Canada. The public lecture of 9 April 1912 and the two addresses to Russian members have been previously published as appendices to an edition of the GA 136 Helsinki course by Anthroposophic Press, Hudson, New York 1992. The address of 31 December 1914 was included in the translation of GA 275 entitled *Art as Seen in the Light of Mystery Wisdom*, published in 1984/1996 by Rudolf Steiner Press. The other lectures and addresses have never been published in English before, although typescript translations exist of the majority of them. The present translation has been made with reference to these previous versions, although—except where specifically noted—it is essentially a new translation in every case. The translator wishes to acknowledge with gratitude the valuable work of previous translators.

1. See also Rudolf Steiner's notes for this lecture and the invitation to the lecture cycle.
2. In 1913 the German Section of the Theosophical Society—of which Rudolf Steiner was the secretary from 1902 to 1912—for the most part separated itself off from it and established the Anthroposophical Society. There is a

passage in the introduction to Rudolf Steiner's book *Theosophy. An Introduction to the Supersensible Knowledge of the World and the Destination of Man* (GA 9) which sheds some light on the question of the general use of the words 'theosophical' or 'spiritual-scientific': 'Hence that wisdom that reaches out beyond the sense-perceptible and reveals to him [man] his own being, and with this his final goal, may be called "divine wisdom" or *theosophy*. The study of the spiritual processes in human life and in the cosmos may be referred to by the term *spiritual science*.'

3. *Spiritual Beings in the Heavenly Bodies and in the Kingdoms of Nature*, GA 136, given between 3 and 14 April 1912.

4. The second public lecture (on 'Occultism and Initiation') took place on 12 April 1912 and is included in GA 136.

5. The runes of the *Kalevala*, previously handed down by oral tradition, were published for the first time in 1835 by Elias Lönnrot (1802–84). See note 15.

6. Ninth century BC, author of the two great epics of the *Iliad* and the *Odyssey*.

7. Herman Grimm, *Homer's Iliad*, 2nd edition Stuttgart and Berlin 1907; first edition (in two volumes), Berlin 1890 and 1895. See Rudolf Steiner's page references in his notes for this lecture. Regarding Herman Grimm, see note 31.

8. Jakob Grimm (1785–1863), see note 33.

9. In his study of the sixth canto Herman Grimm writes (p. 148, op. cit.): 'Who would not insist that Homer must have been a shepherd, or a huntsman, or a sailor, or that he was an expert in something else—the favourite suggestion being that he was an old soldier. And yet he was nothing more than an ordinary human being who, wherever he turned his eyes, discerned in every situation the very essence of what people did, which is why he is recognized as an "expert". Dante was also an expert in this sense. Napoleon, Frederick the Great and Goethe had a similar ability, as did a few others.' And with regard to the sixteenth canto (p. 330) he writes: 'We imagine that he must have spent his life observing lions fighting in remote mountains, or with shepherds and woodcutters, while other passages lead one to think that he was a seafarer and still others that he lived as a citizen or farmer on the plain.'

10. Napoleon Bonaparte, 1769–1821, Emperor of France and legendary commander. His military expeditions led as far as Egypt and Russia (1812). The latter campaign signified the turning point of his career: the Russian winter forced him to retreat, the large part of his army perished through cold and hunger. *Writings* (Paris 1821/22); *Correspondance de Napoleon I* (Paris 1858–70, 32 vols; a selection in 3 vols 1909/10 and an extract entitled *Correspondance militaire* (Paris 1875–7, 10 vols).

11. A translation of Herman Grimm's version of the first canto could be as follows: 'Goddess, sing the anger of Achilles, the pernicious one/Who inflicted utter disaster upon the Achaeans.' The translation by J.H. Voss, that Grimm thought very highly of, could be rendered thus: 'Sing the anger, O Goddess, of Achilles son of Peleus,/He who through his passions caused the Achaeans unspeakable sorrow.'

12. See *Kalevala*, rune 50.

13. See the chapter 'The World Conception of the Greek Thinkers' in Rudolf

Steiner's book *The Riddles of Philosophy* (1914), GA 18.

14. *Theosophy. An Introduction to the Supersensible Knowledge of the World and the Destination of Man*, 1904 (GA 9).

15. Rudolf Steiner is referring here to a folk song with which Elias Lönnrot (1802–84), Professor in Helsinki, doctor, specialist in the national culture and language of Finland and editor of the *Kalevala*, prefaced his collection *Kanteletar, die Volkslyrik der Finnen* (The Folk Lyric Poetry of the Finns), Helsinki 1840 (translated into German by Hermann Paul, Helsinki 1882). It has not been possible to discover whose translation Rudolf Steiner has used or if the version here rendered into English is his own. In addition to the Finnish original edited by Lönnrot and an English translation, a German translation by Hermann Paul (Helsinki 1885) and several editions of the translation by Anton Schiefner—edited, augmented and introduced by Martin Buber—were found in his library. Buber refers to the folk song in a note to the 40th rune, the subject of which is the origin of the kantele.

16. GA 10 (1904–5).

17. The fourth post-Atlantean period, the Graeco-Roman, which followed the three previous periods designated as the Indian, Persian and Egypto-Chaldean, began in 747 BC and ended in 1413. Regarding the cultural epochs, see also the chapter 'The Evolution of the World and Man' in *Occult Science—An Outline* (GA 13) and the lectures of 7 and 14 June 1906 in *An Esoteric Cosmology* (GA 94).

18. Compare the lecture of 31 August 1909 in *The East in the Light of the West. The Children of Lucifer and the Brothers of Christ*, GA 113.

19. Lecture of 9 April 1912, included in this volume.

20. See the previous note.

21. The name of the Swedish Vikings who, by way of the eastern coast of the Baltic Sea towards Russia, brought the East-European lowlands as far as the Black Sea under their sway.

22. See note 37.

23. *The Secrets of the Threshold*, 24–31 August 1913, GA 147.

24. See the sixth scene in Rudolf Steiner's Mystery Play *The Souls' Awakening* (GA 14).

25. See especially the cycle entitled *Michael's Mission* (GA 194).

26. In *Four Mystery Plays*, GA 14.

27. See the first scene in *The Portal of Initiation*, GA 14.

28. GA 17 (1913).

29. This is a reference to the architraves of the wooden columns in the great hall of the First Goetheanum, which was under construction from 1913 and, when still unfinished, burnt down on New Year's Eve 1922. See further in *Ways to a New Style in Architecture*, GA 286, *The Building in Dornach as a Symbol of Historical Development and Artistic Transformation*, GA 287, *The Architectural Conception of the Goetheanum* and *The Goetheanum as a Synthesis of the Arts*.

30. These lectures were given in Dornach between 3 and 6 October 1914 (GA 156). The added lecture in question is entitled 'Times of Expectation' and is included in the English volume of the lectures which is published under the title *Inner Reading and Inner Hearing*.

31. Herman Grimm, 1828–1901, literary and art historian, son of the linguistic

214 * OUR CONNECTION WITH THE ELEMENTAL WORLD

researcher and fairy tale collector Wilhelm Grimm, Professor in Berlin. Regarding Herman Grimm see also Rudolf Steiner's essays/articles *Eine vielleicht zeitgemässe persönliche Erinnerung* ('A personal recollection with some bearing on today'), *Wie sich heute "Gegenwart" schnell in "Geschichte" wandelt* ('How "Present" rapidly becomes "History" today'), *Der notwendige Wandel im Geistesleben der Gegenwart* ('The necessary change in modern intellectual life'), *Der Geist von gestern und der Geist von heute* ('The spirit of yesterday and the spirit of today') in *Gesammelte Aufsätze* (Collected Essays), 1921–5, GA 36; *Herman Grimm zu seinem siebzigsten Geburtstage* ('To mark Herman Grimm's 70th birthday') and the obituary of Herman Grimm in *Methodische Grundlagen der Anthroposophie* (Methodical Foundations of Anthroposophy), GA 30; and the lecture about Herman Grimm of 16 January 1913 in *Ergebnisse der Geistesforschung* (Results of Spiritual Research), GA 62.

32. From 24 June to 7 July 1909: *The Gospel of St John in its Relation to the Other Three Gospels*, GA 112.

33. Wilhelm Grimm (1786–1859) and Jakob Grimm (1785–1863) are regarded as the founders of German philology. They worked tirelessly to assemble elements of the linguistic heritage of Germany and were the editors and publishers of the *Deutsches Wörterbuch* (German Dictionary), *Deutsche Mythologie* (German Mythology) and above all the world-famous *Kinder- und Hausmärchen* (Fairy Tales) (1812).

34. Dorothea Grimm (1785–1867), known as 'Dortchen', née Wild, the wife of Wilhelm Grimm. Many of the 'Grimm's Fairy Tales' that the brothers collected derive from what was handed down through her and her sister Margareta (Gretchen) Wild (1787–?).

35. Rudolf Wild (1747–1814).

36. 'A Brief Outline of an Approach to Anthroposophy', *The Riddles of Philosophy, Presented in an Outline of its History*, GA 18 (1914).

37. Ralph Waldo Emerson, 1803–82, American writer. Nature was for him both the symbol of his ideal world-conception—based on his study of the mystics, ancient Greek and German philosophy—and a revelation of the spirit. He was a leading member of the transcendental movement in America. His later works came increasingly to explore topical social issues. In 1857 Herman Grimm translated two essays by Emerson on Shakespeare and Goethe (see the following note) and expressed his appreciation of him again in 1861 ('Ralph Waldo Emerson' in *Fünfzehn Essays, Erste Folge* (Fifteen Essays, First Series), third edition Gütersloh 1884). After Emerson's death in 1882 he wrote an obituary, published in the Third Series of his *Fünfzehn Essays* (1882). Regarding Emerson's karmic connections, especially his connection with Herman Grimm, see the lecture of 23 April 1924 in GA 236 (*Karmic Relationships*, vol. 2).

38. In the course of a visit to England in 1847–8 Emerson gave lectures on 'Representative Men', which he published in 1850 as *Essays on Representative Men*. The individual essays are concerned with the following individuals: Plato, 429–347: 'Plato: or the Philosopher'; Emanuel Swedenborg, 1688–1772: 'Swedenborg: or the Mystic'; Michel Eyquem de Montaigne, 1533–92: 'Montaigne: or the Sceptic'; William Shakespeare, 1564–1616: 'Shakespeare:

or, the Poet'; Napoleon Bonaparte, 1769–1821: 'Napoleon: or, the Man of the World'; and Johann Wolfgang Goethe, 1749–1832: 'Goethe: or, the Writer'. Herman Grimm published a German translation of the essays on Shakespeare and Goethe in 1857, together with a critical appreciation of Emerson's writings. They were included in the Third Series of his *Fünfzehn Essays*.

39. 'I will ... offer ... a word or two to explain how my love began and grew for this admirable gossip. A single odd volume of Cotton's translation of the Essays remained to me from my father's library, when a boy. It lay long neglected, until, after many years, when I was newly escaped from college, I read the book, and procured the remaining volumes. I remember the delight and wonder in which I lived with it. It seemed to me as if I had myself written the book, in some former life, so sincerely it spoke to my thought and experience' (p. 277 of the 1903 World Classics edition of *English Traits and Representative Men*). A—heavily annotated—copy of K. Federn's 1896 German translation of *Representative Men* was in Rudolf Steiner's library.

40. Albrecht Dürer (1471–1528): 'Der grosse Hercules' (The great Hercules), copperplate engraving. See illustration 295 in the volume of illustrations for *Art History as a Reflection of Inner Spiritual Impulses*, GA 292, lecture of 17 January 1917.

41. Lecture of 14 November 1914 (in the present volume).

42. Lecture of 9 November 1914, included in the present volume.

43. In another version of the transcript this passage runs as follows: 'But the opposite pole—the ego—must here become strong, that which works not from without but from within; the ahrimanic element must be taken into man's being and put into its right place.'

44. *Faust*, Part One, 'Night'.

45. Lecture of 14 November 1914 (in the present volume).

46. Cf. note 29.

47. A Viennese cake.

48. In the cycle *The Secrets of the Threshold*, 24–31 August 1913, GA 147.

49. GA 17 (1913).

50. See, for example, the chapter from *Occult Science* (GA 13) entitled 'Present and Future in the Evolution of Mankind' and the lecture of 3 January 1915 in *Art as Seen in the Light of Mystery Wisdom* (GA 275).

51. It has not been possible to identify the source of the following narrative.

52. Immanuel Kant (1724–1804). The most important works of the Königsberg philosopher are: *Critique of Pure Reason* (1781/1786; *Critique of Practical Reason* (1788); and *Critique of Judgement* (1790). The quotation is taken from the *Critique of Practical Reason*, part I, third section, 'Concerning the Motives underlying Pure Practical Reason'. This is the relevant passage in full: ' Duty, you great and exalted name, you do not court popularity or curry favours but demand subjection; but neither do you make threats in order to engage the will, which would provoke a natural aversion, but simply put forward a law which gains access out of itself to people's hearts, while instilling a sense of reverence (although not always subservience) in the will which bridles all desires that work within it in secrecy. What is the source that is worthy of you,

and where can one find the roots of your noble heritage, which proudly eradicates all affinity with desires and from which derives the inalienable nature of that precious quality with which human beings alone are able to endow themselves?'

53. In a satirical essay, e.g. in the poem 'The Philosophers': *Scruples of conscience* 'I gladly serve my friends, though I unfortunately like doing so,/And so it often rankles with me that I am not virtuous'. *Verdict* 'The only advice is that you must seek to despise them,/And then out of your repugnance do what duty bids you.'

54. Friedrich Schiller (1759–1805), *Über die ästhetische Erziehung des Menschen in einer Reihe von Briefen* (1795). The letters that were sent after November 1791 in respect of the honorary gift offered to Schiller—an annual pension of 1000 thalers which was paid for five years—from Jena and Ludwigsburg to Duke Friedrich Christian von Schleswig Holstein-Sonderburg-Augustenburg were lost in the fire at the Christiansburg in Copenhagen in February 1794. At the wish of the Duke, Schiller recreated the letters from his drafts and published them in an expanded form in 1795 in his periodical *Die Horen* (The Horae). Regarding the question referred to by Rudolf Steiner, see for example the 23rd letter: 'Just as a person is humiliated and dishonoured if he does something out of sensual motives which he should have undertaken out of pure motives of duty, so does it do him credit and enhance his honour to aspire towards legitimate aims, harmony and absolute principles in situations where the ordinary person merely satisfies his desires.' And in a note to this letter he adds: 'The moral philosopher teaches us that one can never do more than one's duty, and he is perfectly right if he is referring to the relationship that actions have to the moral law. But in the case of actions that merely relate to a purpose, to go *beyond this purpose* out into the supersensible (which can here mean none other than to carry out something physical in an aesthetic way) means at the same time to go out *beyond duty*, in that duty can merely stipulate that the *will* should be holy, and also that *nature* should have been sanctified [by it]. Hence while it is not possible to go beyond duty in moral terms, this can be done aesthetically; and such conduct may be deemed noble.'

55. A dualistic teaching named after its founder Manes (216–76), which concerned itself especially with the question of evil; two eternal fundamental elements, one that is good and light and one evil and dark, are in conflict with one another. Christian Manichaeism taught that the good God sent the Sun Spirit Christ down to the Earth in an outwardly perceptible body in order once again to take up the portion of the light that had been cast down in the battle. Cf. especially the lecture of 11 November 1904 in *The Temple Legend* (GA 93) and also the lectures of 29 August 1906 in *At the Gates of Spiritual Science/ Founding a Science of the Spirit* (GA 95), 25 June 1908 in *The Apocalypse of St John* (GA 104), 26 December 1914 in *Inner Reading and Inner Hearing* (GA 156) and 19 April 1917 in *Building Stones for an Understanding of the Mystery of Golgotha* (GA 175).

56. See the cycle *Art as Seen in the Light of Mystery Wisdom* (GA 275), held in Dornach from 28 December 1914 until 4 January 1915.

57. Rudolf Steiner spoke about the Norwegian Dream Song of Olaf Åsteson on 1

January 1912, 7 January 1913 and 31 December 1914. On each occasion his observations were accompanied by a recitation of the Dream Song by Marie Steiner-von Sivers. That this very remarkable folk epic has acquired such an important place in the anthroposophical movement is largely due to the initiative of Ingeborg Møller-Lindholm, the Norwegian poetess (1878–1964), who drew Rudolf Steiner's attention to the old legend. Her kind cooperation has enabled us to append the record that she made of her conversations with Rudolf Steiner.

Notes on the Dream Song by Ingeborg Møller, Lillehammer

In June 1910 Dr Steiner gave a cycle of lectures in Oslo entitled *The Mission of the Individual Folk Souls in Relation to Teutonic Mythology*. I took the opportunity to invite approximately 40 anthroposophical friends to tea, as I lived in Oslo at the time and had a large room at my disposal. Dr and Frau Marie Steiner had also agreed to come. On the previous day I had asked Dr Steiner whether he could say something about the remarkable Norwegian folk song The Dream Song of Olaf Åsteson. He smiled amiably and said that he would first have to have read or heard the song. I saw the point of this. He then himself suggested that he should arrive the following day an hour before the other guests, so that I could recite the song and make a rough translation for him. This is what happened.

During the reading Dr Steiner sat with his eyes closed and listened intently. He was obviously deeply affected by the remarkable content of the song. After everyone had had tea the Dream Song was recited in Norwegian by a member of the Society. Dr. Steiner then gave a short but moving lecture about the song. He dwelt especially upon the fact that the events in the song take place during the time of the twelve Holy Nights, when extra-terrestrial influences are at their strongest. He also referred especially to the name of Olaf Åsteson. Olaf or Oleifr means 'the one who has remained' or 'has been left behind' after his ancestors are no longer there. He is the one who passes on the blood of the fathers of the generations. Åst means love; so he is the 'son of love'.

Dr Steiner asked me to translate the song into German. He himself did not know Norwegian, let alone the old dialect in which the Dream Song had been written down, which poses difficulties even for modern Norwegians. I first apologized for the fact that my knowledge of German was not adequate to enable me to convey the wonderful musical rhythm. Dr Steiner said that this did not matter—I should simply translate the song literally word for word so that he could acquire a more precise overall impression of the content. I did this in the course of the autumn and sent him the translation, which was very prosaic and in many respects thoroughly inadequate. Rudolf Steiner subsequently put the song into its own characteristic rhythms and went on to give several lectures about it. It was also used for eurythmy performances, especially at Christmas time.

In 1913 Dr Steiner told me that I should not think that St Olaf was the original Olaf Åsteson. (St Olaf, a Norwegian king, was killed in AD 1035 at the battle of Stiklestad, championing the cause of Christianity.) There had been several 'Olaf Åstesons', said Dr Steiner. It was a kind of mystery title.

After the First World War Dr Steiner again visited Norway, in 1921 and 1923. On these occasions he stayed with an engineer by name of Ingerö. His wife,

Ragnild Ingerö, who died a few years ago, told me that Dr Steiner had spoken with her about the Dream Song. He had in the meantime explored it further and had made some new discoveries. One of these was that the song is much older than was generally supposed. It originated around AD 400. At that time there had been a great Christian initiate in this country. He founded a mystery school in southern Norway; the place was not named. His mystery name was Olaf Åsteson, and the song describes his initiation. According to Dr Steiner, the song had originally been much longer and had twelve sections, one for each sign of the zodiac. The song describes Olaf Åsteson's journey through the whole zodiac and what he saw and experienced there. Today we have only fragments of the original song. The mystery school referred to existed until the early Middle Ages. The leader was always called Olaf Åsteson.

Dr Steiner said that in course of time he would make these facts publicly known, together with other important matters connected with the song. However, he did not want to do so until he had found certain outward proofs of his findings. He thought that he would be able to find these. But the burning of the Goetheanum, excessive work and finally illness and his death prevented this intention being realized. Now these indications are all that we have.

Personal observations

I have given much thought to what I learnt from Dr Steiner and have come to the conclusion that this mystery school was possibly in Skiringssal. This place is, or rather was, in Vestfold, a region in the south-western part of Norway. In the old legends it is always described as a holy place. Vikings who died on foreign soil wished to be buried in Skiringssal. There was also a 'kaupang' (market) there. Archaeologists are currently excavating what they assume to be the remains of this commercial centre. However, no one has hitherto been able to ascertain with any certainty where Skiringssal is. At the time in question it was on the coast; but loam deposits have led to the location being 'pushed' further inland. Skiringssal means 'hall of purification'. 'Skirn' means baptism or purification (old Norwegian).

Where did the first Olaf Åsteson come from? It has been historically proved that Irish and Scottish monks were in this country long before the official introduction of Christianity. According to the legend, Joseph of Arimathaea came to the British Isles in the first century AD and began his missionary work there. There have been mystery centres in Ireland since very early times. The neighbouring islands were inhabited by heathen tribes. The Irish and Scottish Church, also called the Culdee Church, emerged from the activity of Christian missionaries, which was imbued with ancient Druid wisdom. It flourished in many places between AD 300 and 400. There were churches, schools and monasteries, even though they were constantly vulnerable to attacks from the powerful neighbouring heathen tribes. Many priests and monks died a martyr's death. This Culdee Church was based in particular on the Gospel of St John and the preaching of the Apostle John. It bore a similarity to the communities of the early Church and contrasted strongly with the Petrine or Roman Catholic Church. But the latter was victorious. The Culdee Church was destroyed and dissolved in the year AD 664. Both before and after this outward destruction it sent many missionaries to various European countries. This Church was of a distinctly esoteric nature. There is much to suggest that the first Olaf Åsteson was a representative of this spiritual stream.

(Translation based on that by Pauline Wehrle in *Art as Seen in the Light of Mystery Wisdom*, RSP 1996.)

58. This address was given at a New Year Festival during the lecture cycle *The World of the Senses and the World of the Spirit* (GA 134), which took place from 27 December 1911 until 1 January 1912 in Hanover.

59. This refers to the address given on 26 December 1911 in Hanover, included in *Die Mission der neuen Geistesoffenbarung. Das Christus-Ereignis als Mittelpunktsgeschehen der Erdenevolution* (The Mission of the New Spiritual Revelation. The Christ Event as the Middle-Point of Earth Evolution), GA 127. This rendering of the relevant part of the address is based on the translation by Dorothy Osmond, published in *The Festivals and Their Meaning*, RSP, 1981: 'Thus it is correct to associate the 6th of January with the day of Christ's birth and these thirteen nights with the time during which the powers of seership in the human soul discern and perceive what man must undergo through his life in the incarnations from Adam and Eve to the Mystery of Golgotha.

'During my visit to Christiania last year, it was interesting to me to discover this thought, which I have expressed in somewhat different words in so many lectures on the Christ mystery, embodied in a beautiful saga, the so-called Dream Legend which has in a remarkable way appeared in Norway during the last ten to fifteen years and has become familiar to the people, although its origin is, of course, very much earlier. It is a legend which in a wonderfully beautiful way relates how Olaf Åsteson is initiated, as it were by natural forces, in that he falls asleep on Christmas Eve, sleeps through the thirteen days and nights until the 6th of January, and lives through all the terrors which a human being must experience from the Earth's beginning until the Mystery of Golgotha; and how, when the 6th of January has come, Olaf Åsteson has a vision of Christ's intervention in human evolution, the spirit of Michael being His forerunner. I hope that on some other occasion in the course of these days we shall be able to present this poem to you, for then you will realize that an awareness of such a visionary quality during the thirteen days and nights survives even today and is, in fact, being revivified. I shall merely quote some characteristic lines from the beginning of the poem:

> Hearken all, a song I have to sing,
> The song of a wondrous youth.
> I'll sing of Olaf Åsteson
> Who slept so long a sleep.
> Yea, Olaf Åsteson it was
> Who slept a sleep so long, so deep.
>
> He lay him down on Christmas Eve
> And fell in a slumber deep,
> He woke not till the thirteenth day

When folk to church did go.
Yea, Olaf Åsteson it was
Who slept a sleep so long, so deep.

(Translation derived from Benedict Wood and John Wood, see below.)

And so the poem goes on, until in his dream during the thirteen days and nights Olaf Åsteson is led through all that man must experience, on account of Lucifer's temptation. A vivid picture is given of Olaf Åsteson's journey through the spheres where human beings have the experiences which I have so often described in connection with Kamaloka, and of how the Christ Spirit, preceded by Michael, streams into this vision of Kamaloka.

'Thus with the coming of Christ in the spirit, it will become more and more possible for human beings to know how spiritual forces exert their influence and that the festivals have not been instituted arbitrarily but, rather, by the cosmic wisdom whose influence prevails through history, even though people are so often unaware of it.'

60. *The Mission of the Individual Folk Souls in Relation to Teutonic Mythology*, Christiania (Oslo), 7–17 June 1910 (GA 121). See also the memorandum by Ingeborg Møller.

61. M.B. Landstad, a well-known Norwegian psalmist and publisher of psalters. He was a clergyman in Telemark, at the time a remote valley where old habits and customs, traditional costumes and ancient languages had been preserved in a largely unchanged state since time immemorial. Landstad was strongly influenced by Grundtvig (1783–1872, the Danish poet and teacher of folk customs) and, like most of Grundtvig's followers, journeyed about in the countryside and wrote down ancient legends and folk-tunes. He arranged for these to be told and sung by elderly people. Landstad was often accompanied by Olea Kröger, a clergyman's daughter who was very musical. Moreover, she had the quite remarkable capacity of familiarizing herself with the old melodies and songs and then writing down these often difficult melodies, which were in the form of ancient scales. Olea Kröger was born and grew up in Telemark and knew the language and customs of that part of the country as well as anyone. She modestly passed on what she acquired through her own work as a collector to Landstad or to other 'scholars'. Her work is little known outside a limited circle of researchers, but the value of her contribution cannot be over-estimated. (Ingeborg Møller)

62. Olaf II, also known as the Fat or Saint Olaf, 995–1030. In 1016 he seized the throne of Norway, which since 1000 had been under Danish and Swedish sovereignty. He had to flee from Canute the Great and from the rebellious Norwegian nobility and was killed in 1030 in the course of his attempt to re-establish his authority and regain his dominions. In 1164 he was named as the patron saint of Norway because of his efforts to Christianize the country.

63. Marie Steiner, née von Sivers (1867–1948). She came from a German Baltic family and grew up in Petersburg. She trained in the arts of recitation and drama in Petersburg, Paris and Berlin, where in 1900 she met Rudolf Steiner for the first time. From 1902 onwards she was his closest colleague. She was

responsible for the structure of the Society, worked towards the development of the anthroposophical art of drama and established a publishing house for Rudolf Steiner's literary works. After his death she continued publishing his works and founded the Rudolf Steiner-Nachlassverwaltung (literary estate) in furtherance of this aim.

64. Ingeborg Møller-Lindholm (1878–1964), Norwegian author, editor of Marian legends and stories about the Apostles. Regarding her life and works see the obituaries by S.R. Wikberg (issue no. 19, 1964) and K. Ruths (issue no. 10, 1979) in the (German) newsletter of the weekly journal *Das Goetheanum* and also the obituary by E. Froböse in *Blätter für Anthroposophie*, issue no. 3, 1964.

65. Rudolf Steiner never gave a final version of the text.

66. *Draumkvaedet*, see the anthology *Norske Folkeviser*, ed. Thorwald Lammers, H. Aschehoug & Co., Christiania 1910. The most widely known English translation of the Dream Song is the one made by Eleanor Merry (see, for example, the edition published by Floris Books in 2007, with illustrations by Janet Jordan, a preface by Jonathan Stedall and a substantial introduction by Andrew Welburn). Eleanor Merry, whose version is essentially poetic in character, also made her own illustrations; and some of these were included in the edition of the Dream Song published by New Knowledge Books and Rudolf Steiner Press (1961/1988). A translation by Pauline Wehrle, which adheres more closely to Rudolf Steiner's German version, was published by Rudolf Steiner Press in 1984/1996 as part of *Art as Seen in the Light of Mystery Wisdom* (GA 275). Meanwhile, further work has been done in the German language by Erich Trummler and Dan Lindholm (son of Ingeborg Møller-Lindholm) in conjunction with the old Norwegian text; and indeed, Eleanor Merry made her translation from the version by Erich Trummler. It strikes the present translator that what is lacking in published form in English is a version which, while reflecting the content of Rudolf Steiner's text and also its ancient Norwegian source, can be sung to the very beautiful original melodies. Such an English translation was made from Erich Trummler's version by Benedict Wood for the purpose of singing the verses; and his translation was subsequently revised by John Wood, who continued Benedict Wood's tradition of singing the Dream Song in this way (and then passed this on to the present translator). John Wood may therefore be acknowledged as the author of the translation printed here. The spaces between the sections of the Dream Song indicate where a new melody begins. There are four different melodies, two of which are related to two sections of the text.

67. The Gjaller Bridge spans the mystical river Gjoll, which divides the realms in the spiritual world. (Ingeborg Møller)

68. Olaf goes on to relate how he journeyed through the zodiac. It is especially clear at this point that, as Landstad has also indicated in his commentaries, a large part of the song is missing. The only constellation that is mentioned here is the Dog (Canis major), which, however, lies outside the zodiac (as does the Serpent, Serpens). Nevertheless, the Bull (Taurus), which is in the zodiac, is an important image for him. After journeying through the zodiac, Olaf is prompted to take another path; and he proceeds to the Milky Way

(Vintergaten). There is an old notion that the Milky Way leads to the realm of the blessed, to paradise. (Ingeborg Møller)

69. 'Brooksvalin' is an old and unusual word which Landstad translates as 'the forecourt of distress'. It is apparent from the song that Olaf now returns to the zodiac and arrives at the sign of the Scales. (Ingeborg Møller)

70. Grutte Graubart = Ahriman (Ingeborg Møller). In Rudolf Steiner's version the reference is to the 'Prince of Hell'.

71. Wherever Christianity had spread there were images of Michael holding a pair of scales in one hand. In the other hand he often has a lance or a sword, with which he pierces the dragon. He is depicted in this way in countless church paintings and sculptures, for example on the north portal of the Cathedral Church in Trondheim. This essentially concludes the epic part of the song. It is followed by a few verses where Olaf gives his fellow human beings warnings along the lines of the Scriptures: 'They shall rest from their labours, but their deeds will follow them.' Landstad relates that he had heard that the Dream Song was formerly used for vigils for the dead. The song was supposed to help the soul at the start of its journey in the other world. (Ingeborg Møller)

72. The lecture of 7 January 1913 consisted of two parts, the first of which is printed here. In this first part, Rudolf Steiner accompanied a first presentation to the members in Berlin of the Dream Song of Olaf Åteson, which was recited by Marie von Sivers, with a study of the spiritual experience of the seasons. The second part of the lecture forms the sixth of ten lectures in *Life between Death and New Birth in Relationship to Cosmic Facts* (GA 141).

73. See the address of 1 January 1912 in the present volume.

74. In connection with the cycle *The Mission of Individual Folk Souls in Relation to Teutonic Mythology*, Christiania (Oslo), 7 to 17 June 1910 (GA 121). See also the notes by Ingeborg Møller (note 57).

75. This is probably a reference to, in particular, the lecture given in Cologne on 7 May 1912 (included in the volume *Erfahrungen des Übersinnlichen. Die Wege der Seele zu Christus*, GA 143: 'Experiences of the Supersensible. The Paths of the Soul to Christ'). Additionally, at Easter 1912 the *Anthroposophical Calendar of the Soul* appeared for the first time (included in GA 40 and available separately in numerous English translations), through which, according to Rudolf Steiner, 'the weaving of one's own soul' can be 'pictorially sensed through the impressions of the course of the year'. In 1923 Rudolf Steiner gave substantial descriptions of this relationship between spiritual processes and the cycle of the year in the lectures *The Cycle of the Year as a Breathing Process of the Earth and the Four Great Festivals* (GA 223), 'The Human Soul and its Connection with Divine-Spiritual Individualities. The Internalization of the Festivals of the Year' (GA 224) and 'The Experience of the Course of the Year in Four Cosmic Imaginations' (GA 229).

76. Hugo Bergmann (1883–1975), school friend of Franz Kafka, studied philosophy in Prague and Berlin. He was deeply affected by his acquaintances with the philosopher Marti and his teacher Franz Brentano, on the one hand, and Rudolf Steiner on the other hand. In 1920 Bergmann went to Jerusalem and in 1935 become the rector of its university. To mark Rudolf Steiner's centenary he gave a lecture in 1961 to the Philosophical Society of the Hebrew

University (published in the journal *Die Drei*, vol. 1/1962, pp. 16 ff.). Right up until his death he was working on a five-volume *Geschichte der neueren Philosophie* ('History of Modern Philosophy'), where he allots a significant place to Goethe. More can be found about Hugo Bergmann in Benjamin Ben-Zadok's article 'Reine Idee und sittliche Tat—Hugo Bergmann zum Gedenken ('Pure Idea and Moral Deed—in Memory of Hugo Bergmann') in *Die Drei*, vol. 10/ 1984, pp. 737 ff. See also his *Tagebücher & Briefe 1901–1975* ('Diaries and Letters 1901–1975', 2 vols Königstein 1985).

77. See in this connection Rudolf Steiner's lectures entitled *Study of Man/Foundations of Human Experience* (GA 293), where he gives a detailed analysis of human nature at each of these three levels. Regarding the threefold nature of the body, see in particular 'Die physischen und geistigen Abhängigkeiten der Menschen-Wesenheit', translated under the title 'Principles of Psychosomatic Physiology' (*The Case for Anthroposophy*, RSP, 1970), from *Von Seelenrätseln* (*The Riddles of the Soul*), GA 21 (1918).

78. In the lectures entitled *From Symptom to Reality in Modern History* (GA 185), and in particular that of 3 November 1918, these three concepts are related respectively to the physical plane (fraternity), the soul world (freedom) and the spirit land (equality). In *Die Kernpunkte der sozialen Frage* (*Towards Social Renewal*, GA 23) we find a way of regarding the threefold ordering of social life that differs from the one presented here; while the *Essays concerning the Threefold Division of the Social Organism and the Period 1915–1921* (GA 24) together with the series *Beiträge zur Rudolf Steiner Gesamtausgabe*, vols 24/25, 27/28, 88 and 106 may also be consulted.

79. GA 15 (1911).

80. From an undated manuscript originating from Rudolf Steiner.

81. Rudolf Steiner had been invited to give these lectures by Finnish theosophists. The lecture cycle took pace in Helsingfors (Helsinki) from 3 to 14 April 1912. In addition to these lectures for members he also gave two public lectures, one of which, 'The Essential Nature of National Epics with special reference to the *Kalevala*' (9 April 1912) is included in this volume. See also Margarita Woloschin's recollections *The Green Snake*, English edition Floris Books 2010, the chapter entitled 'Philadelphia'.

82. Helena Petrovna Blavatsky (1831–91) was the daughter of a Mecklenburg family bearing the name of Hahn that had settled in Russia. From childhood she exhibited strongly psychic powers, but was also very independent-minded. As an act of rebellion against her family she married Nikifor von Blavatsky, who was over 30 years older than herself, but then separated from him immediately afterwards. After long journeys through various continents, in August 1851 she met Mahatma M.—the Master with whom she had had a spiritual bond since the visions of her childhood—in London. In accordance with his instructions, she prepared herself through studies and occult training to work in a society devoted to occult research. In 1873 she went to New York in order to counteract a tendency towards confusion in the spiritistic movement there. Here—together with Colonel Olcott—she founded the Theosophical Society in 1875, the headquarters of which were moved to India in 1879. In 1886 she left India and until her death lived for the most part in

London. Principal works: *Isis Unveiled* (1877); *The Secret Doctrine* (1888). Rudolf Steiner frequently spoke about H.P. Blavatsky, for example in the lectures *The Occult Movement in the Nineteenth Century and its Relation to Modern Culture* (GA 254); in the lectures of 7 May 1906 in *Original Impulses for the Science of the Spirit* (GA 96); 28 March 1916 in *The Human Spirit* (GA 167); 12 March 1916 in *Die geistigen Hintergründe des Ersten Weltkrieges* (GA 174b); and 9 and 16 December 1916 in *The Karma of Untruthfulness*, vol.1 (GA 173).

83. This is a paraphrase of I Corinthians 3:19.

84. GA 146. See the introductory remarks to this edition.

85. On the occasion of the first of the lecture-cycles held in Helsinki from 3 to 14 April 1912 (*Spiritual Beings in the Heavenly Bodies and in the Kingdoms of Nature*, see note 81). In her memoirs entitled *The Green Snake* (note 81) the painter Margarita Woloschin recalls this incident as follows: 'After the lecture on Easter Saturday, Rudolf Steiner was to go with us Russians and a few Germans to the Russian Orthodox Church, for the Easter night mass and stay after-wards for the traditional Easter meal. The church we attended was unfortu-nately a garrison church; the congregation consisted only of soldiers with dour faces. The choruses were sung, boringly and rather pitifully, by sleepy boys. Rudolf Steiner joined us in standing throughout this service, and also at the mass which followed, which was rather tiring for the remaining Germans, not used to standing for so long. We did not arrive at the hotel till around three o'clock in the morning. There the good Kleopatra Christoforova, the hotel owner, had ordered the Easter meal for us. We arrived in the joyful mood which animates every Russian on Easter night, especially glad to have Rudolf Steiner celebrate with us. He stood at the door of the dining hall and shook hands with each of us. The rapturous enthusiasm with which we were filled encountered his very earnest, stringent, questioning look. When we had taken our seats at the table, he cut the Easter bread into a hexagram, shared it out among us, stood up and held an address, the meaning of which was as follows: "The whole history of mankind is the Entombment of the Godhead. We, with our consciousness, are only capable of celebrating the Entombment on Good Friday. We do not have the ability to comprehend Easter with our intellect. We can only celebrate Easter in vowing to follow the path to the spirit." ' (Translation by Peter Stebbing from the English edition.)

86. Matthew 8:22.

87. Thomas Woodrow Wilson (1856–1924), President of the United States from 1913 until 1921, Professor of Law and Politics in Princeton. Regarding Wilson, see Rudolf Steiner's *Das Goetheanum* article 'Wilsons Erbe' ('Wilson's legacy') in GA 36; and the lectures of 13 May 1917, 24 February and 26 April 1918 in GA 174b (the latter two are available in typescript form in English) and 4 and 19 May 1917 (that of 19 May is translated and is available as a typescript). With regard to karmic connections see the lectures of 5 April 1924 in GA 239 (*Karmic Relationships*, vol. 5) and 9 April 1924 in GA 240 (*Karmic Relationships*, vol. 6).

88. See *Mere Literature and Other Essays*, Houghton Mifflin Company, Boston and New York, 1896. Thus, for example, he writes in the chapter entitled 'A Calendar of Great Americans': 'Liberty, among us, is not a sentiment, but a

product of experience; its derivation is not rationalistic, but practical . . . The American spirit is something more than the old, the immemorial Saxon spirit of liberty from which it has sprung. It has been bred by the conditions attending the great task which we have all the century been carrying forward: the task, at once material and ideal, of subduing a wilderness and covering all the wide stretches of a vast continent with a single free and stable polity' (from an edition published in London and Boston, 1914). See also the twelfth chapter of Wilson's book *The New Freedom*: 'What is liberty? I have long had an image in my mind of what constitutes liberty. Suppose that I were building a great piece of powerful machinery, and suppose that I should so awkwardly and unskilfully assemble the parts of it that every time one part tried to move it would be interfered with by the others, and the whole thing would buckle up and be checked. Liberty for the several parts would consist in the best possible assembling and adjustment of them, would it not? . . . Human freedom consists in perfect adjustment of human interests and human activities and human energies to one another' (originally published in 1913; quotation taken from an expanded edition published by J.M. Dent in London, 1916).

89. Friedrich Schiller in the *Xenien* about knowledge: 'To one it is a high, heavenly goddess, to another/A capable cow that provides him with butter.'

90. After the fifth lecture of the cycle *Spiritual Beings in the Heavenly Bodies and in the Kingdoms of Nature*, GA 136, 3–14 April 1912 in Helsinki.

91. *The Mission of the Individual Folk Souls in Relation to Teutonic Mythology*, Christiania (Oslo), 7–17 June 1910, GA 121. See also the notes of Ingeborg Møller (note 57).

92. Lecture of 9 April 1912 on 'The Essential Nature of National Epics, with particular reference to the *Kalevala*', included in the present volume.

93. See the chapter entitled 'The Nature of Man' in *Theosophy* (GA 9), especially the sub-section 'Body, Soul and Spirit'.

94. This theme can be found in a great variety of ancient sagas, for example in the Egyptian myths as the dismembering of the corpse of Osiris or as the dismembering of Dionysos Zagreus, the older Dionysos, who was a son of Zeus and Persephone and was mutilated by the Titans at the instigation of Hera. His still twitching heart was rescued from them by Pallas and was swallowed by Zeus (according to other versions of the story by Semele), thus giving rise to the younger Dionysos. See in this connection Rudolf Steiner's lectures *Wonders of the World, Ordeals of the Soul and Revelations of the Spirit*, GA 129, especially the lecture of 22 August 1911.

95. In Greek mythology, Uranus is the sky, the son and at the same time the husband of Gaia, the Earth, with whom he procreates the Titans and the Titanids. Uranus is castrated by his son Kronus; Aphrodite, the one born from foam, comes into being from the contact of his drops of blood with the sea.

RUDOLF STEINER'S COLLECTED WORKS

The German Edition of Rudolf Steiner's Collected Works (the *Gesamtausgabe* [GA] published by Rudolf Steiner Verlag, Dornach, Switzerland) presently runs to 354 titles, organized either by type of work (written or spoken), chronology, audience (public or other), or subject (education, art, etc.). For ease of comparison, the Collected Works in English [CW] follows the German organization exactly. A complete listing of the CWs follows with literal translations of the German titles. Other than in the case of the books published in his lifetime, titles were rarely given by Rudolf Steiner himself, and were often provided by the editors of the German editions. The titles in English are not necessarily the same as the German; and, indeed, over the past seventy-five years have frequently been different, with the same book sometimes appearing under different titles.

For ease of identification and to avoid confusion, we suggest that readers looking for a title should do so by CW number. Because the work of creating the Collected Works of Rudolf Steiner is an ongoing process, with new titles being published every year, we have not indicated in this listing which books are presently available. To find out what titles in the Collected Works are currently in print, please check our website at www.rudolfsteinerpress.com (or www.steinerbooks.org for US readers).

Written Work

Public Lectures

Lectures to the Members of the Anthroposophical Society

SIGNIFICANT EVENTS IN THE LIFE OF
RUDOLF STEINER

1829:   June 23: birth of Johann Steiner (1829–1910)—Rudolf Steiner's father—in Geras, Lower Austria.

1834:   May 8: birth of Franciska Blie (1834–1918)—Rudolf Steiner's mother—in Horn, Lower Austria. 'My father and mother were both children of the glorious Lower Austrian forest district north of the Danube.'

1860:   May 16: marriage of Johann Steiner and Franciska Blie.

1861:   February 25: birth of *Rudolf Joseph Lorenz Steiner* in Kraljevec, Croatia, near the border with Hungary, where Johann Steiner works as a telegrapher for the South Austria Railroad. Rudolf Steiner is baptized two days later, February 27, the date usually given as his birthday.

1862:   Summer: the family moves to Mödling, Lower Austria.

1863:   The family moves to Pottschach, Lower Austria, near the Styrian border, where Johann Steiner becomes stationmaster. 'The view stretched to the mountains ... majestic peaks in the distance and the sweet charm of nature in the immediate surroundings.'

1864:   November 15: birth of Rudolf Steiner's sister, Leopoldine (d. November 1, 1927). She will become a seamstress and live with her parents for the rest of her life.

1866:   July 28: birth of Rudolf Steiner's deaf-mute brother, Gustav (d. May 1, 1941).

1867:   Rudolf Steiner enters the village school. Following a disagreement between his father and the schoolmaster, whose wife falsely accused the boy of causing a commotion, Rudolf Steiner is taken out of school and taught at home.

1868:   A critical experience. Unknown to the family, an aunt dies in a distant town. Sitting in the station waiting room, Rudolf Steiner sees her 'form,' which speaks to him, asking for help. 'Beginning with this experience, a new soul life began in the boy, one in which not only the outer trees and mountains spoke to him, but also the worlds that lay behind them. From this moment on, the boy began to live with the spirits of nature...'

1869:   The family moves to the peaceful, rural village of Neudörfl, near Wiener-Neustadt in present-day Austria. Rudolf Steiner attends the village school. Because of the 'unorthodoxy' of his writing and spelling, he has to do 'extra lessons.'

1870:   Through a book lent to him by his tutor, he discovers geometry: 'To grasp something purely in the spirit brought me inner happiness. I know that I first learned happiness through geometry.' The same tutor allows him to draw, while other students still struggle with their reading and writing. 'An artistic element' thus enters his education.

1871: Though his parents are not religious, Rudolf Steiner becomes a 'church child,' a favourite of the priest, who was 'an exceptional character.' 'Up to the age of ten or eleven, among those I came to know, he was far and away the most significant.' Among other things, he introduces Steiner to Copernican, heliocentric cosmology. As an altar boy, Rudolf Steiner serves at Masses, funerals, and Corpus Christi processions. At year's end, after an incident in which he escapes a thrashing, his father forbids him to go to church.

1872: Rudolf Steiner transfers to grammar school in Wiener-Neustadt, a five-mile walk from home, which must be done in all weathers.

1873–75: Through his teachers and on his own, Rudolf Steiner has many wonderful experiences with science and mathematics. Outside school, he teaches himself analytic geometry, trigonometry, differential equations, and calculus.

1876: Rudolf Steiner begins tutoring other students. He learns bookbinding from his father. He also teaches himself stenography.

1877: Rudolf Steiner discovers Kant's *Critique of Pure Reason*, which he reads and rereads. He also discovers and reads von Rotteck's *World History*.

1878: He studies extensively in contemporary psychology and philosophy.

1879: Rudolf Steiner graduates from high school with honours. His father is transferred to Inzersdorf, near Vienna. He uses his first visit to Vienna 'to purchase a great number of philosophy books'—Kant, Fichte, Schelling, and Hegel, as well as numerous histories of philosophy. His aim: to find a path from the 'I' to nature.

October 1879–1883: Rudolf Steiner attends the Technical College in Vienna—to study mathematics, chemistry, physics, mineralogy, botany, zoology, biology, geology, and mechanics—with a scholarship. He also attends lectures in history and literature, while avidly reading philosophy on his own. His two favourite professors are Karl Julius Schröer (German language and literature) and Edmund Reitlinger (physics). He also audits lectures by Robert Zimmermann on aesthetics and Franz Brentano on philosophy. During this year he begins his friendship with Moritz Zitter (1861–1921), who will help support him financially when he is in Berlin.

1880: Rudolf Steiner attends lectures on Schiller and Goethe by Karl Julius Schröer, who becomes his mentor. Also 'through a remarkable combination of circumstances,' he meets Felix Koguzki, a 'herb gatherer' and healer, who could 'see deeply into the secrets of nature.' Rudolf Steiner will meet and study with this 'emissary of the Master' throughout his time in Vienna.

1881: January: '... I didn't sleep a wink. I was busy with philosophical problems until about 12:30 a.m. Then, finally, I threw myself down on my couch. All my striving during the previous year had been to research whether the following statement by Schelling was true or not: *Within everyone dwells a secret, marvelous capacity to draw back from the stream of time—out of the self clothed in all that comes to us from outside—into our innermost being and there, in the immutable form of the Eternal, to look into ourselves.* I believe, and I am still quite certain of it, that I discovered this capacity in myself; I had long had an inkling of it. Now the whole of idealist philosophy stood before me in modified form. What's a sleepless night compared to that!'

Rudolf Steiner begins communicating with leading thinkers of the day, who send him books in return, which he reads eagerly.

July: 'I am not one of those who dives into the day like an animal in human form. I pursue a quite specific goal, an idealistic aim—knowledge of the truth! This cannot be done offhandedly. It requires the greatest striving in the world, free of all egotism, and equally of all resignation.'

August: Steiner puts down on paper for the first time thoughts for a 'Philosophy of Freedom.' 'The striving for the absolute: this human yearning is freedom.' He also seeks to outline a 'peasant philosophy,' describing what the worldview of a 'peasant'—one who lives close to the earth and the old ways—really is.

1881–1882: Felix Koguzki, the herb gatherer, reveals himself to be the envoy of another, higher initiatory personality, who instructs Rudolf Steiner to penetrate Fichte's philosophy and to master modern scientific thinking as a preparation for right entry into the spirit. This 'Master' also teaches him the double (evolutionary and involutionary) nature of time.

1882: Through the offices of Karl Julius Schröer, Rudolf Steiner is asked by Joseph Kürschner to edit Goethe's scientific works for the *Deutschen National-Literatur* edition. He writes 'A Possible Critique of Atomistic Concepts' and sends it to Friedrich Theodor Vischer.

1883: Rudolf Steiner completes his college studies and begins work on the Goethe project.

1884: First volume of Goethe's *Scientific Writings* (CW 1) appears (March). He lectures on Goethe and Lessing, and Goethe's approach to science. In July, he enters the household of Ladislaus and Pauline Specht as tutor to the four Specht boys. He will live there until 1890. At this time, he meets Josef Breuer (1842–1925), the co-author with Sigmund Freud of *Studies in Hysteria*, who is the Specht family doctor.

1885: While continuing to edit Goethe's writings, Rudolf Steiner reads deeply in contemporary philosophy (Eduard von Hartmann, Johannes Volkelt, and Richard Wahle, among others).

1886: May: Rudolf Steiner sends Kürschner the manuscript of *Outlines of Goethe's Theory of Knowledge* (CW 2), which appears in October, and which he sends out widely. He also meets the poet Marie Eugenie Delle Grazie and writes 'Nature and Our Ideals' for her. He attends her salon, where he meets many priests, theologians, and philosophers, who will become his friends. Meanwhile, the director of the Goethe Archive in Weimar requests his collaboration with the *Sophien* edition of Goethe's works, particularly the writings on colour.

1887: At the beginning of the year, Rudolf Steiner is very sick. As the year progresses and his health improves, he becomes increasingly 'a man of letters,' lecturing, writing essays, and taking part in Austrian cultural life. In August–September, the second volume of Goethe's *Scientific Writings* appears.

1888:   January–July: Rudolf Steiner assumes editorship of the 'German Weekly' (*Deutsche Wochenschrift*). He begins lecturing more intensively, giving, for example, a lecture titled 'Goethe as Father of a New Aesthetics.' He meets and becomes soul friends with Friedrich Eckstein (1861–1939), a vegetarian, philosopher of symbolism, alchemist, and musician, who will introduce him to various spiritual currents (including Theosophy) and with whom he will meditate and interpret esoteric and alchemical texts.

1889:   Rudolf Steiner first reads Nietzsche (*Beyond Good and Evil*). He encounters Theosophy again and learns of Madame Blavatsky in the Theosophical circle around Marie Lang (1858–1934). Here he also meets well-known figures of Austrian life, as well as esoteric figures like the occultist Franz Hartmann and Karl Leinigen-Billigen (translator of C.G. Harrison's *The Transcendental Universe*). During this period, Steiner first reads A.P. Sinnett's *Esoteric Buddhism* and Mabel Collins's *Light on the Path*. He also begins travelling, visiting Budapest, Weimar, and Berlin (where he meets philosopher Eduard von Hartmann).

1890:   Rudolf Steiner finishes volume 3 of Goethe's scientific writings. He begins his doctoral dissertation, which will become *Truth and Science* (CW 3). He also meets the poet and feminist Rosa Mayreder (1858–1938), with whom he can exchange his most intimate thoughts. In September, Rudolf Steiner moves to Weimar to work in the Goethe-Schiller Archive.

1891:   Volume 3 of the Kürschner edition of Goethe appears. Meanwhile, Rudolf Steiner edits Goethe's studies in mineralogy and scientific writings for the *Sophien* edition. He meets Ludwig Laistner of the Cotta Publishing Company, who asks for a book on the basic question of metaphysics. From this will result, ultimately, *The Philosophy of Freedom* (CW 4), which will be published not by Cotta but by Emil Felber. In October, Rudolf Steiner takes the oral exam for a doctorate in philosophy, mathematics, and mechanics at Rostock University, receiving his doctorate on the twenty-sixth. In November, he gives his first lecture on Goethe's 'Fairy Tale' in Vienna.

1892:   Rudolf Steiner continues work at the Goethe-Schiller Archive and on his *Philosophy of Freedom*. *Truth and Science*, his doctoral dissertation, is published. Steiner undertakes to write introductions to books on Schopenhauer and Jean Paul for Cotta. At year's end, he finds lodging with Anna Eunike, née Schulz (1853–1911), a widow with four daughters and a son. He also develops a friendship with Otto Erich Hartleben (1864–1905) with whom he shares literary interests.

1893:   Rudolf Steiner begins his habit of producing many reviews and articles. In March, he gives a lecture titled 'Hypnotism, with Reference to Spiritism.' In September, volume 4 of the Kürschner edition is completed. In November, *The Philosophy of Freedom* appears. This year, too, he meets John Henry Mackay (1864–1933), the anarchist, and Max Stirner, a scholar and biographer.

1894:   Rudolf Steiner meets Elisabeth Förster Nietzsche, the philosopher's sister, and begins to read Nietzsche in earnest, beginning with the as yet unpublished *Antichrist*. He also meets Ernst Haeckel (1834–1919). In the fall, he begins to write *Nietzsche, A Fighter against His Time* (CW 5).

1895:   May, *Nietzsche, A Fighter against His Time* appears.

1896:   January 22: Rudolf Steiner sees Friedrich Nietzsche for the first and only time. Moves between the Nietzsche and the Goethe-Schiller Archives, where he completes his work before year's end. He falls out with Elisabeth Förster Nietzsche, thus ending his association with the Nietzsche Archive.

1897:   Rudolf Steiner finishes the manuscript of *Goethe's Worldview* (CW 6). He moves to Berlin with Anna Eunike and begins editorship of the *Magazin für Literatur*. From now on, Steiner will write countless reviews, literary and philosophical articles, and so on. He begins lecturing at the 'Free Literary Society.' In September, he attends the Zionist Congress in Basel. He sides with Dreyfus in the Dreyfus affair.

1898:   Rudolf Steiner is very active as an editor in the political, artistic, and theatrical life of Berlin. He becomes friendly with John Henry Mackay and poet Ludwig Jacobowski (1868–1900). He joins Jacobowski's circle of writers, artists, and scientists—'The Coming Ones' (*Die Kommenden*)— and contributes lectures to the group until 1903. He also lectures at the 'League for College Pedagogy.' He writes an article for Goethe's sesquicentennial, 'Goethe's Secret Revelation,' on the 'Fairy Tale of the Green Snake and the Beautiful Lily.'

1898–99:   'This was a trying time for my soul as I looked at Christianity. . . . I was able to progress only by contemplating, by means of spiritual perception, the evolution of Christianity. . . . Conscious knowledge of real Christianity began to dawn in me around the turn of the century. This seed continued to develop. My soul trial occurred shortly before the beginning of the twentieth century. It was decisive for my soul's development that I stood spiritually before the Mystery of Golgotha in a deep and solemn celebration of knowledge.'

1899:   Rudolf Steiner begins teaching and giving lectures and lecture cycles at the Workers' College, founded by Wilhelm Liebknecht (1826–1900). He will continue to do so until 1904. Writes: *Literature and Spiritual Life in the Nineteenth Century; Individualism in Philosophy*; *Haeckel and His Opponents; Poetry in the Present;* and begins what will become (fifteen years later) *The Riddles of Philosophy* (CW 18). He also meets many artists and writers, including Käthe Kollwitz, Stefan Zweig, and Rainer Maria Rilke. On October 31, he marries Anna Eunike.

1900:   'I thought that the turn of the century must bring humanity a new light. It seemed to me that the separation of human thinking and willing from the spirit had peaked. A turn or reversal of direction in human evolution seemed to me a necessity.' Rudolf Steiner finishes *World and Life Views in the Nineteenth Century* (the second part of what will become *The Riddles of Philosophy*) and dedicates it to Ernst Haeckel. It is published in March. He continues lecturing at *Die Kommenden*, whose leadership he assumes after the death of Jacobowski. Also, he gives the Gutenberg Jubilee lecture before 7,000 typesetters and printers. In September, Rudolf Steiner is invited by Count and Countess Brockdorff to lecture in the Theosophical Library. His first lecture is on Nietzsche. His second lecture is titled 'Goethe's Secret Revelation.' October 6, he begins a lecture cycle on the mystics that will become *Mystics after Modernism* (CW 7). November–December: 'Marie von Sivers appears in the audience. . . .' Also in November, Steiner gives his first lecture at the Giordano Bruno Bund (where he will continue to lecture until May, 1905). He speaks on Bruno and modern Rome, focusing on the importance of the philosophy of Thomas Aquinas as monism.

1901: In continual financial straits, Rudolf Steiner's early friends Moritz Zitter and Rosa Mayreder help support him. In October, he begins the lecture cycle *Christianity as Mystical Fact* (CW 8) at the Theosophical Library. In November, he gives his first 'Theosophical lecture' on Goethe's 'Fairy Tale' in Hamburg at the invitation of Wilhelm Hubbe-Schleiden. He also attends a gathering to celebrate the founding of the Theosophical Society at Count and Countess Brockdorff's. He gives a lecture cycle, 'From Buddha to Christ,' for the circle of the *Kommenden*. November 17, Marie von Sivers asks Rudolf Steiner if Theosophy needs a Western-Christian spiritual movement (to complement Theosophy's Eastern emphasis). 'The question was posed. Now, following spiritual laws, I could begin to give an answer. . . .' In December, Rudolf Steiner writes his first article for a Theosophical publication. At year's end, the Brockdorffs and possibly Wilhelm Hubbe-Schleiden ask Rudolf Steiner to join the Theosophical Society and undertake the leadership of the German section. Rudolf Steiner agrees, on the condition that Marie von Sivers (then in Italy) work with him.

1902: Beginning in January, Rudolf Steiner attends the opening of the Workers' School in Spandau with Rosa Luxemburg (1870–1919). January 17, Rudolf Steiner joins the Theosophical Society. In April, he is asked to become general secretary of the German Section of the Theosophical Society, and works on preparations for its founding. In July, he visits London for a Theosophical congress. He meets Bertram Keightly, G.R.S. Mead, A.P. Sinnett, and Annie Besant, among others. In September, *Christianity as Mystical Fact* appears. In October, Rudolf Steiner gives his first public lecture on Theosophy ('Monism and Theosophy') to about three hundred people at the Giordano Bruno Bund. On October 19–21, the German Section of the Theosophical Society has its first meeting; Rudolf Steiner is the general secretary, and Annie Besant attends. Steiner lectures on practical karma studies. On October 23, Annie Besant inducts Rudolf Steiner into the Esoteric School of the Theosophical Society. On October 25, Steiner begins a weekly series of lectures: 'The Field of Theosophy.' During this year, Rudolf Steiner also first meets Ita Wegman (1876–1943), who will become his close collaborator in his final years.

1903: Rudolf Steiner holds about 300 lectures and seminars. In May, the first issue of the periodical *Luzifer* appears. In June, Rudolf Steiner visits

London for the first meeting of the Federation of the European Sections of the Theosophical Society, where he meets Colonel Olcott. He begins to write *Theosophy* (CW 9).

1904: Rudolf Steiner continues lecturing at the Workers' College and elsewhere (about 90 lectures), while lecturing intensively all over Germany among Theosophists (about 140 lectures). In February, he meets Carl Unger (1878–1929), who will become a member of the board of the Anthroposophical Society (1913). In March, he meets Michael Bauer (1871–1929), a Christian mystic, who will also be on the board. In May, *Theosophy* appears, with the dedication: 'To the spirit of Giordano Bruno.' Rudolf Steiner and Marie von Sivers visit London for meetings with Annie Besant. June: Rudolf Steiner and Marie von Sivers attend the meeting of the Federation of European Sections of the Theosophical Society in Amsterdam. In July, Steiner begins the articles in *Luzifer-Gnosis* that will become *How to Know Higher Worlds* (CW 10) and *Cosmic Memory* (CW 11). In September, Annie Besant visits Germany. In December, Steiner lectures on Freemasonry. He mentions the High Grade Masonry derived from John Yarker and represented by Theodore Reuss and Karl Kellner as a blank slate 'into which a good image could be placed.'

1905: This year, Steiner ends his non-Theosophical lecturing activity. Supported by Marie von Sivers, his Theosophical lecturing—both in public and in the Theosophical Society—increases significantly: 'The German Theosophical Movement is of exceptional importance.' Steiner recommends reading, among others, Fichte, Jacob Boehme, and Angelus Silesius. He begins to introduce Christian themes into Theosophy. He also begins to work with doctors (Felix Peipers and Ludwig Noll). In July, he is in London for the Federation of European Sections, where he attends a lecture by Annie Besant: 'I have seldom seen Mrs. Besant speak in so inward and heartfelt a manner....' 'Through Mrs. Besant I have found the way to H.P. Blavatsky.' September to October, he gives a course of thirty-one lectures for a small group of esoteric students. In October, the annual meeting of the German Section of the Theosophical Society, which still remains very small, takes place. Rudolf Steiner reports membership has risen from 121 to 377 members. In November, seeking to establish esoteric 'continuity,' Rudolf Steiner and Marie von Sivers participate in a 'Memphis-Misraim' Masonic ceremony. They pay forty-five marks for membership. 'Yesterday, you saw how little remains of former esoteric institutions.' 'We are dealing only with a "framework"... for the present, nothing lies behind it. The occult powers have completely withdrawn.'

1906: Expansion of Theosophical work. Rudolf Steiner gives about 245 lectures, only 44 of which take place in Berlin. Cycles are given in Paris, Leipzig, Stuttgart, and Munich. Esoteric work also intensifies. Rudolf Steiner begins writing *An Outline of Esoteric Science* (CW 13). In January, Rudolf Steiner receives permission (a patent) from the Great Orient of the Scottish A & A Thirty-Three Degree Rite of the Order of the Ancient

Freemasons of the Memphis-Misraim Rite to direct a chapter under the name 'Mystica Aeterna.' This will become the 'Cognitive-Ritual Section' (also called 'Misraim Service') of the Esoteric School. (See: *Freemasonry and Ritual Work: The Misraim Service*, CW 265). During this time, Steiner also meets Albert Schweitzer. In May, he is in Paris, where he visits Edouard Schuré. Many Russians attend his lectures (including Konstantin Balmont, Dimitri Mereszkovski, Zinaida Hippius, and Maximilian Woloshin). He attends the General Meeting of the European Federation of the Theosophical Society, at which Col. Olcott is present for the last time. He spends the year's end in Venice and Rome, where he writes and works on his translation of H.P. Blavatsky's *Key to Theosophy*.

1907: Further expansion of the German Theosophical Movement according to the Rosicrucian directive to 'introduce spirit into the world'—in education, in social questions, in art, and in science. In February, Col. Olcott dies in Adyar. Before he dies, Olcott indicates that 'the Masters' wish Annie Besant to succeed him: much politicking ensues. Rudolf Steiner supports Besant's candidacy. April-May: preparations for the Congress of the Federation of European Sections of the Theosophical Society—the great, watershed Whitsun 'Munich Congress,' attended by Annie Besant and others. Steiner decides to separate Eastern and Western (Christian-Rosicrucian) esoteric schools. He takes his esoteric school out of the Theosophical Society (Besant and Rudolf Steiner are 'in harmony' on this). Steiner makes his first lecture tours to Austria and Hungary. That summer, he is in Italy. In September, he visits Edouard Schuré, who will write the introduction to the French edition of *Christianity as Mystical Fact* in Barr, Alsace. Rudolf Steiner writes the autobiographical statement known as the 'Barr Document.' In *Luzifer-Gnosis*, 'The Education of the Child' appears.

1908: The movement grows (membership: 1,150). Lecturing expands. Steiner makes his first extended lecture tour to Holland and Scandinavia, as well as visits to Naples and Sicily. Themes: St. John's Gospel, the Apocalypse, Egypt, science, philosophy, and logic. *Luzifer-Gnosis* ceases publication. In Berlin, Marie von Sivers (with Johanna Mücke (1864–1949) forms the *Philosophisch-Theosophisch* (after 1915 *Philosophisch-Anthroposophisch*) *Verlag* to publish Steiner's work. Steiner gives lecture cycles titled *The Gospel of St. John* (CW 103) and *The Apocalypse* (104).

1909: *An Outline of Esoteric Science* appears. Lecturing and travel continues. Rudolf Steiner's spiritual research expands to include the polarity of Lucifer and Ahriman; the work of great individualities in history; the Maitreya Buddha and the Bodhisattvas; spiritual economy (CW 109); the work of the spiritual hierarchies in heaven and on earth (CW 110). He also deepens and intensifies his research into the Gospels, giving lectures on the Gospel of St. Luke (CW 114) with the first mention of two Jesus children. Meets and becomes friends with Christian Morgenstern (1871–1914). In April, he lays the foundation stone for the Malsch model—the building that will lead to the first Goetheanum. In May, the International Congress of the Federation of European Sections of the

Theosophical Society takes place in Budapest. Rudolf Steiner receives the Subba Row medal for *How to Know Higher Worlds*. During this time, Charles W. Leadbeater discovers Jiddu Krishnamurti (1895–1986) and proclaims him the future 'world teacher,' the bearer of the Maitreya Buddha and the 'reappearing Christ.' In October, Steiner delivers seminal lectures on 'anthroposophy,' which he will try, unsuccessfully, to rework over the next years into the unfinished work, *Anthroposophy (A Fragment)* (CW 45).

1910: New themes: *The Reappearance of Christ in the Etheric* (CW 118); *The Fifth Gospel; The Mission of Folk Souls* (CW 121); *Occult History* (CW 126); the evolving development of etheric cognitive capacities. Rudolf Steiner continues his Gospel research with *The Gospel of St. Matthew* (CW 123). In January, his father dies. In April, he takes a month-long trip to Italy, including Rome, Monte Cassino, and Sicily. He also visits Scandinavia again. July–August, he writes the first mystery drama, *The Portal of Initiation* (CW 14). In November, he gives 'psychosophy' lectures. In December, he submits 'On the Psychological Foundations and Epistemological Framework of Theosophy' to the International Philosophical Congress in Bologna.

1911: The crisis in the Theosophical Society deepens. In January, 'The Order of the Rising Sun,' which will soon become 'The Order of the Star in the East,' is founded for the coming world teacher, Krishnamurti. At the same time, Marie von Sivers, Rudolf Steiner's co-worker, falls ill. Fewer lectures are given, but important new ground is broken. In Prague, in March, Steiner meets Franz Kafka (1883–1924) and Hugo Bergmann (1883-1975). In April, he delivers his paper to the Philosophical Congress. He writes the second mystery drama, *The Soul's Probation* (CW 14). Also, while Marie von Sivers is convalescing, Rudolf Steiner begins work on *Calendar 1912/1913*, which will contain the 'Calendar of the Soul' meditations. On March 19, Anna (Eunike) Steiner dies. In September, Rudolf Steiner visits Einsiedeln, birthplace of Paracelsus. In December, Friedrich Rittelmeyer, future founder of the Christian Community, meets Rudolf Steiner. The *Johannes-Bauverein*, the 'building committee,' which would lead to the first Goetheanum (first planned for Munich), is also founded, and a preliminary committee for the founding of an independent association is created that, in the following year, will become the Anthroposophical Society. Important lecture cycles include *Occult Physiology* (CW 128); *Wonders of the World* (CW 129); *From Jesus to Christ* (CW 131). Other themes: esoteric Christianity; Christian Rosenkreutz; the spiritual guidance of humanity; the sense world and the world of the spirit.

1912: Despite the ongoing, now increasing crisis in the Theosophical Society, much is accomplished: *Calendar 1912/1913* is published; eurythmy is created; both the third mystery drama, *The Guardian of the Threshold* (CW 14) and *A Way of Self-Knowledge* (CW 16) are written. New (or renewed) themes included life between death and rebirth and karma and reincarnation. Other lecture cycles: *Spiritual Beings in the Heavenly Bodies and in the Kingdoms of Nature* (CW 136); *The Human Being in the Light of Occultism, Theosophy, and Philosophy* (CW 137); *The Gospel of St. Mark* (CW 139); and *The Bhagavad Gita and the Epistles of Paul* (CW 142). On May 8, Rudolf Steiner celebrates White Lotus Day, H.P. Blavatsky's death day, which he had faithfully observed for the past decade, for the last time. In August, Rudolf Steiner suggests the 'independent association' be called the 'Anthroposophical Society.' In September, the first eurythmy course takes place. In October, Rudolf Steiner declines recognition of a Theosophical Society lodge dedicated to the Star of the East and decides to expel all Theosophical Society members belonging to the order. Also, with Marie von Sivers, he first visits Dornach, near Basel, Switzerland, and they stand on the hill where the Goetheanum will be built. In November, a Theosophical Society lodge is opened by direct mandate from Adyar (Annie Besant). In December, a meeting of the German section occurs at which it is decided that belonging to the Order of the Star of the East is incompatible with membership in the Theosophical Society. December 28: informal founding of the Anthroposophical Society in Berlin.

1913:   Expulsion of the German section from the Theosophical Society. February 2–3: Foundation meeting of the Anthroposophical Society. Board members include: Marie von Sivers, Michael Bauer, and Carl Unger. September 20: Laying of the foundation stone for the *Johannes Bau* (Goetheanum) in Dornach. Building begins immediately. The third mystery drama, *The Soul's Awakening* (CW 14), is completed. Also: *The Threshold of the Spiritual World* (CW 147). Lecture cycles include: *The Bhagavad Gita and the Epistles of Paul* and *The Esoteric Meaning of the Bhagavad Gita* (CW 146), which the Russian philosopher Nikolai Berdyaev attends; *The Mysteries of the East and of Christianity* (CW 144); *The Effects of Esoteric Development* (CW 145); and *The Fifth Gospel* (CW 148). In May, Rudolf Steiner is in London and Paris, where anthroposophical work continues.

1914:   Building continues on the *Johannes Bau* (Goetheanum) in Dornach, with artists and co-workers from seventeen nations. The general assembly of the Anthroposophical Society takes place. In May, Rudolf Steiner visits Paris, as well as Chartres Cathedral. June 28: assassination in Sarajevo ('Now the catastrophe has happened!'). August 1: War is declared. Rudolf Steiner returns to Germany from Dornach—he will travel back and forth. He writes the last chapter of *The Riddles of Philosophy*. Lecture cycles include: *Human and Cosmic Thought* (CW 151); *Inner Being of Humanity between Death and a New Birth* (CW 153); *Occult Reading and Occult Hearing* (CW 156). December 24: marriage of Rudolf Steiner and Marie von Sivers.

1915:   Building continues. Life after death becomes a major theme, also art. Writes: *Thoughts during a Time of War* (CW 24). Lectures include: *The Secret of Death* (CW 159); *The Uniting of Humanity through the Christ Impulse* (CW 165).

1916:   Rudolf Steiner begins work with Edith Maryon (1872–1924) on the sculpture 'The Representative of Humanity' ('The Group'—Christ, Lucifer, and Ahriman). He also works with the alchemist Alexander von Bernus on the quarterly *Das Reich*. He writes *The Riddle of Humanity* (CW 20). Lectures include: *Necessity and Freedom in World History and Human Action* (CW 166); *Past and Present in the Human Spirit* (CW 167); *The Karma of Vocation* (CW 172); *The Karma of Untruthfulness* (CW 173).

1917: Russian Revolution. The U.S. enters the war. Building continues. Rudolf Steiner delineates the idea of the 'threefold nature of the human being' (in a public lecture March 15) and the 'threefold nature of the social organism' (hammered out in May-June with the help of Otto von Lerchenfeld and Ludwig Polzer-Hoditz in the form of two documents titled *Memoranda*, which were distributed in high places). August–September: Rudolf Steiner writes *The Riddles of the Soul* (CW 20). Also: commentary on 'The Chymical Wedding of Christian Rosenkreutz' for Alexander Bernus (*Das Reich*). Lectures include: *The Karma of Materialism* (CW 176); *The Spiritual Background of the Outer World: The Fall of the Spirits of Darkness* (CW 177).

1918: March 18: peace treaty of Brest-Litovsk—'Now everything will truly enter chaos! What is needed is cultural renewal.' June: Rudolf Steiner visits Karlstein (Grail) Castle outside Prague. Lecture cycle: *From Symptom to Reality in Modern History* (CW 185). In mid-November, Emil Molt, of the Waldorf-Astoria Cigarette Company, has the idea of founding a school for his workers' children.

1919: Focus on the threefold social organism: tireless travel, countless lectures, meetings, and publications. At the same time, a new public stage of Anthroposophy emerges as cultural renewal begins. The coming years will see initiatives in pedagogy, medicine, pharmacology, and agriculture. January 27: threefold meeting: ' We must first of all, with the money we have, found free schools that can bring people what they need.' February: first public eurythmy performance in Zurich. Also: 'Appeal to the German People' (CW 24), circulated March 6 as a newspaper insert. In April, *Towards Social Renewal* (CW 23) appears— 'perhaps the most widely read of all books on politics appearing since the war.' Rudolf Steiner is asked to undertake the 'direction and leadership' of the school founded by the Waldorf-Astoria Company. Rudolf Steiner begins to talk about the 'renewal' of education. May 30: a building is selected and purchased for the future Waldorf School. August–September, Rudolf Steiner gives a lecture course for Waldorf teachers, *The Foundations of Human Experience (Study of Man)* (CW 293). September 7: Opening of the first Waldorf School. December (into January): first science course, the *Light Course* (CW 320).

1920: The Waldorf School flourishes. New threefold initiatives. Founding of limited companies *Der Kommende Tag* and *Futurum A.G.* to infuse spiritual values into the economic realm. Rudolf Steiner also focuses on the sciences. Lectures: *Introducing Anthroposophical Medicine* (CW 312); *The Warmth Course* (CW 321); *The Boundaries of Natural Science* (CW 322); *The Redemption of Thinking* (CW 74). February: Johannes Werner

Klein—later a co-founder of the Christian Community—asks Rudolf Steiner about the possibility of a 'religious renewal,' a 'Johannine church.' In March, Rudolf Steiner gives the first course for doctors and medical students. In April, a divinity student asks Rudolf Steiner a second time about the possibility of religious renewal. September 27–October 16: anthroposophical 'university course.' December: lectures titled *The Search for the New Isis* (CW 202).

1921: Rudolf Steiner continues his intensive work on cultural renewal, including the uphill battle for the threefold social order. 'University' arts, scientific, theological, and medical courses include: *The Astronomy Course* (CW 323); *Observation, Mathematics, and Scientific Experiment* (CW 324); the *Second Medical Course* (CW 313); *Colour*. In June and September-October, Rudolf Steiner also gives the first two 'priests' courses' (CW 342 and 343). The 'youth movement' gains momentum. Magazines are founded: *Die Drei* (January), and—under the editorship of Albert Steffen (1884–1963)—the weekly, *Das Goetheanum* (August). In February–March, Rudolf Steiner takes his first trip outside Germany since the war (Holland). On April 7, Steiner receives a letter regarding 'religious renewal,' and May 22–23, he agrees to address the question in a practical way. In June, the Klinical-Therapeutic Institute opens in Arlesheim under the direction of Dr. Ita Wegman. In August, the Chemical-Pharmaceutical Laboratory opens in Arlesheim (Oskar Schmiedel and Ita Wegman are directors). The Clinical Therapeutic Institute is inaugurated in Stuttgart (Dr. Ludwig Noll is director); also the Research Laboratory in Dornach (Ehrenfried Pfeiffer and Günther Wachsmuth are directors). In November–December, Rudolf Steiner visits Norway.

1922: The first half of the year involves very active public lecturing (thousands attend); in the second half, Rudolf Steiner begins to withdraw and turn toward the Society—'The Society is asleep.' It is 'too weak' to do what is asked of it. The businesses—*Der Kommende Tag* and *Futurum A.G.*—fail. In January, with the help of an agent, Steiner undertakes a twelve-city German lecture tour, accompanied by eurythmy performances. In two weeks he speaks to more than 2,000 people. In April, he gives a 'university course' in The Hague. He also visits England. In June, he is in Vienna for the East–West Congress. In August–September, he is back in England for the Oxford Conference on Education. Returning to Dornach, he gives the lectures *Philosophy, Cosmology, and Religion* (CW 215), and gives the third priests' course (CW 344). On September 16, The Christian Community is founded. In October–November, Steiner is in Holland and England. He also speaks to the youth: *The Youth Course* (CW 217). In December, Steiner gives lectures titled *The Origins of Natural Science* (CW 326), and *Humanity and the World of Stars: The Spiritual Communion of Humanity* (CW 219). December 31: Fire at the Goetheanum, which is destroyed.

1923: Despite the fire, Rudolf Steiner continues his work unabated. A very hard year. Internal dispersion, dissension, and apathy abound. There is conflict—between old and new visions—within the Society. A wake-up call is needed, and Rudolf Steiner responds with renewed lecturing vitality. His focus: the spiritual context of human life; initiation science; the course of the year; and community building. As a foundation for an artistic school, he creates a series of pastel sketches. Lecture cycles: *The Anthroposophical Movement; Initiation Science* (CW 227) (in England at the Penmaenmawr Summer School); *The Four Seasons and the Archangels* (CW 229); *Harmony of the Creative Word* (CW 230); *The Supersensible Human* (CW 231), given in Holland for the founding of the Dutch society. On November 10, in response to the failed Hitler-Ludendorff putsch in Munich, Steiner closes his Berlin residence and moves the *Philosophisch-Anthroposophisch Verlag* (Press) to Dornach. On December 9, Steiner begins the serialization of his *Autobiography: The Course of My Life* (CW 28) in *Das Goetheanum*. It will continue to appear weekly, without a break, until his death. Late December–early January: Rudolf Steiner re-founds the Anthroposophical Society (about 12,000 members internationally) and takes over its leadership. The new board members are: Marie Steiner, Ita Wegman, Albert Steffen, Elisabeth Vreede, and Günther Wachsmuth. (See *The Christmas Meeting for the Founding of the General Anthroposophical Society*, CW 260). Accompanying lectures: *Mystery Knowledge and Mystery Centres* (CW 232); *World History in the Light of Anthroposophy* (CW 233). December 25: the Foundation Stone is laid (in the hearts of members) in the form of the 'Foundation Stone Meditation.'

1924: January 1: having founded the Anthroposophical Society and taken over its leadership, Rudolf Steiner has the task of 'reforming' it. The process begins with a weekly newssheet ('What's Happening in the Anthroposophical Society') in which Rudolf Steiner's 'Letters to Members' and 'Anthroposophical Leading Thoughts' appear (CW 26). The next step is the creation of a new esoteric class, the 'first class' of the 'University of Spiritual Science' (which was to have been followed, had Rudolf Steiner lived longer, by two more advanced classes). Then comes a new language for Anthroposophy—practical, phenomenological, and direct; and Rudolf Steiner creates the model for the second Goetheanum. He begins the series of extensive 'karma' lectures (CW 235–40); and finally, responding to needs, he creates two new initiatives: biodynamic agriculture and curative education. After the middle of the year, rumours begin to circulate regarding Steiner's health. Lectures: January–February, *Anthroposophy* (CW 234); February: *Tone Eurythmy* (CW 278); June: *The Agriculture Course* (CW 327); June–July: *Speech Eurythmy* (CW 279); *Curative Education* (CW 317); August: (England, 'Second International Summer School'), *Initiation Consciousness: True and False Paths in Spiritual Investigation* (CW 243); September: *Pastoral Medicine* (CW 318). On September 26, for the first time, Rudolf Steiner cancels a lecture. On September 28, he gives his last lecture. On September 29, he withdraws to his studio in the carpenter's shop; now he is definitively ill. Cared for by Ita Wegman, he continues working, however, and writing the weekly installments of his *Autobiography* and *Letters to the Members/Leading Thoughts* (CW 26).

1925: Rudolf Steiner, while continuing to work, continues to weaken. He finishes *Extending Practical Medicine* (CW 27) with Ita Wegman.

On March 30, around ten in the morning, Rudolf Steiner dies

INDEX

as Yahweh, 158–159, 161–162
Jesus (of Nazareth), 137
John, St, Gospel of, 56
judgement, 75, 201
  judgement day, 147
Jupiter (future stage), 122
justice, 144–146

Kalevala (folk poem), xiii, xvii–xviii, 3,
    5, 9–11, 19, 23–28, 36–40,
    51, 53, 74–75, 100, 203–205
Kamaloka, 136
Kant, 128
kantele (instrument), 28
karma/karmic, 81, 126, 131, 176–179,
    182
  world, 131
knowledge, 4, 31, 55, 63–64, 66–67,
    69–70, 77, 81, 85, 96, 99, 115,
    155, 158, 164, 167–168, 175,
    177
  ancient, 154, 156, 167, 189
  clairvoyant, 163
  cosmic, 166
  occult, 202–203
  spiritual, 100, 163, 165, 168
  spiritual science, 30, 163
Kriemhilde, 8, 18–19

Laius, 97
Landstad, 137–138
legends (sagas), 4, 9, 94–95, 155, 157,
    170, 202
Lemminkäinen, 9, 24, 36, 51–53, 74,
    100, 108, 203–204
liberty, 164
light, 7, 27, 30, 37, 105, 108,
    120–121, 129, 135–136,
    155–156, 166, 200
  light-filled, 203
  occult, 203
  soul light, 168

Lindholm, Frau, 139
liver, 107
logic/logical, 63, 70, 116, 177
love, 23–24, 80, 129–131, 137–138,
    161
  as inner fire, 131
  self-love, 129, 130–131
Lucifer/luciferic, xvii, 87–92, 95,
    97–98, 105–112, 114–123,
    126–132
lungs, 60

macrocosm, 154–157, 161, 163, 168
magnetism, 22
Manichaeism, 132
Marjatta, 10–11, 26
materialism/materialistic, 27–28, 46,
    81, 87, 90, 93–94, 100–102,
    115, 153, 155, 158–159, 163,
    167–168, 177–180, 195–197
maya, 47, 49–51, 55, 58, 61, 81,
    103–105, 111
meditation/meditatively, 75, 192
medium, 178
memory, 17, 42, 74, 170–171
  folk-memories, 138
Mephistopheles, xvii, 91–99
metamorphosis. *See transformation*
metaphysical, 192
Michael/Michaelic, 44–46, 146, 171
  as archangel, 137
  as countenance of Jehovah, 137
  his rulership, 44
  as St Michael, 145
microcosm, 154–156, 168
'midnight', 44
migrations, 72
mind, 21
modesty, 197
monism, 132
Montaigne, 65–66
Moon (sphere), 151
  spiritual region, 170